AN MIS CASE STUDY:
ZIMCO ENTERPRISES

About the Author

Dr. Larry Long, a partner at Long and Associates, is a lecturer, author, columnist, consultant, and educator in the computer and information services fields. His many books cover a broad spectrum of MIS related topics from programming to MIS strategic planning. Dr. Long addresses a breadth of management, computer, and MIS issues in his "Turnaround Time" column in *Computerworld* and in his executive seminars. He has served as a consultant to all levels of management in virtually every major type of industry. Dr. Long has over a decade of classroom experience at the University of Oklahoma and at Lehigh University, where he continues to be an active lecturer. The author received his Ph.D., M.S., and B.S. degrees in Industrial Engineering at the University of Oklahoma.

Photo by Marty Chamberlain

AN MIS CASE STUDY: ZIMCO ENTERPRISES

LARRY LONG

PRENTICE-HALL, INC., Englewood Cliffs, NJ 07632

Library of Congress Cataloging-in-Publication Data

LONG, LARRY E.
  An MIS case study, Zimco Enterprises.

  Includes index.
  1. Management information systems. I. Title.
T58.6.L665 1988   658.4′038   87-11542
ISBN 0-13-585837-2

Editorial/production supervision: Colleen Brosnan
Cover design: Ben Santora
Manufacturing buyer: Barbara Kelly Kittle

These case studies also appeared in Larry Long, *Computers in Business* © 1987, pp. 29,
58, 90, 116, 141, 174, 209, 237, 268, 296, 331, 363, 386. Reprinted by permission of Prentice-
Hall, Englewood Cliffs, N.J.

Printed in the United States of America

10 9 8 7 6 5 4 3 2 1

ISBN 0-13-585837-2 025

Prentice-Hall International (UK) Limited, *London*
Prentice-Hall of Australia Pty. Limited, *Sydney*
Prentice-Hall of Canada Inc., *Toronto*
Prentice-Hall Hispanoamericana, S.A., *Mexico*
Prentice-Hall of India Private Limited, *New Delhi*
Prentice-Hall of Japan, Inc., *Tokyo*
Prentice-Hall of Southeast Asia Pte. Ltd., *Singapore*
Editora Prentice-Hall do Brasil, Ltda., *Rio de Janeiro*

Contents

**Case Study 7:   Information Systems at Zimco:
Finance and Accounting**

Case Study 8:   Zimco's Computer Network

Case Study 9:   Information Systems at Zimco: Personnel

Case Study 10:   Information Systems at Zimco: Operations

**Case Study 11:   Information Systems at Zimco:
Sales and Marketing**

Preface

Only a few years ago access to computers was limited to computer specialists—now, computers are commonplace in every business endeavor, from materials management on the shop-room floor to strategic planning in the board room. To make the most effective use of this valuable business tool, members of the business community need both a fundamental understanding of computers and an ability to apply them within the context of the business environment. *An MIS Case Study: Zimco Enterprises* is designed to help those aspiring to or involved in a career in business to bridge the gap between *computer/MIS concepts* and *business practice*.

INTENDED AUDIENCE

This case book is designed to serve as the primary text for a course that emphasizes MIS concepts (and, as an option, micro software skills) within the context of business practice *or* it can be a readings or supplemental text for an upper division or graduate course in MIS. It could also serve as the primary reading material for in-house seminars. The student who would benefit the most from this case book would have an understanding of computer/MIS fundamentals or be acquiring this knowledge concurrent with the study of this case book.

ORGANIZATION

This case book is organized into two parts. The first part is a comprehensive case study of Zimco Enterprises. The second section provides instruction on the function, concepts, and use of microcomputer productivity software within the context of Zimco Enterprises.

The Zimco Enterprises Case Study. The case study focuses on Zimco Enterprises, a fictitious medium-sized manufacturer of handy consumer products. The Zimco case study is presented in 13 topical segments. Each case study focuses on some facet of how computers are used at Zimco.

The case studies are relatively independent. The first two case studies are designed to familiarize you with Zimco's background, product line, management philosophy, organization, and people. After completing these you can go to any of the following case studies: 3, 4, 5, 8, 12, or 13. Case Studies 7, 9, 10, and 11 are subordinate to Case Study 3 (these focus on the flow of information within Zimco). Case Study 6 is subordinate to Case Study 5 (both are on micros).

The case studies, individually and collectively, provide the basis for discussion at any or all levels of activity—clerical, operational, tactical, or strategic. This flexibility makes this case book applicable to a broad range of undergraduate and graduate courses, as well as in-house seminars in industry.

By the time you finish this book, you will probably feel some affection for Zimco and may even come to know its employees as your friends. Zimco is, of course, a fictional company, but it is very real in that its people, systems, methods, and planning mirror that of other successful businesses. In fact, the company as well as its people are composites of real companies and real people.

Microcomputer Productivity Software. The *Microcomputer Productivity Software* section is positioned at the end of the text so that hands-on skills can be introduced at any point in the course. This section on micro software provides generic yet detailed coverage of word processing, electronic spreadsheet (oriented to Lotus 1-2-3), data management (oriented to dBASE III), graphics, idea processor, and communications software. Once the student has read and understood the principles, the student can easily relate what has been learned to the specifics of your hardware/software environment. With a little practice, the student has a computer skill.

The sections within this skills section are relatively independent. Once you have completed Sections S-1 and S-2, you can go directly to any of those sections that deal with a specific type of micro software (Sections S-3 through S-8).

SUPPORT PACKAGE

Instructor's Resource Manual with Test Item File and Transparency Masters. An *Instructor's Resource Manual* or *IRM* accompanies this case book. The *IRM* contains (for each topical case study): Teaching Hints, Lecture Notes, Answers to the Discussion Questions, and Review Exercises. The lecture notes are in an outline format. Boldface terms, in-class discussion questions, and references to appropriate transparencies are embedded in the outline. The section on "Microcomputer Productivity Software" follows a similar format.

The *test item file*, which is included in the *Instructor's Resource Manual*, has three types of questions (true/false, multiple choice, and essay) for each case study and for the special skills section on micro software.

Black-line *transparency masters*, which support material in the text and the *IRM*, are provided to facilitate in-class explanation and discussion.

Software Supplement. SuperSoftware, which contains 30-plus hours of hands-on lab activity for the IBM PC version (15-plus hours for the Apple version), is designed to instruct, intrigue, and motivate. The design philosophy of this supplement is to actively involve students through interactive communication with the computer. Graphic images and icons enhance the software's "user friendliness."

Scores of interesting and graphic programs, such as "Introduction to the PC," encourage students to become familiar with the computer. There are many business applications, such as airline reservation systems and home banking.

SuperSoftware interactively demonstrates micro software (electronic spreadsheet, word processing, database, and so on) concepts through imaginative simulations.

ACKNOWLEDGMENTS

I wish to extend my heartfelt gratitude to the entire Prentice-Hall team, and especially Marcia Horton, Colleen Brosnan, and Janet Schmid. I am forever grateful to my wife Nancy and my colleague Marty Chamberlain for their significant contributions to the case book and the support package.

DEDICATION

I would like to dedicate this book to those proponents of computers and MIS who have literally risked their careers to make their respective organizations more competitive and a better place to work.

Larry Long, Ph.D.

PART I

CASE STUDY 1

Background, Function, and Organization of Zimco Enterprises

BACKGROUND SUMMARY

Zimco was founded in 1876 during the post–Civil War era by Ezekiel "Zeke" F. Zimmers. Zeke, an immigrant from Europe, was an upholsterer by trade. Much of his day was spent stretching fabric over wooden furniture frames. He secured the fabric to the frame with small tacks. Over the years, these menacing little tacks caused Zeke a lot of pain. He and other upholsterers had trouble holding the tightly stretched fabric and hammering in the tack at the same time. Zeke and his upholstery friends were constantly complaining to their wives about smashed thumbs.

Zeke's wife, Bertha, sympathized with him, but she had no desire to spend the rest of her life hearing complaints about black-and-blue fingers. So she did something about it. She converted a small magnet, which she had been using to hold her sewing needles, into a combination tack and fabric holder. First, she notched the magnet with a small "V," then she placed a glue-and-sand mixture on the bottom of the magnet. Then she affixed a small eight-inch handle to the magnet and *voilá*, a new industry was born.

One year later, Zeke perfected the tool, named it the *Stib* (see Figure Z1–1), founded Zimco Enterprises, and created the now famous slogan, "Don't be dumb and hit your thumb, buy a Stib." The Stib was an instant success.

Fascinated with cowboys and the "wild west," Zeke moved his small but growing business to Dallas, Texas, in 1890. Zimco is still headquartered

1

in Dallas. Ezekiel F. Zimmers, Jr. became president in 1900 upon his father's retirement. Under Zeke, Jr., Zimco continued to thrive in an economy that relied more and more on tacks and, therefore, the need for Stibs. In 1935, Ezekiel F. Zimmers III inherited Zimco Enterprises, but he was simply not cut out for management. He wanted the money, not the responsibility of a company. In 1936, Zimco Enterprises went public and is now owned by shareholders from every walk of life.

Oldtimers at Zimco still tell stories about Ezekiel III. For several decades he was a mainstay with the jet set and was often photographed with budding starlets. Eventually, the money ran out and he returned to the trade of his grandfather—he became a master upholsterer.

THE MODERN ERA

Zimco's new management continued to focus on the sale of Stibs to the upholstery industry until the late 1950s and the introduction of staple guns. The upholsterers embraced the staple gun with the same fervor that they had embraced the Stib 75 years earlier. Many industry analysts thought that the staple gun would be the "death nail" (or "tack") to the Stib. Such was not the case. Aggressive Zimco managers were among the first to recognize the beginning of the "do it yourself" era. They knew that eventually just about every handy man and handy woman would smash a thumb in an attempt to hammer in a tack, so they initiated an aggressive marketing campaign to let consumers know that they had a product that would eliminate black-and-blue thumbs.

Before staple guns, Zimco didn't even have a marketing department. The product sold itself in the upholstery industry. In the 1950s, the consumer public had never heard of a Stib—but they certainly have now. Via every medium, including billboards, newspapers, and television, consumers read or heard "Don't be dumb and hit your thumb, buy a Stib." Frustrated tack-hammering consumers rushed to buy Stibs, and the rest is business history.

ZIMCO MANAGEMENT PHILOSOPHY

Zimco management adopted a simple entrepreneurial philosophy: Produce a limited line of high-quality consumer products that are innovative and for which there is relatively little (or no) competition. Management figured that if they could identify a need early and produce the right product at the right price, they could corner the market, just as founder Zeke Zimmers did with Stibs 75 years earlier.

THE ZIMCO PRODUCT LINE TODAY

Today, Zimco produces and sells four very successful consumer products. These are the Stib, Farkle, Tegler, and Qwert.

- *Stib*. Even after 100 years, the Stib (see Figure Z1–1) is relatively unchanged. It still holds tacks and saves thumbs. The slogan remains the same, "Don't be dumb and hit your thumb, buy a Stib."

- *Farkle*. Like the Stib, the Farkle (see Figure Z1–2) was born of need. Commuters wanted relief from the hard plastic seats in buses and subways on their journeys to and from work. Zimco researchers produced a portable inflatable cushion that could be blown up with a few breaths of air, then collapsed to the size of a pocket calendar for ease of carrying. Millions of commuters are now believers in Farkle comfort. Commuters often tout the wonders of the Farkle to non-Farkle users by repeating its slogan: "Farkles add sparkle."

- *Tegler*. Teachers, parents, friends, and colleagues have cautioned others that chewing on ball-point pen caps is unsightly and socially unacceptable. Nevertheless, millions of "closet" chewers unconsciously nibble on these caps at every opportunity. Pen-cap addicts are found from grammar school classrooms to corporate boardrooms. Zimco's market research identified the need and Zimco's research department developed a product.

   In 1978, Teglers hit the market with a bang. Teglers (see Figure Z1–3) are flavored pen caps that add a little zip to the enjoyment of habitual pen-cap chewers. The one-size-fits-all Teglers are sold everywhere in packages of five: licorice, peppermint, cherry, lemon, and avocado. The beauty of Teglers is that the flavor comes through without

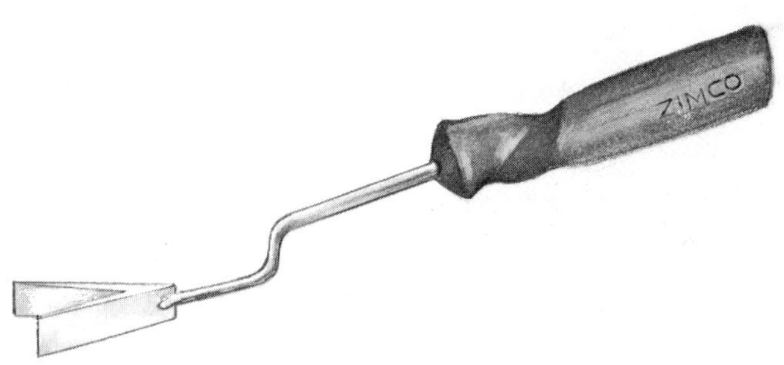

FIGURE Z1–1
Stib
Zimco Enterprises' Stib, a tack holder.

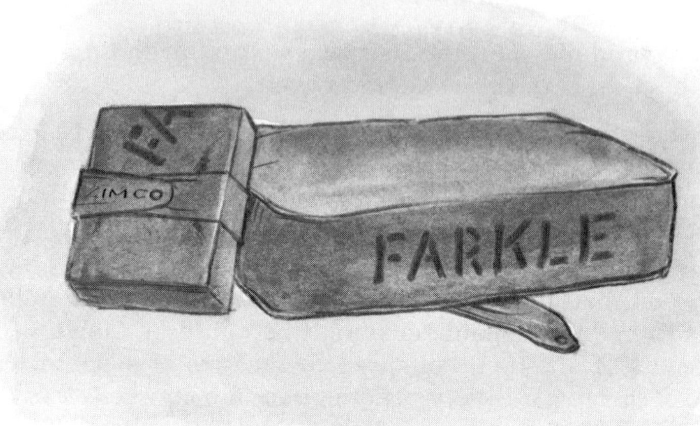

FIGURE Z1–2
Farkle
Zimco Enterprises' Farkle, an inflatable commuter cushion.

leaving telltale teeth marks on the caps. As the slogan says, "Any time is Tegler time."

■ *Qwert.* The Qwert, introduced in 1987, is Zimco's most recent product. After five years of intense research and development, Zimco became a high-tech company with the introduction of the Qwert (Figure Z1–4), a watchlike biofeedback mechanism. When placed around the wrist, the Qwert measures the variations in galvanic skin response

FIGURE Z1–3
Tegler
Zimco Enterprises' Tegler, a flavored open cap.

FIGURE Z1–4
Qwert
Zimco Enterprises' Qwert, a watchlike
biofeedback mechanism.

and heart rate. A tiny computer in the Qwert (which doubles as a digital watch), continuously collects and analyzes the galvanic and heart rate data. These data are analyzed by the computer, then a digital readout of a person's physical and, to some extent, emotional well-being, is displayed.

The readout varies from 1 to 10, with 1 being extreme lethargy and 10 being extreme anxiety. With a little practice and the Qwert providing the biofeedback, Qwert users can learn to adjust their body chemistry to optimize their mental acuity and reduce stress and tension (readouts of 4, 5, or 6). As the saying goes, "Do smart work with a Qwert."

ZIMCO'S SIZE AND ORGANIZATIONAL STRUCTURE

Zimco is a $150 million (annual sales) company with about 1500 employees nationwide. Except for 100 field representatives, all employees work out of the Dallas, Texas, headquarters office or one of the four regional plants, located at Dallas, Becker (Minnesota), Eugene (Oregon), and Reston

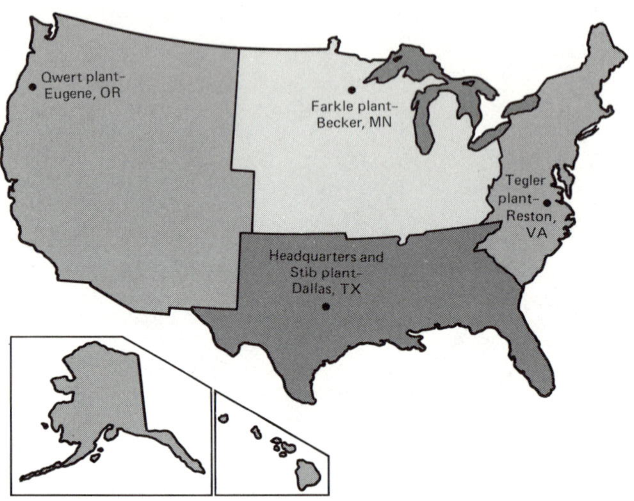

FIGURE Z1–5
Zimco Headquarters and Plant Sites

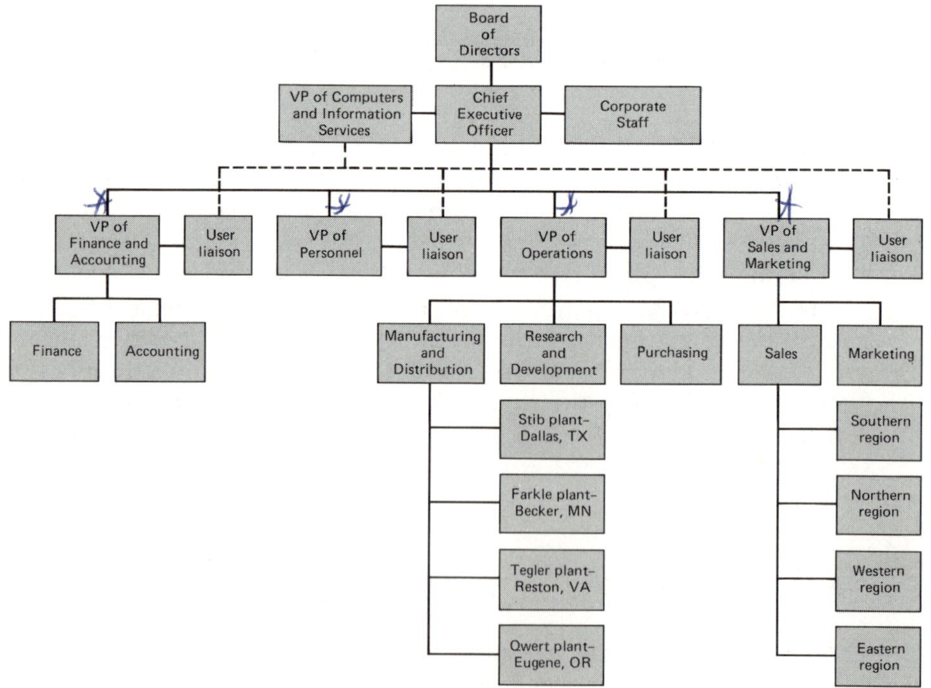

FIGURE Z1–6
Zimco Organizational Chart

(Virginia). Stibs are manufactured at Dallas, Farkles at Becker, Qwerts at Eugene, and Teglers at Reston. Each of the four plant sites is also a *regional distribution center* and a *regional sales office* for all Zimco products (Figure Z1–5).

Figure Z1–6 illustrates the basic structural organization of Zimco. It is classically organized into four *line* divisions and one *staff* division. The line divisions are the Finance and Accounting Division, Sales and Marketing Division, Personnel Division, and Operations Division [which includes manufacturing, distribution, research and development (R and D), and purchasing.] The Computer and Information Services Division, which is commonly abbreviated CIS, provides services to all areas of corporate operation. All division heads are vice-presidents and report directly to the president, *Preston Smith*. The corporate staff, which includes legal affairs, public relations, and other support groups, also reports to the president.

The function and operation of each of the divisions is described briefly below. Details of how these divisions interact with one another via integrated computer systems (e.g., information flow) are illustrated and discussed in later segments of the Zimco case study.

Computer and Information Services Division (CIS)

The VP of the Computer and Information Services (CIS) Division, *Conrad Innis*, is charged with the support of all Zimco Enterprises information processing requirements that are consistent with corporate objectives. Specific responsibilities include:

- The development, ongoing operation, and maintenance of information systems
- Serving as a catalyst for the development of new information systems
- Coordinating systems integration
- Evaluating and selecting hardware and software
- Setting of standards and policy relating to computers and information processing

Finance and Accounting Division

The head of the Finance and Accounting Division, *Monroe Green*, oversees the Finance and Accounting Departments. The Accounting Department collects and manipulates monetary data to provide information that reflects Zimco's monetary activity. For example, accounting systems generate the profit and loss statements, allocate expenses to various accounts, and reflect the value of finished goods inventory. The Finance Department seeks to optimize Zimco's cash flow. They make sure that Zimco is liquid enough to meet short-term financial obligations while investing extra funds until they are needed.

Sales and Marketing Division

Sally Marcio, the VP of the Sales and Marketing Division, is responsible for the activities of the Sales and Marketing Departments. Zimco relies exclusively on field sales representatives to sell their products. The Sales Department field reps work out of the four regional sales offices (southern, northern, western, eastern) and call on thousands of retailers and wholesalers throughout the country. Over 95 percent of the Zimco products are sold to drugstores, supermarkets, hardware stores, specialty stores, department stores, and mail-order companies. The Marketing Department is concerned primarily with making consumers aware of the spectacular products that Zimco has to offer.

Personnel Division

The VP of the Personnel Division, *Peggy Peoples*, has the responsibility for all personnel accounting functions. Peggy's division hires people to meet work force requirements, then provides services to individuals and departments regarding personnel benefits, compensation, and other personnel matters. The department also maintains a skills inventory and does the background work for internal training sessions.

Operations Division

Otto Manning, VP for the Operations Division, sees that the products are made and delivered to customers. The plant managers in Dallas, Eugene, Becker, and Reston report to the manager of Manufacturing and Distribution, who, in turn, reports to Otto Manning. Associated with each plant is a regional distribution center for all Zimco products. Managers of the Research and Development Department and the Purchasing Department also report to Otto.

User Liaisons

The intensity of computer and information processing activity is very heavy in companies that seek to take full advantage of the potential of automation. Zimco, being one of these companies, has assigned a user liaison to work directly with each of the four "functional area" vice-presidents. The user liaison is a "live-in" computer specialist who coordinates all computer-related activities within a particular division. The user liaison is intimately familiar with the functional area (e.g., marketing, accounting, etc.) as well as the technical end of computers and information processing. The user liaison is the catalyst for new system development and coordinates system conversions.

THE BUSINESS SYSTEM

The focus of this running case study is to describe how Zimco Enterprises uses available computing and information resources. So that you can better understand future discussions of Zimco operations, let's look at Zimco as a business system. Figure Z1–7 graphically illustrates how some of the pieces fit together.

The heart of any company is its people (the pyramid in Figure Z1–7). Like most medium-sized and large companies, Zimco has three levels

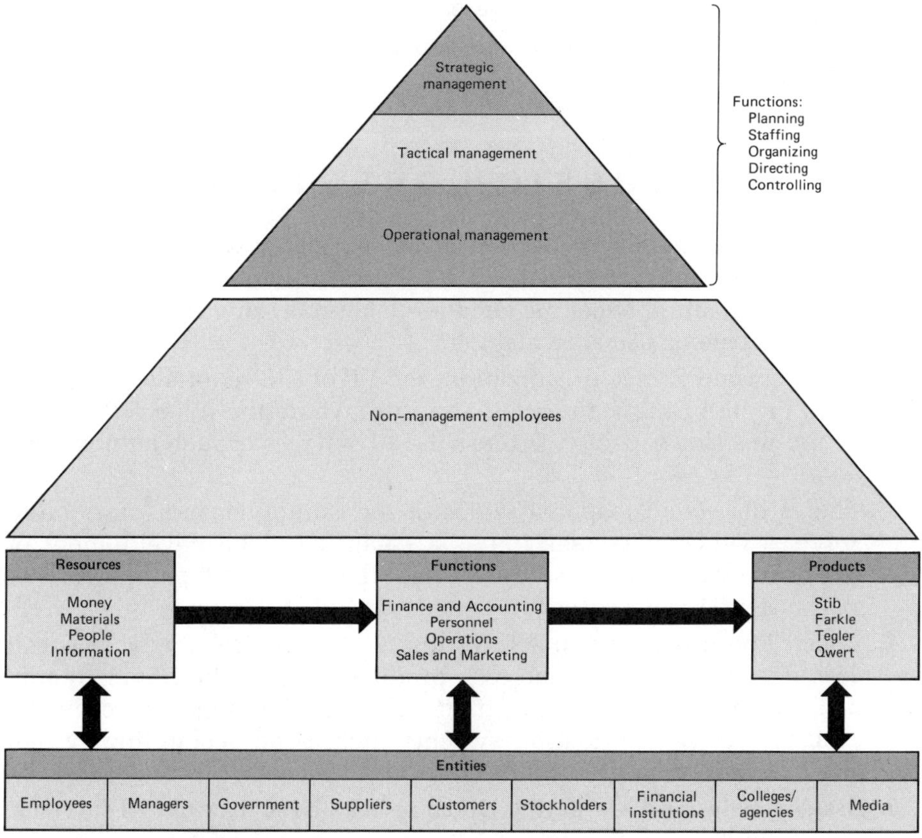

FIGURE Z1–7
A Business System Model for Zimco Enterprises

of management: operational, tactical, and strategic. Managers at each level have an ongoing need for information that will enable them to better use the resources at their disposal to meet corporate objectives and to perform the management functions of *planning, staffing, organizing, directing,* and *controlling.* These resources are *money, materials* (to include facilities and equipment), *people,* and *information.* As illustrated in Figure Z1–7, these resources become "input" to the various functional units of Zimco (operations, sales, etc.). The people at Zimco use their talent and knowledge, together with these resources, to produce the Zimco products (Stibs, Farkles, Teglers, and Qwerts).

The business system acts in concert with several *entities.* An entity is the source or destination of information flow, or an entity can be the source or destination of materials or product flow. For example, suppliers are both a source of information and materials. They are also the destination of payments for materials. The customer entity is the destination of products and the source of orders. *Flow diagrams* in later case studies detail direct interaction between all departments and entities in the business system.

DISCUSSION QUESTIONS

1. What special challenges faced Zimco management when Zimco transitioned from a privately held to a public corporation in 1936? How did this transition affect the need for data processing and information for management decision making?

2. In the current Zimco organization, the VP of CIS reports to the president, Preston Smith, in a staff capacity, where the other VPs report to him in a line capacity. Discuss the advantages of such an organization.

3. One of the stated responsibilities of the Computer and Information Services Division is "serving as a catalyst for the development of new information systems." How might the VP of the Operations Division interpret this charge?

4. Zimco Enterprises manufactures and sells three relatively low-tech products and one very high-tech product. Discuss the effects, if any, that the mixing of low- and high-tech products might have on the design of basic information systems such as an accounting system or an inventory control system.

5. Zimco's Sales and Marketing Division is a heavy user of CIS services. Speculate on how the field sales representatives might use Zimco's corporate data base at Dallas.

6. Discuss the advantages and disadvantages of having user liaisons in each of Zimco's four functional divisions.

7. For each of the three levels of management illustrated in the business system model in Figure Z1–7, what would be the horizon (time span) for planning decisions? Explain.

8. Top managers at Zimco have always treated money, materials, and people as valuable resources, but only recently have they recognized that information is also a valuable resource. Why do you think they waited so long?

CASE STUDY 2

Zimco's Computer and Information Services Division

HISTORY

Ever since Zimco went public in 1936, Zimco management has taken pride in the fact that they have always kept pace with the technology. Zimco relied on various types of punched-card-oriented accounting machines until 1959. During the period 1936 to 1945, the entire data processing, or DP, staff consisted of one manager and one combination keypunch/machine operator. Together, they wired the control panels for the various punch-card machines and maintained automated payroll, accounts receivable, and general ledger systems. In 1945, they added an accounts payable and an inventory control system, and one more keypunch/machine operator. The DP department stayed at three people until 1959, even though Zimco grew from 200 employees in 1945 to 450 in 1959.

In 1959, electronic accounting machines were commonplace, even in small companies, but expensive computers were used almost exclusively by very large companies. Zimco was one of the first relatively small companies to purchase an electronic computer. It was even written up in the *Business Weekly* and called "one of the country's most aggressive users of emerging computer technology." During the second generation of computers, most of the medium-sized companies adopted a "wait and see" attitude toward computers—but not Zimco.

Zimco ordered a small third-generation computer the day they were announced and took delivery 20 months later in December 1965. Early third-generation computers were made to order and they were in great demand. It was not uncommon for a company to wait more than a year to receive a computer! Each computer manufactured had a customer's name on it. Zimco's president at the time visited the factory and spent a couple of hours watching "his" computer being built.

The Computer Arrives

The 20 months following the order were busy times for the DP department. Management was confident that this new generation of computers would make life a breeze for the people in the DP department. But as Conrad Innis, the current VP of CIS, often says, "Confidence is that feeling you get before you fully understand the situation." Eventually, life would be easier with third-generation computers, but for the present, the conversion from second- to third-generation computers involved more than replacing one computer with a faster one.

Since existing programs did not run on the new generation of computers, all systems had to be redesigned and the programs rewritten—all 243 of them! The situation was further complicated by the fact that the people in the DP department had to learn a new programming language called COBOL. The DP manager hired two new programmers to help with the conversion and an expected increased demand for services from nonfinancial departments.

The DP Department Comes of Age

By 1972, Zimco had taken delivery on a fourth-generation computer, increased their staff to 10, and was providing computing support for all of Zimco's departments. In 1976, the DP manager, who reported to the VP of Finance, was promoted and the "data processing" function was made a division. The new vice-president of the Computer and Information Services (CIS) Division reported directly to the president in a staff position. The name was changed to better reflect the role that CIS played in the overall operation of Zimco Enterprises.

The CIS staff, which now numbered 30, was constantly involved in developing systems to support all aspects of a rapidly expanding and very successful company.

The Integration of Zimco's Information Systems

The demand for CIS services was so great that the division seemed to be growing out of control. In 1981, a new VP of CIS was hired to put some semblance of order back into CIS operation. The new VP, Conrad Innis, later observed that the "chaos in CIS was a result of an understaffed organization trying desperately to meet the seemingly endless information needs of the user departments." Conrad was a firm believer in order. He believed that each step forward should be well planned and cost justified.

Before Conrad arrived, systems were developed and files were created to meet a specific need. The result was dozens of autonomous information systems and a lot of data redundancy. Conrad shifted the emphasis from *autonomous* systems to *integrated* information systems. Before the movement to integrated information systems, CIS maintained autonomous systems for accounting, sales, marketing, and manufacturing, each of which had at least one computer-based file containing order information. Now order information is available to accounting, sales, marketing, manufacturing, or any other part of the company via a *centralized* integrated data base. Today, the VP of CIS has a staff of 51 in Dallas, and five at each of the three plant sites.

ROLES AND RESPONSIBILITIES

When Conrad Innis arrived at Zimco in 1981, the first thing he noticed was that CIS had no well-defined direction or purpose. Programmers and systems analysts "barely had time to catch their breath, much less know where they are heading and what they are supposed to be doing." Being a man of order, Conrad established a CIS charter that clarified *roles* and *responsibilities* of the CIS Department. The following charter was approved by the president, Preston Smith, in July 1982.

CIS is charged with the support of those information processing requirements that are consistent with corporate objectives. CIS responsibilities complementary to this charge include:

1. Development, ongoing operation, and maintenance of production information systems
2. Acting as an advisor to users throughout Zimco on computer-related matters
3. Serving as a catalyst for improving operations through system enhancements or new systems development
4. Coordinating data and systems integration throughout Zimco
5. Establishing standards, policy, and procedures relating to computers and information processing
6. Evaluating and selecting hardware and software
7. Conducting end-user education programs

With the CIS charter in place, there is seldom any question about who does what. This is often a problem in other companies.

ORGANIZATION

Background.   In most businesses, the information services departments evolved as part of the accounting/finance function, and so it was with Zimco. As accounting systems, such as payroll and accounts receivable, proved the worth of the computer, other Zimco departments, such as personnel and marketing, began to request that systems be developed for them. From the beginning, Zimco's DP department was centralized to take advantage of the economies of scale. But rapid growth caused some information services departments, including Zimco's CIS, to become cumbersome and unnecessarily complex.

By the early 1980s, a *lack of responsiveness* to the regional plants and the *availability of small, cost-effective computers* was beginning to reverse Zimco's trend toward centralization. In order to be more responsive to user information requirements, Conrad Innis decentralized parts of the information services function through *distributed processing*. However, he remained committed to a centralized CIS so that he could effectively coordinate all the activities involving information resources, such as hardware acquisition, information planning, and so on.

In effect, distributed processing is moving hardware, software, data, and computer specialists closer to where they are needed—the user areas. For example, each of the three plants outside of Dallas (Reston, Eugene, and Becker) has their own computer systems and computer specialists. These "distributed" computer systems are linked to Zimco's centralized computer system in Dallas.

Current CIS Organization.   CIS is the data and information "nerve center" of Zimco. The *data* are supplied by the various user groups. In return, the Computer and Information Services Division provides the software and operational support needed to produce *information*. Recognizing how important it is to be responsive to the company's information processing needs, Conrad Innis identified two basic objectives when he set out to reorganize the CIS Department in 1986. His first objective was to be responsive to the information needs of CIS users. The other objective was to have an organization that could operate efficiently to accomplish the responsibilities set forth in the CIS charter. The resultant organization is shown in Figure Z2–1.

Notice that CIS is divided into six groups, each with a manager. These groups are *systems analysis, programming, technical support, data communications, operations,* and *education.* The managers of the three regional computer centers at Eugene, Becker, and Reston also report to the VP of CIS. Conrad Innis also has "dotted line" responsibility for the user liaisons in each of the four functional divisions: finance and accounting, sales and marketing, personnel, and operations. The role of the VP

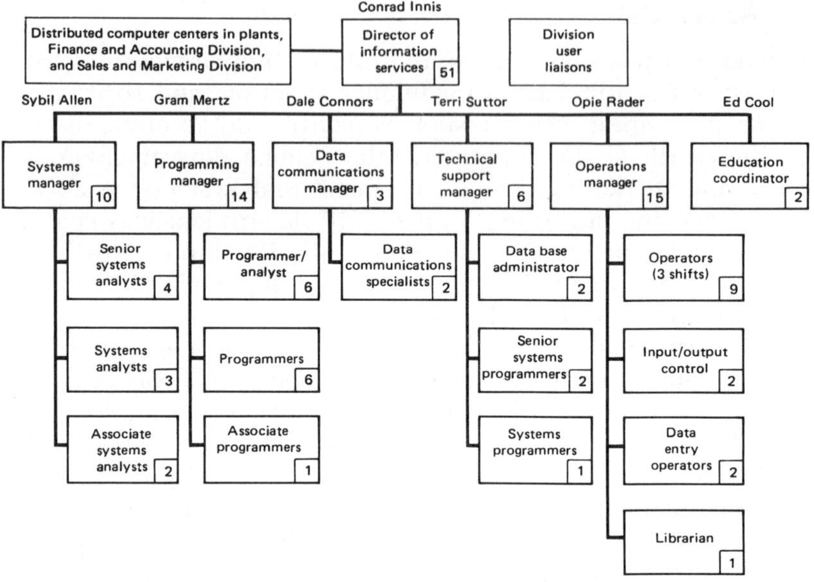

FIGURE Z2–1
Organization Chart for Zimco's Computer and Information Services Division

of CIS and each of the six departments in CIS and the regional computing centers is described below.

The Role of the Vice-President of CIS

Conrad Innis, the VP of CIS, is the chief information officer (CIO) and has responsibility for all computer and information systems activity at Zimco. At least half of his time is spent interacting with user managers and executives. In this capacity, Conrad coordinates the integration of data and information systems and serves as the catalyst for new systems development. The remainder of his time is devoted to managing the Computer and Information Services Division.

Systems Analysis Department

Sybil Allen heads the Systems Analysis group and has a staff of nine **systems analysts** working for her. The systems analysts, or simply "analysts," do the analysis, design, and implementation of information systems. The analysts work closely with people in the four user areas to

Systems analysts at Zimco work with users to ensure that they get the information they need in a format that they can easily understand. This analyst recommended presenting productivity data in the form of a color-coded pie chart.
(Dataproducts Corporation)

design information systems that meet their data processing and information needs. These "problem solvers" are assigned a variety of tasks, which might include feasibility studies, system reviews, security assessments, long-range planning, and hardware/software selection.

The role of these "problem solvers" is expanding with the technology. For example, with recent innovations in programming languages, users and analysts can work together at a workstation to design *and* implement certain information systems—without programmer involvement!

Programming Department

Gram Mertz manages the Programming Department. The **applications programmers** in his group, or simply **programmers,** translate analyst-prepared system and input/output specifications into programs. Programmers design the logic, then code, debug, test, and document the programs.

Gram's people write programs for a certain application, such as market analysis or inventory management.

Sometimes called "implementers" or "miracle workers," programmers are charged with turning system specifications into an information system. To do this, they must exhibit logical thinking and overlook nothing. Gram characterizes a good programmer as "*perceptive, patient, persistent, picky,* and *productive*: the five Ps of programming."

Some companies distinguish between *development* and *maintenance* programmers. Development programmers create *new* systems. Maintenance programmers enhance existing systems by *modifying* programs to meet changing needs. At Zimco, all programmers do both. About 50 percent of the applications programming tasks are related to maintenance and 50 percent to new development.

A person holding a **programmer/analyst** position performs the functions of both a programmer and a systems analyst. At Zimco, the more senior people in the Programming Department are programmer/analysts.

Data Communications Department

The **data communications specialists,** managed by *Dale Conners,* design and maintain computer networks that link computers and workstations for data communications. This involves selecting and installing appropriate hardware, such as modems, data PBXs, and front-end processors, as well as selecting the transmission media. Data communications specialists also develop and implement the software that controls the flow of data between computing devices.

Technical Support Department

The Technical Support Department, managed by *Terri Suttor,* designs, develops, maintains, and implements *systems software.* Systems software is fundamental to the general operation of the computer; that is, it does not address a specific business or scientific problem.

The types of positions that report to Terri are systems programmers and the data base administrator. **Systems programmers** develop and maintain systems software. The **data base administrator (DBA)** position evolved with the need to integrate information systems. The data base administrator designs, creates, and maintains Zimco's integrated data base. The DBA coordinates discussions between user groups to determine the content and format of the data base so that data redundancy is kept to a minimum. Accuracy and security of the data base are also responsibilities of the data base administrator.

Operations Department

Opie Rader is the manager of the Operations Department and of people who perform a variety of jobs, each of which is described in the following paragraphs.

Computer Operator.   The **computer operators** at Zimco perform those hardware-based activities that are needed to keep production information systems operational. An operator works in the machine room, initiating software routines and mounting the appropriate magnetic tapes, disks, and preprinted forms. The operator is in constant communication with the computer while monitoring the progress of a number of simultaneous production runs, initiating one-time jobs, and troubleshooting. If the computer system fails, the operator initiates restart procedures to "bring the system up."

Control Clerk.   The **control clerk** accounts for all input to and output from the computer center. Control clerks follow standard procedures to validate the accuracy of the output before it is distributed to the user department.

Data Entry Operator.   **Data entry operators,** sometimes called key operators, use key entry devices to transcribe data into machine-readable format. At Zimco, only a small data entry group is attached to CIS because the majority of the data entry operators are "distributed" to the user areas.

Librarian.   The **librarian** selects the appropriate interchangeable magnetic tapes and disks and delivers them to the operator. The operator mounts the tapes and disks on the storage devices for processing, then returns them to the librarian for storage. The librarian maintains a status log on each tape and disk. Zimco, like other companies its size, has hundreds of tapes and disks.

The librarian is also charged with maintaining a reference library filled with computer books, periodicals, and manuals, as well as internal system and program documentation (i.e., logic diagrams, program listings).

Education Department

Ed Cool is the **education coordinator** at Zimco. He and his assistant coordinate all computer-related educational activities. Ed says that "anyone who works with computers or selects a computer-related career automatically adopts a life of continuing education. Computer technology is changing rapidly and you have to run pretty fast just to stand still!" He schedules users and computer specialists for technical update seminars, video training programs, computer-assisted instruction, and others, as needed. Ed often conducts the training sessions himself.

"Distributed" Computer Centers

It's not unusual for people working in small computer centers and distributed computer centers, such as those in Reston, Eugene, and Becker, to be accomplished at a variety of jobs. Both small and large "shops" (a slang term for information services departments) must accomplish the functions of systems analysis, programming, technical support, data communications, operations, and education. In larger shops, such as Zimco's CIS in Dallas, the people are highly specialized; but in the small distributed shops, each person must be a generalist, capable of doing whatever needs to be done. The three people in each of the distributed centers at the remote plants double-up on duties. For example, one person who does primarily applications programming is also the data base administrator at the Reston plant.

Zimco has six distributed computer centers which are linked to the central computer center in Dallas. Because only a few people work at each of the distributed computer centers, each must acquire skills in a variety of computer specialists positions, from operations to data communications.
(Honeywell, Inc.)

HIRING PRACTICES

Zimco has had great success hiring recent college graduates. New hires go through an 18-month training program. Most people with associate or bachelor's degrees begin work as programmers. Technical school graduates and some associate-degree holders begin working as operators, control clerks, librarians, and data entry operators, depending on their qualifications. After gaining operations experience, those with associate degrees and programming education often are promoted to programming positions.

Like most companies, Zimco doesn't recruit recent graduates to fill *systems analyst* positions. They prefer their analysts to have programming experience. Occasionally, CIS hires a *programmer/analyst*, but assignments for a rookie programmer/analyst are usually programming tasks for the first couple of years.

Zimco's rationale behind starting people as programmers is well founded. Gram Mertz explained their policy. "Programming not only develops logic and design skills, but it also provides real-world insight into the capabilities and limitations of a computer system. We want our computer specialists to know what a computer system can and cannot do and programming is about the best way for them to acquire this knowledge."

Once a Zimco employee has a solid foundation in programming (18 months to three years), he or she can pursue a career as a programmer or branch out into other information services careers. There is no traditional career path at Zimco; two people rarely advance through the ranks in the same manner. Most are faced with the luxury of having several promotion alternatives at each level.

SUMMARY OF ZIMCO'S CIS ORGANIZATION

The central focus of the Computer and Information Services Division is the development and ongoing operation of information systems. Figure Z2–2 graphically summarizes the relationship between the positions that have been described and the development and operation of an information system. A *user* request for a computer-related service, called a **service request,** is compiled and submitted to the CIS department. Because resources are limited, the VP of CIS, Conrad Innis, approves those requests that appear to offer the greatest benefits to the organization.

A project team made up of *systems analysts, programmers, user liaisons,* and possibly the *data base administrator* is formed to develop and implement the information system. *Systems programmers* and *data com-*

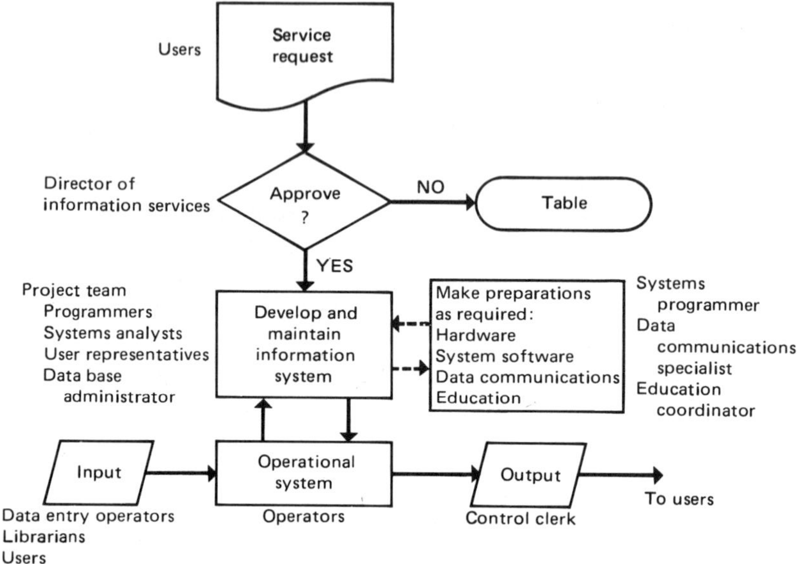

FIGURE Z2–2
Position Functions and Information Systems at Zimco
This chart summarizes the relationship between the various positions in
the Computer and Information Services Division and user personnel
in the development and operation of an information system.

munications specialists make changes to the hardware configuration, data
communications network, and systems software, as required. The *education coordinator* schedules needed training sessions for both computer
specialists and users. Once the system is implemented and becomes operational, operations people handle the routine input, processing, and output
activities. *Data entry operators* transcribe the raw data to machine-readable
format. The *librarian* readies magnetic storage media for processing. *Operators* initiate and monitor computer runs and distribute the output to
control clerks, who then check the output for accuracy before delivering
it to the *users*.

DISCUSSION QUESTIONS

1. Zimco's Data Processing Department consisted of three people from
   1945 to 1959, even though the company grew from 200 to 450 people.
   Why did all departments, except DP, expand markedly during this
   period?

2. Why do you think Zimco skipped the first and second generations
   of computers?

3. The people in the DP Department had a 20-month lead time prior to the delivery of their first computer in 1965. What did they do in preparation for its arrival?

4. In 1981, why did Conrad Innis want to shift the emphasis from autonomous information systems to an integrated information system?

5. During the formation of the CIS charter, several items in the charter were debated heavily. Which charter items do you think are the most controversial, and why?

6. What prompted Conrad Innis to decentralize certain operations through distributed processing?

7. Sybil Allen has suggested on several occasions to Conrad Innis that both programmers and systems analysts should report to a single manager. Discuss the pros and cons of her suggestion.

8. Gram Mertz uses the "five Ps of programming" to describe a "good programmer." Discuss desirable characteristics of a good systems analyst.

9. Zimco encourages the hiring of recent college graduates. Other companies prefer hiring those with experience. Discuss the advantages and disadvantages of each approach.

CASE STUDY 3

Management Information Systems at Zimco

DOCUMENTING INFORMATION AND WORK FLOW

The four functional divisions at Zimco Enterprises (Finance and Accounting, Sales and Marketing, Operations, and Personnel) work together as a unit to accomplish the goals of the corporation. Each division is very much dependent on information derived from the others. In this Zimco case study, we'll take a *top-down* view of Zimco's overall management information system. To do this, we'll start at the "top" (general overview) and examine a diagram that illustrates the basic information flow between the four divisions. In subsequent extensions of the Zimco case study, we'll move "down" the ladder and take a closer look (greater detail) at the information flow within each of the four divisions. The design tool that Zimco uses to graphically illustrate the flow of information, at both the overview and detailed levels, is the **data flow diagram.**

There are a number of techniques that aid systems analysts and programmers in the design and documentation of an information system, but Sybil Allen, the manager of the Systems Analysis Department, feels that data flow diagrams, or **DFDs,** are perfect for Zimco. Sybil says, "DFDs are particularly well suited to our purposes because we encourage top-down design and they can be easily understood by management at all levels." DFDs enable an MIS to be portrayed graphically at several levels of generality.

Only four symbols are needed for data flow diagrams: *entity, process, flow line*, and *data store*. The symbols are summarized in Figure Z3–1 and their use is illustrated in Figure Z3–2. The entity symbol ⌐, a square with a darkened border on the top and left sides, is the source or destination of data or information flow. An entity can be a person, a group of persons (e.g., customers or employees), a department, or even a place (e.g., First National Bank). Each process symbol ⌐, a rectangle with rounded corners, contains a description of a function to be performed. Sybil says that "we use the process symbol to show processes associated with data entry, verification, calculation, storage, creation, and production." Process symbol identification numbers are assigned in levels. The first-level processes are labeled 1, 2, 3, and so on. Second-level processes that are subordinate to process 1 are labeled 1.1, 1.2, 1.3, and so on. The flow lines ⟶ indicate the flow and direction of data or information. Data storage symbols ⌐, open-ended rectangles, identify storage locations for data. A storage location could be a file drawer, a shelf, a data base on magnetic disk, and so on.

A diagonal line in the lower right corner of the entity symbols indicates that the entity is repeated elsewhere on the same diagram. When the same data store is repeated on the same chart, the left end of the data store symbol is drawn to be diagonal rather than vertical.

"At Zimco, DFDs were our primary documentation tool even during the days of autonomous, function-based systems," says Sybil Allen. Zimco's "old" (i.e., before implementation of their current MIS) systems are easy to understand and provide good examples of the principles of data flow diagrams. For example, Figure Z3–2 shows that portion of a payroll system that produces payroll checks. Processes 1 and 2 deal with the employee data base, but in Process 3 the actual payroll checks are produced. In the bottom portion of Figure Z3–2, Process 3 is *exploded* to show greater detail. Notice that the *second-level* processes within the explosion of Process 3 are numbered 3.1, 3.2, 3.3, and 3.4. Process 3.1 could be exploded to a third level of processes to show even greater detail (e.g., 3.1.1, 3.1.2, etc.).

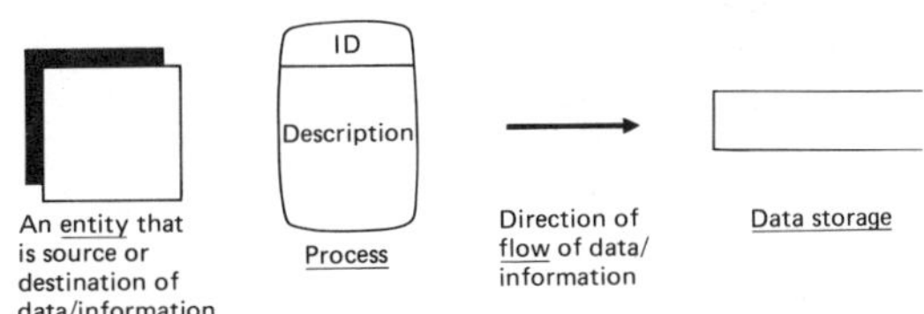

FIGURE Z3–1
Data Flow Diagram Symbols

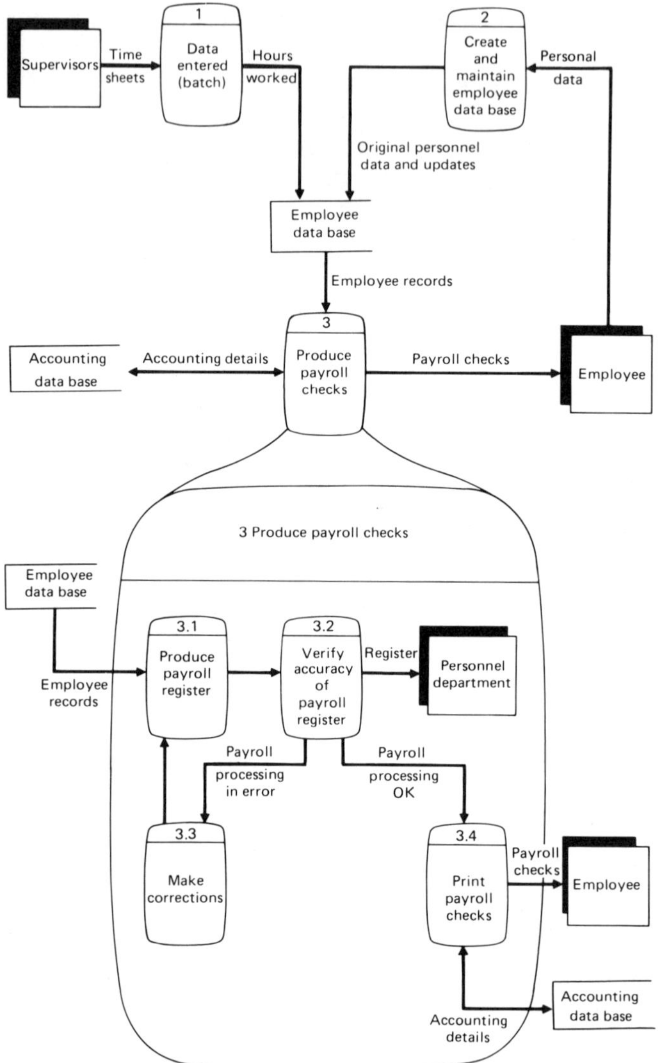

FIGURE Z3–2
Data Flow Diagram
In the example data flow diagram of a payroll system, process 3 is exploded to show greater detail.

STRATEGIC-LEVEL INFORMATION FLOW

Conrad Innis, VP of CIS, with help from Sybil Allen, compiled the "MIS overview" of Figure Z3–3 to provide top management with a strategic overview of the information flow within Zimco Enterprises. Conrad had another reason. People in CIS are always enhancing existing systems or

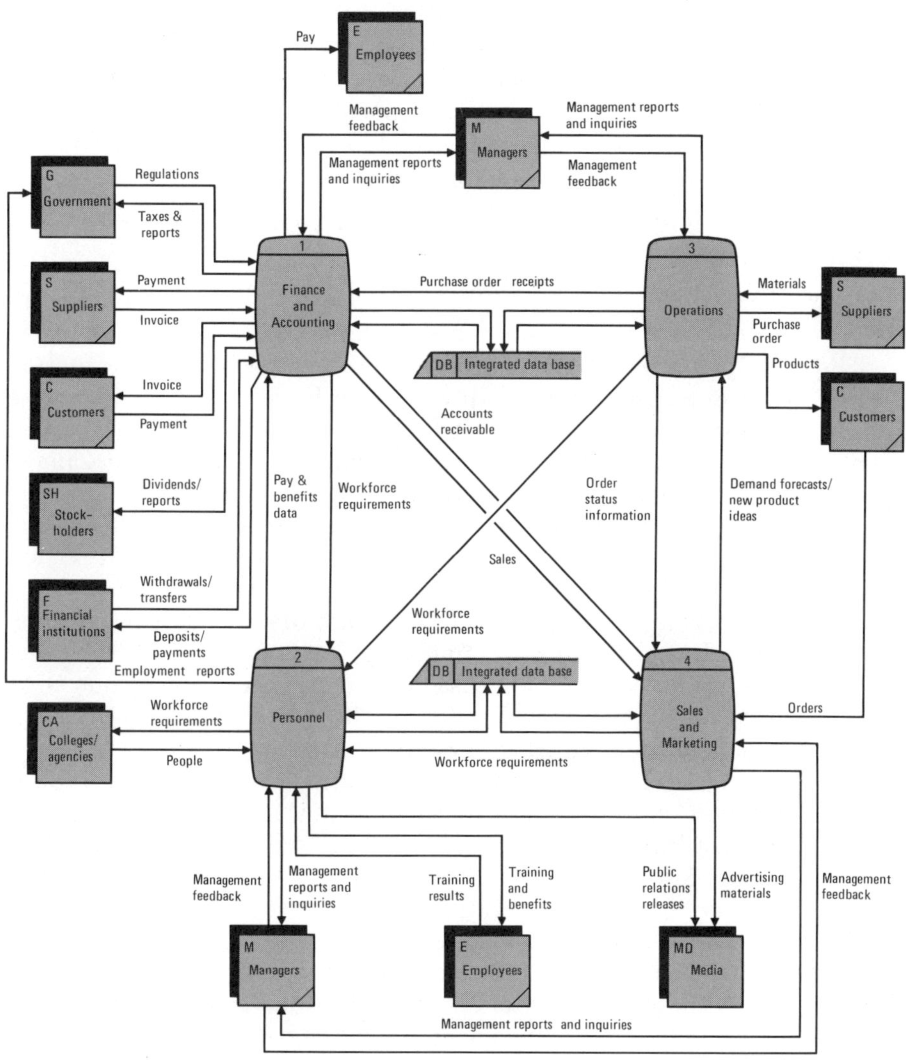

FIGURE Z3–3
MIS Overview for Zimco Enterprises

developing new systems, so he wanted to document Zimco's information systems. Conrad has a saying: "If you don't know where you are, how can you know where you're going?"

In the "business system" model (Figure Z1–7) presented in the Zimco case study following Chapter 1, the corporate resources (money, material, people, and information), the corporate functions, and the products are shown to interact with a variety of "entities," both within and outside of Zimco. These interactions, as well as the basic information flow between the four functional areas, are graphically portrayed in the overview data flow diagram of Figure Z3–3. These interactions are further expanded, or "exploded," in tactical- and operational-level DFDs in the "Information Systems at Zimco" case studies.

- Zimco Case Study 7 (Finance and Accounting)
- Zimco Case Study 9 (Personnel)
- Zimco Case Study 10 (Operations)
- Zimco Case Study 11 (Sales and Marketing)

The function of the CIS Division is to facilitate the flow of information within Zimco Enterprises. Since all computer-based information at one time or another passes through the CIS division (or its computers), you might say that CIS is the nucleus of information flow within Zimco. However, to simplify things, the intermediate flow of information through CIS is omitted in the overview data flow diagram of Figure Z3–3 such that information is shown to flow directly from one functional division to the next.

The MIS overview (Figure Z3–3) highlights the interdependence between the four line divisions at Zimco. For example, the Finance and Accounting Division receives purchase orders from the Operations Division, accounts receivable data from the Sales and Marketing Division, and pay and benefits data from the Personnel Division. In turn, the Finance and Accounting Division provides cost information to the Operations Division, gross sales information to Sales and Marketing Division, and information regarding the division's work force requirements to the Personnel Division. Information flows to and from the other three divisions are illustrated in Figure Z3–3.

The two entities internal to Zimco are *employees* and *managers*. The employees entity encompasses all employees, including managers. The managers entity includes managers at the operational, tactical, and strategic levels. The interaction between Zimco's integrated MIS and the employees entity generally falls into the areas of pay, benefits, and training. The interaction between the MIS and managers entity is primarily in the areas of management inquiries, reports, and directives. For example, in the Sales and Marketing Division, management routinely makes inquiries regarding the progress of sales of certain products. The system also supplies forecasts of potential sales. These forecasts eventually become input to the Operations Division.

There are many external entities from which the Zimco MIS receives input and to which it must provide output. These external entities include the *government* (all levels), *suppliers, customers, stockholders, financial institutions, colleges/agencies*, and the *media*.

Zimco's primary interaction with the government is in the area of taxes. Payment is made to suppliers for the materials that they provide. Zimco's customers, who are primarily retailers and wholesalers, are the primary source of revenue (and "headaches," so says Cullen Certain, manager of the Customer Service Department). The stockholders own Zimco and therefore are interested in its ongoing well-being and its dividends. The financial institutions service Zimco in much the same way that they service individuals; that is, Zimco deposits, withdraws, transfers, and invests money as needed to meet the company's liquidity requirements. Colleges and employment agencies are the primary source of Zimco's people resources. Zimco routinely uses the media, primarily newspapers, magazines, radio, and television, to advertise their products. Also, promotions and Zimco news items are released to local newspapers.

THE INTEGRATED DATA BASE

The only data store (the open-ended boxes) in Figure Z3–3 is Zimco's integrated data base. The data base symbol is repeated to simplify the presentation of the DFD. The diagonal line on the left end of the data-store symbols indicates that the data store is repeated elsewhere in the DFD.

To explain the concept of an integrated data base, we need to back up a few years and discuss Zimco's data base as it was prior to 1980. At that time, Zimco had several dozen files, each designed to meet a specific user group's requirements. When a file was designed and created, very little thought was given to how it would benefit Zimco as a whole. As a result, many very similar, but different files were created. For example, basic customer data were collected and maintained in separate files for the headquarters sales office, for the Distribution Department, for the Accounting Department, and for the Customer Service Department. Imagine, when customer data changed (e.g., the name of the purchasing agent), each file would have to be updated separately!

Conrad Innis recognized that *data redundancy* is costly. When he joined Zimco, he said, "data redundancy can be minimized by designing an *integrated data base* to serve Zimco as a whole, not a single department.

Over 300 workstations throughout Zimco Enterprises provide authorized persons with ready access to the integrated data base.
(Honeywell, Inc.)

To do this we'll need **database management system (DBMS)** software." DBMS software is discussed in more detail in Zimco Case Study 10.

Zimco first installed DBMS software in 1981 and has upgraded it several times since. The four categories of data included as part of Zimco's integrated data base are: *manufacturing/inventory, customer/sales, personnel,* and *general accounting.* The Technical Support Department, managed by Terri Suttor, is responsible for maintaining the integrated data base. Terri says, "Zimco employees are authorized access to all or part of the data base, depending on their need to know."

Zimco's integrated data base provides its managers with enormous flexibility in the types of reports that can be generated and the types of on-line inquiries that can be made. Otto Manning, VP of Operations, said recently that "the greater access to information provided by Zimco's integrated data base enables me to make better decisions. As a result, we are able to produce a quality product at less cost than our competitors."

DISCUSSION QUESTIONS

1. Identify the data elements that would provide the links between the four categories of data in Zimco's integrated data base (*manufacturing/ inventory, customer/sales, personnel, and general accounting*). For example, the customer account number data element is common to all data categories except personnel.

2. Describe the information flow between Zimco Enterprises and all levels of government, and between its suppliers, customers, and stockholders.

3. Describe the information flow between Zimco Enterprises and those financial institutions, colleges/agencies, and media organizations with whom they have business relations.

4. In the example of Figure Z3–2, identify and describe processes that would be subordinate to Process 2, "Create and Maintain Employee Data Base."

5. Conrad Innis and Sybil Allen created the MIS overview in Figure Z3–3 while using a software package that enabled them to interactively create a data flow diagram directly on the workstation display. Discuss the advantages of using an automated design tool versus pencils, templates, and paper to create the DFD.

6. Prior to the implementation of Zimco's integrated data base in 1981, CIS maintained 113 separate computer-based files. Most of these files supported autonomous, departmental information systems and had numerous instances of redundant data. Discuss the impact that redundant data have on the integrity or accuracy of data.

7. Would it be possible for Zimco Enterprises to maintain a skeleton information services department of about 10 people and use commercially available packaged software for all their computer application needs? Explain.

8. In Figure Z3–3, Zimco's MIS is logically organized into four major processes. Discuss an alternative organization that would involve five, six, or seven major processes. Discuss the advantages of such an organization.

CASE STUDY 4

Office Automation at Zimco

THE AUTOMATED OFFICE

One Monday morning last April, Sally Marcio, Zimco's VP of Sales and Marketing, came to work as usual in the Dallas office and greeted her assistant, Lynn Lester. "Good morning. Did you have a nice weekend?"

Lynn responded, "Very nice, thank you."

"Lynn, have you finished that report for the Burpo account? I'd like to make a few quick changes."

"Sure have. You can call it up on your workstation."

Sally was obviously happy that the report was ready. She replied, "I'll make those changes and route it via electronic mail to Burpo headquarters in St. Paul. If we don't have it to them by noon today, we may lose their business."

"Oh, by the way Sally, this new ad piece for the Qwert just arrived from the Art Department."

Seeing the finished product, Sally voiced her personal approval. "Wow! That new presentation graphics equipment has certainly improved the quality of work coming out of the Art Department. Before we send this to the Printing Department, we need to get approval from the four regional sales managers. Would you send each of them a facsimile copy for approval. Ask them to reply by electronic mail no later than 10 o'clock tomorrow morning."

"Also, Lynn, would you set up an emergency teleconference meeting with the plant managers in Reston, Becker, and Eugene. The topic will be the third-quarter production forecast."

"Consider it done. Each of them will have the message suggesting possible meeting times in their electronic mailboxes in a couple of minutes."

"Lynn, we'll also need to put a notice on Z-Buzz (Zimco's electronic bulletin board) about the availability of that new position in market research. That reminds me, don't let me forget to sit down this afternoon and run statistical summaries on the Stib research data. With our on-line statistics package, it shouldn't take more than a few minutes. It's hard to believe that I used to spend all day on these summaries." As Sally leaned back in her chair, she said, "You know Lynn, our automated office has sure made life a lot easier."

Secure in the fact that the day won't be all memos, calling, adding figures, and paper shuffling, Lynn responds, "I couldn't agree more."

As she sat down at her workstation to look over the Burpo report, Sally reminded Lynn, "I won't be in the office Friday. I'm going to telecommute and work on the annual market summary report."

OFFICE AUTOMATION APPLICATIONS

As you could probably gather from the scenario between Sally Marcio and Lynn Lester in the Sales and Marketing Division, Zimco Enterprises is a showplace for application of **office automation.** This case study is devoted to describing applications of office automation at Zimco. The term "office automation" refers collectively to those computer-based applications associated with general office work. Office automation applications include *word processing, electronic mail, image processing, voice processing, office information systems,* and *telecommuting.* All of these applications are available on both micro and mainframe computer systems at Zimco.

Peggy Peoples, VP of Personnel, did a study of the effects of office automation on the Personnel Division. The study revealed an increase in office productivity of almost 100 percent. The other divisions report improvements in office productivity of 50 to 75 percent. Preston Smith, the president, takes pride in the fact that "we are taking advantage of the potential of office automation." In the sections that follow, each of the applications of office automation is discussed in the context of how it is used at Zimco.

At Zimco, all office workers, including executives, are trained to use word processing and to send messages via electronic mail. Executives prefer editing their reports using word processing to making red-pencil revisions to a hard copy for a secretary to key in. They also like having the option of sending a memo electronically, thereby circumventing the time-consuming step of producing a hard copy.
(Quotron Systems, Inc.)

WORD PROCESSING

Word processing, the cornerstone of office automation, revolves around written communication and is found virtually everywhere at Zimco. Managers, secretaries, engineers, and just about everyone else who has a need to write a memo, a letter, a report, or just jot down ideas has become a word processing addict. Word processing means using the computer to enter, store, manipulate, and print text in letters, memos, reports, books, and so on.

Peggy Peoples explained: "The word is out on word processing. People love it! With word processing, managers and secretaries alike have only to key in the initial draft of whatever they are doing, be it a memo or a report; then they make revisions and corrections to the disk-based draft until it is ready to be printed in final form."

The fundamental concepts of word processing are discussed briefly below. These concepts are discussed in more detail in the special skills section of this text entitled, "Microcomputer Productivity Software."

Formatting a Document. When you *format* a document, you are describing the size of the print page and how you want the document to look when printed. As with the typewriter, you must set the left and right margins, the tab settings, line spacing, and character spacing. You can even justify on both the left and the right margins, such as in newspapers and books. Depending on the software, some or all of these specifications are made in a *layout line*.

Entering Text. To begin preparation of the document, all you have to do is start keying-in the text. Text is entered in **replace mode** or **insert mode.** When in replace mode, the character that you enter *overstrikes* the character in the cursor position. When in insert mode, you can enter *additional* text. Word processing permits *full-screen editing*. That is, you can move the **cursor** (the blinking character that indicates the location of the next input) to any position in the document to insert or replace text.

Features. Word processing features presented here are common to most word processing software packages. Two of the handiest features are the *copy* and *move* commands. With the copy feature, you can select a word, a phrase, or as much contiguous text as you desire, and copy it to another portion of the document. To do this, you simply issue the copy command, then tell the computer what to copy and where to put it. At the end of the copy procedure, two exact copies of the text are present in the document. The move command works in a similar manner, except that the text you select is moved to the location that you designate and the original text is deleted.

George Brooks, the Northern Regional Sales Manager, uses word processing to generate memos to his staff. Figure Z4–1 illustrates how George edited a memo to the field staff to make it more readable. He did this by "moving" the last sentence from the end of the memo to just after the first sentence.

The *search* or *find* feature permits George to search through the entire document and identify all occurrences of a particular character string. For example, George decided to switch the meeting announced in the memo of Figure Z4–1 from Thursday to Friday. If he wanted to search the memo for all occurrences of "Thursday", he would simply initiate the search command and type in "Thursday". The cursor would be immediately positioned at the first occurrence of "Thursday". He can also *search and replace*. For example, he can selectively replace "Thursday" with "Friday". George, however, selected the option that allows him to *replace* all occurrences instantly with a *global search and replace* (see Figure Z4–2).

Several years ago, a letter to employees went out over President Preston Smith's signature. A couple of "typos" resulted in misspelled words and

```
To:       Field Sales Staff
From:     G. Brooks, Northern Sales Manager
Re:       Weekly Briefing Session

     The Sales Department's weekly briefing session will be
held at 9:00 a.m. this Thursday.  Last month's sales figures
and new sales strategies for the Tegler and Qwert will be
discussed.  See you Thursday!  We'll meet in the second floor
conference room.
```

```
To:       Field Sales Staff
From:     G. Brooks, Northern Sales Manager
Re:       Weekly Briefing Session

     The Sales Department's weekly briefing session will be
held at 9:00 a.m. this Thursday.  We'll meet in the second
floor conference room.  Last month's sales figures and new
sales strategies for the Tegler and Qwert will be discussed.
See you Thursday!
```

FIGURE Z4–1
The Move Command in Word Processing

In the first screen, the text to be moved is identified. The cursor is then positioned at the "move to" location—in our example, after the first sentence. In the second screen, the move command is issued and the designated text is "moved" to a location following the first sentence.

```
To:       Field Sales Staff
From:     G. Brooks, Northern Sales Manager
Re:       Weekly Briefing Session

     The Sales Department's weekly briefing session will be
held at 9:00 a.m. this Friday.  We'll meet in the second
floor conference room.  Last month's sales figures and new
sales strategies for the Tegler and Qwert will be discussed.
See you Friday!
- - - - - - - - - - - - - - - - - - - - - - - - - - - - - - -
Search for: Thursday
Replace with: Friday
Manual or Automatic (M/A): A
Number of replacements: 2
```

FIGURE Z4–2
The Global Search and Replace Command in Word Processing

All occurrences of the word "Thursday" in the memo of Figure Z4–1 are replaced with "Friday" when a global search and replace command is issued.

an embarrassment to Preston Smith. After that unfortunate mishap, Preston declared that "all letters must be checked electronically for misspelled words before they are sent." People use the *spell* feature to do this. The spell feature checks every word in the text against an electronic dictionary (usually from 75,000 to 150,000 words), then alerts the user if a word is not in the dictionary.

Other word processing features, such as *centering* of titles *indenting*, *boldface*, *underline*, *header* and *trailer labels*, and *pagination* (numbering of pages), are discussed in the special skills section, "Microcomputer Productivity Software."

Merging Text with a Data Base. Besides providing a faster and easier way to type, the text generated by word processing can be merged with data from a data base. For example, a typical word processing application could involve the preparation of the same letter that is to be sent to a number of people.

When Zimco announced the enhanced version of the Qwert, each regional sales manager sent a "personal" letter to every Zimco customer in their respective regions. There are thousands of customers in each region. The secretary with a regular typewriter would have only two choices: either type thousands of separate letters or type one letter and photocopy it. In the business world in general and at Zimco in particular, the latter is not acceptable. Using word processing, a secretary can type the letter once, store it on the disk, then simply merge the customer name-and-address file (also stored on the disk) with the letter. The letters are then printed with the proper addresses and salutations. Figure Z4–3 illustrates how the Qwert announcement letter is merged with the customer name-and-address file to produce a "personalized" letter.

ELECTRONIC MAIL

Because Zimco's computers, including PCs, are linked together in a *computer network*, employees are able to route messages to each other via **electronic mail.** A message can be a note, letter, report, chart, or even a procedures manual. Each person at Zimco is assigned an "electronic mailbox" on disk storage in which messages are received and stored. Preston Smith, or any other employee at Zimco, "opens" and "reads" his electronic mail by simply going to the nearest workstation and recalling the message(s) from storage.

Recently, Monroe Green, the VP of Finance and Accounting, asked his assistant to call a meeting for the purpose of discussing recent revisions to the federal tax code. She sent a message to each accounting manager via electronic mail, thereby avoiding the time-consuming ritual of "tele-

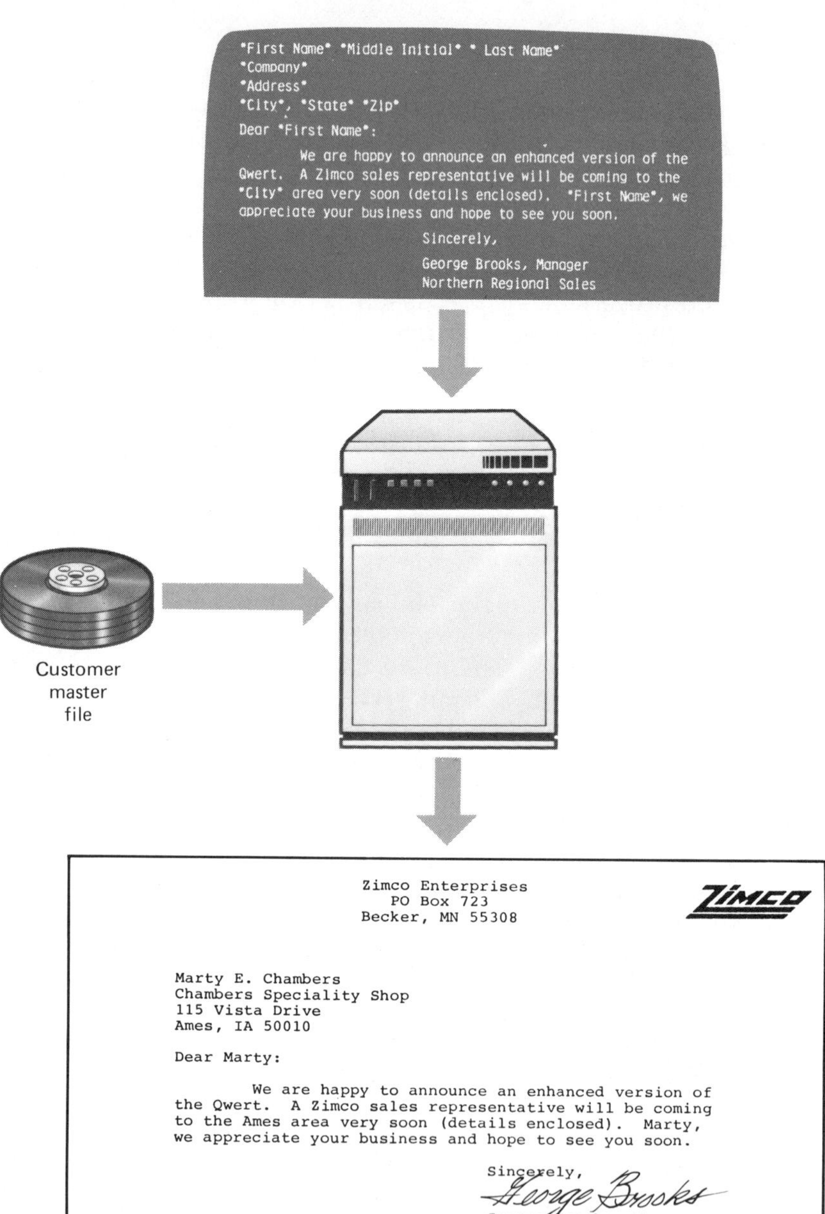

FIGURE Z4–3
Merging Data with Word Processing

The names and addresses from a customer master file are retrieved from secondary storage and merged with the text of a letter. In the actual letter, the appropriate data items are inserted for *First Name*, *Company*, *Address*, *City*, and so on. In this way, a "personalized" letter can be sent to each customer.

phone tag." She entered a single message at her workstation and designated a preassigned routing code (all accounting managers). When sent, the message is routed to the electronic mailboxes of the all accounting managers. Each manager "opens the mail" by displaying the message at his or her workstation. At Zimco, an employee "logs on" by entering a password and authorization code at a workstation. A message, such as "Check mail", is displayed if there is any mail in his or her electronic mailbox.

Electronic mail is a common application at Zimco. It's a lot faster, more effective, and a good deal less expensive than interoffice mail.

IMAGE PROCESSING

Image processing involves the creation, storage, and distribution of pictorial information. There are two levels of image processing sophistication at Zimco.

At the first level, *facsimile* equipment, which has been around since the 1960s, transfers hard-copy documents via telephone lines to another office. The process is similar to making a copy on a copying machine, except that the original is inserted in a facsimile machine at one office and a hard copy is produced on another facsimile machine in another office. In the office automation scenario at the first of this case study, Sally Marcio needed quick approval on a Qwert ad piece, so she sent facsimile copies of the ad piece to the regional sales managers.

Recent technological innovations have expanded the scope of image processing. Conrad Innis, the VP of CIS, has commissioned a feasibility study to assess the feasibility and applicability of offering more sophisticated image processing capabilities to users at Zimco, specifically an *image processor*. An image processor uses a camera to scan and digitize the image; then the digitized image is stored on a disk. The image can be handwritten notes, photographs, drawings, or anything that can be digitized. In digitized form, the image can be retrieved, displayed, altered, merged with text, stored, and sent via data communications to one or several remote locations.

Preliminary indications are that Zimco may remove all facsimile equipment and replace it with image processors. The image processors provide greater flexibility and can be integrated with existing MISs.

VOICE PROCESSING

Voice processing applications at Zimco include *voice message switching* and *teleconferencing*. The workstation for voice message switching (a store-and-forward "voice mailbox" system) is a touch-tone telephone.

Voice message switching accomplishes the same function as electronic mail, except that the hard copy is not available. When a manager sends a message, the voice is digitized and stored on a magnetic disk for later retrieval. The message is routed to the destination(s) the manager designates (using the telephone's keyboard); then it is heard upon request by the intended receiver(s). Zimco's voice store-and-forward system permits any employee to send one or many messages with just one phone call.

Twice a year, Zimco sales reps from the four regional offices meet to discuss sales strategies via teleconferencing. Teleconferencing enables people in different locations to see and talk to each other and to visually share charts and other meeting materials. Zimco doesn't have their own teleconferencing facility, so they use public facilities. Each facility has video cameras, monitors, and a meeting table. The voice and video of teleconferencing are supported by the telephone network. The idea behind teleconferencing is that people who are geographically scattered can meet without the need for time-consuming and expensive travel.

Zimco has elected not to use teleconferencing as a substitute for all travel. Otto Manning, the VP of Operations, observed that "the controlled teleconferencing environment does not transmit subtle nonverbal communication, which is so important to human understanding.

OFFICE INFORMATION SYSTEMS

Zimco has several small information systems that address traditional office tasks. For example, one system allows employees to keep their personal *calendars* on-line. As workers schedule activities, they block out times in their electronic calendars. There are definite advantages to having a central data base of personal calendars. Recently, Preston Smith's assistant scheduled a meeting of the VPs to review the impact of some unfavorable publicity. To do this, his assistant entered the names of the VPs and the expected duration of the meeting. The *conference scheduling* system searched the calendars of vice-presidents and suggested possible meeting times. Preston's assistant then selected a meeting time, and the VPs were notified by electronic mail. Of course, their calendars were automatically updated to reflect the meeting time.

One of the most popular office information systems at Zimco is the company *directory*. The directory contains basic personnel data: name, title, department, location, and phone number. To "look up" someone's telephone number, all an employee has to do is enter the person's name into the nearest workstation. Associated data are displayed within 2 seconds. The beauty of the directory data base is that it is always up to date, unlike the old hard-copy directories that Peggy Peoples said "never seemed to have the current titles or phone numbers."

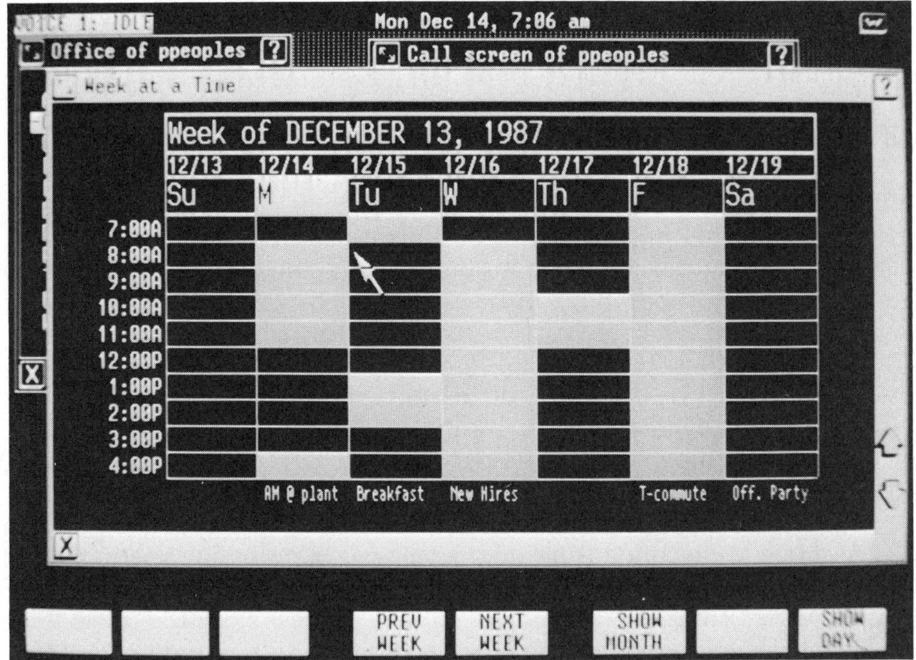

The "calendar" is one of many timesaving office information systems at Zimco.
(Long and Associates)

Other office systems at Zimco allow employees to organize *personal notes*, keep *diaries*, document ideas in a *preformatted outline*, and keep a *tickler* file. When employees log-on in the morning, the tickler file automatically reminds them of "things to do" for that day.

TELECOMMUTING

Each department at Zimco has at least one, and usually a couple, of portable microcomputers. These micros fold up to about the size of an attaché case and can be easily carried between the office and home. Managers often take a micro home with them to take advantage of the peace and quiet. These portable micros can be used as stand-alone computer systems or they can serve as workstations linked to Zimco's mainframe computer system. The latter is known as **telecommuting.**

Zimco's commitment to the support of office automation and on-line access to information systems has made telecommuting very popular and a feasible alternative way to accomplish one's job. Each professional-level employee is permitted to telecommute up to one day per week, as long as the telecommuting is done on Monday or Friday. All group meetings are scheduled on the midweek days. Whenever someone needs a few hours, or perhaps a day, of uninterrupted time to accomplish a task that does not require direct personal interaction, they block out part or all of a Monday or Friday on their personal calendars, then telecommute.

Monroe Green, the VP of Accounting and Finance, says, "I telecommute to prepare the quarterly financial statements." All of the information he needs is at his fingertips and he finishes in one day at home what used to take him a week. Preston Smith stated emphatically: "I got sick and tired of spending nights up in my office. By telecommuting, I'm at least within earshot of my wife and kids. Also, I like to get into more comfortable clothes." Conrad Innis and numerous other Zimco employees have their own PC. Conrad explains one of his many uses of his PC: "Every Monday evening I write out the agenda for my Tuesday morning staff meeting. I then send a summary of the agenda via electronic mail to my managers so that they will see it first thing Tuesday morning when they log in."

At Zimco, telecommuting may never catch on as an alternative to working in the office, but it has proven to be a boon to productivity for many people. Zimco's management feels that telecommuting offers a lot of advantages to motivated workers who want to telecommute occasionally. They encourage telecommuting, but only in those instances where the opportunities for improved productivity are apparent.

DISCUSSION QUESTIONS

1. Identify all of the office automation applications mentioned, directly or indirectly, by Sally Marcio or Lynn Lester in the office scenario at the first of this case study.

2. When doing word processing, under what circumstances would you enter text in replace mode? In insert mode? Which mode would you use most often, and why?

3. Which office automation applications have the potential to reduce the amount of time that Zimco employees spend on the telephone? Explain.

4. After considerable debate, Zimco management decided to allow employees to telecommute one day each week. Some of the benefits of telecommuting were presented in the case study. What do you think were some of management's negative concerns about telecommuting?

5. What advantages does voice message switching have over electronic mail? What advantages does electronic mail have over voice message switching? Why do you suppose that Zimco opted to implement both?

6. How would the manager of the Customer Service Department at Zimco benefit from word processing?

7. Discuss the keystroke-by-keystroke procedures for sending and retrieving electronic mail at your college (your company).

8. What advantages does an image processor have over facsimile equipment?

CASE STUDY 5

Micros at Zimco

MICROCOMPUTER APPLICATIONS AND OPPORTUNITIES

Shortly after Conrad Innis, VP of Computer and Information Services (CIS), began work at Zimco in 1981, he invited the other four VPs and the president, Preston Smith, to spend a Friday and Saturday with him in an informal round-table discussion. The topic was "Computer Applications at Zimco." The six executives met at Beaver Bend State Park in southeastern Oklahoma to get away from the everyday routine (and the telephone) at Zimco headquarters in Dallas.

Conrad's objective was to get Zimco's top management into "thinking computers and automation"—and it worked. Conrad made the point that every system does not have to be designed and developed by the Computer and Information Services Division. He brought the point home by announcing that Zimco was in the top 10 percent of all manufacturing companies in the number of micros per white-collar employee. He said, "Unlike most companies, Zimco has the hardware to support user-developed systems." When Sally Marcio, VP of Sales and Marketing, asked for an example, Conrad talked about using microcomputer-based word processing and database software to announce product promotional campaigns. "These software productivity tools enable us to send 'personalized' letters to our customers."

Conrad told Peggy Peoples of Personnel that "there is no need for us to produce a twice-weekly printout of all personnel records." He said,

"The personnel system could be placed on-line such that records could be accessed and updated from any of the workstations in the Personnel Division."

Conrad came well prepared for the meeting. He had examples of how computers in general, and micros in specific, could be applied in the various divisions *to save time and money*, and *to allow managers to make better decisions*. He encouraged managers to "take advantage of the miracles of modern technology."

Conrad encouraged the VPs to buy micros for their divisions because of their *dual-purpose capabilities*. "You can use micros in stand-alone mode to handle small user-developed systems that are applicable to a particular department or individual. Or they can serve as workstations that can be linked to Zimco's mainframes." At present, Zimco has 345 workstations throughout the enterprise, about 200 of which are microcomputers.

The informal meeting at Beaver Bend State Park focused attention on the potential for computer applications at Zimco. Today, Zimco is a leader in all areas of computer-based automation, both in the office and in the plant. The following sections tell a little about how the four line divisions at Zimco are currently using micros to improve productivity and to provide better and more timely information. Other case studies address Zimco's management information system, which is supported by CIS.

MICROS IN THE SALES
AND MARKETING DIVISION

When the effervescent VP of Sales and Marketing, Sally Marcio, heard about all the things that micros could do for her division, she could hardly contain her excitement. Sally was definitely primed for ideas on further automation of sales and marketing activities. She remarked bluntly that "if we fall behind our competition in the area of customer service, we'll lose market share. To provide the best customer service possible, we must take advantage of what computers have to offer." After that remark, Conrad couldn't resist quoting one of his MIS maxims: "Even if you're on the right track, you'll get run over if you just sit there! "

Today, Zimco is gaining, not losing, market share. Sally attributes their success in sales to "an energetic field staff and effective use of computers." Sally described just one of the many ways that micros are used in the Sales and Marketing Division.

"The Customer Service Department, which reports to me, responds to a variety of customer inquiries, from order status to price information. They do this from their microcomputer workstations, which are linked

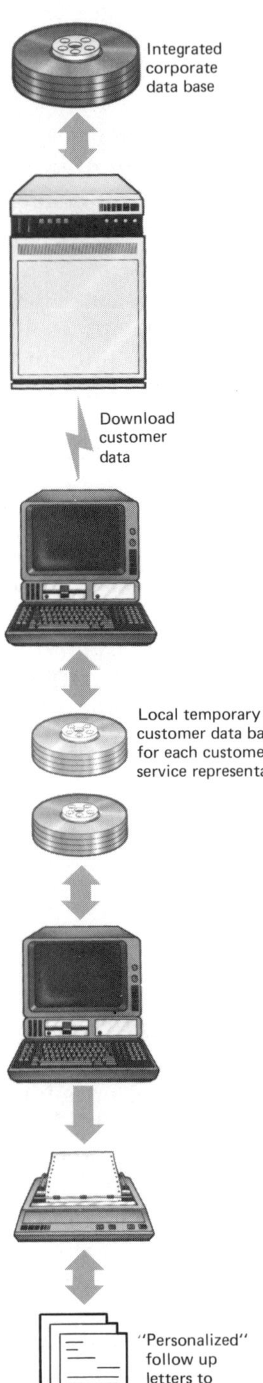

FIGURE Z5–1
Downloading Data to Micro Workstations from the Mainframe

Micros are used as workstations and for stand-alone operation in the Sales and Marketing Division. At the end of the day, customer service representatives request that data be downloaded to their micros. The representatives then use the data to write and send personalized follow-up letters to customers who called in during the day.

to the corporate data base. At the end of the day, each rep requests that the names and addresses of those customers with whom they have interacted be *downloaded* from the corporate data base to disk storage on their microcomputer workstations." She went on to explain that each customer service representative has a micro, with disk storage, and they share a desktop laser printer.

Sally said that during the last hour or so of the day, the customer service workstations become stand-alone computer systems so that representatives can use word processing and mail-merge software to write "personalized" letters to the customers that they talked with during the day. This activity is illustrated graphically in Figure Z5–1.

The basic form letter "confirms Zimco's continuing commitment to customer service." She said that about 50 percent of the time the reps add a sentence or so that relates to the customer's particular situation. The name and address and the body of the letter are on disk. The rep has only to merge the name and address with the appropriate form letter, perhaps add a personal note, then route the letter to the printer.

Sally says that this "immediate and personal follow-up to a customer's inquiry has provided immeasurable goodwill and set us apart from our competitors."

MICROS IN THE FINANCE AND ACCOUNTING DIVISION

The Finance and Accounting Division has been the principal user of computers since the day the first computer arrived at Zimco in 1959. Ironically, prior to the high-level meeting at Beaver Bend, the VP of the Finance and Accounting Division, Monroe Green, was complacent with their level of automation (primarily accounts receivable, accounts payable, general ledger, and payroll) and had no desire to increase his division's "dependence on computers." He was convinced that "mainframe computers are for business and micros are toys."

Well, after Conrad demonstrated the potential of a microcomputer, Monroe changed his tune. Now he is gradually replacing the VDTs in his division with micros so that his people will have the best of both worlds—direct access to the integrated corporate data base on the mainframe and the potential for stand-alone operation as well.

One micro application that Monroe finds particularly helpful is an electronic spreadsheet *template* of Zimco's income statements for the past two years. The template, which is simply a spreadsheet model, contains a column that allows him to produce a pro rata income statement for next year (see Figure Z5–2). Monroe uses the spreadsheet software to create "what if" scenarios. For example, Otto Manning is implementing

A2: 'ZIMCO INCOME STATEMENT ($1000)

	A	B	C	D
1				
2	ZIMCO INCOME STATEMENT ($1000)	Next Year	This Year	Last Year
3				
4	Net sales	$183,600	$153,000	$144,780
5	Cost of sales & op. expenses			
6	Cost of goods sold	116,413	115,260	117,345
7	Depreciation	4,125	4,125	1,500
8	Selling & admin. expenses	19,875	19,875	15,000
9				
10	Operating profit	$43,187	$13,740	$10,935
11	Other income			
12	Dividends and interest	405	405	300
13				
14	TOTAL INCOME	$43,592	$14,145	$11,235
15	Less: interest on bonds	2,025	2,025	2,025
16				
17	Income before tax	41,567	12,120	9,210
18	Provision for income tax	18,777	5,475	4,160
19				
20	NET PROFIT FOR YEAR	$22,790	$6,645	$5,050

A34: 'FORECAST VARIABLES FOR NEXT YEAR'S PRO RATA INCOME STATEMENT

	A	B	C	D
21				
22				
23				
24				
25	Shares outstanding	6,300,000	6,000,000	6,000,000
26	Market price	$21.25	$14.00	$13.00
27	Earnings per share	$3.62	$1.11	$0.84
28				
29	Price-earnings ratio	5.87	12.64	15.45
30				
31				
32				
33				
34	FORECAST VARIABLES FOR NEXT YEAR'S PRO RATA INCOME STATEMENT			
35				
36	Projected change in sales		20.00%	
37	Projected change in cost of goods sold		1.00%	
38	Projected change in administrative expenses		0.00%	
39				
40				

FIGURE Z5–2

An Optimistic Pro Rata Income Statement for Zimco

Electronic spreadsheet software and a spreadsheet template were employed to prepare an optimistic pro rata income statement for Zimco for next year. The spreadsheet user enters only the values of the three forecast variables (sales, cost of goods sold, and administrative expenses); the rest of next year's income statement is filled in automatically.

a number of cost-cutting measures and he anticipates that the Operations Division can hold the "cost of goods sold" to a 1 percent increase, even though more products will be built and shipped. Sally Marcio predicts that next year will be a "great year" and net sales will increase by 20 percent. Preston Smith has asked all managers to "hold the line" on all selling and administrative expenses; therefore, these expenses are expected to remain about the same.

With spreadsheet software, Monroe was able to answer the question: "What if the cost-of-goods-sold increased by 1 percent, sales increased by 20 percent, and everything else remained the same for the coming year?" Monroe entered only the three forecast variables to get the pro rata income statement (the "Next Year" column) printout shown in Figure Z5–2. Other calculations (e.g., sales with a 20 percent increase, net profit, earnings per share, taxes) are performed automatically because the appropriate formulas are built into the spreadsheet template. Some entries are unchanged (e.g., depreciation, dividends, and interest); however, if Monroe wanted to reflect a change in depreciation, he would simply change the value of the "depreciation" entry.

Monroe says, "we at Zimco are very interested in monitoring the _price-earnings ratio,_ or the relationship that exists between the _earnings per share_ and the _market price_ of our stock." Calculations for the price-earnings ratio are shown at the bottom of the spreadsheet in Figure Z5–2. The earnings per share is calculated by dividing the net profit by the number of shares outstanding (e.g., for "This Year," $6,645,000/6,000,000 = $1.11). The price-earnings ratio is calculated by dividing the current market price of Zimco stock by the earnings per share (e.g., for "This Year," $14.00/$1.11 = 12.64).

In the "Next Year" column of the price-earnings ratio section of the spreadsheet, Monroe asked: "What if we issued 300,000 new shares of stock and the market price of Zimco stock reached $21.25; what would the P-E ratio be?" Monroe can easily add other financial ratios (e.g., current ratio, net profit ratio) to the spreadsheet if he so desires because he has the balance sheet data on another part of the same spreadsheet template.

As you can imagine, the president, Preston Smith, was ecstatic with the projected profit and the price-earnings ratio. However, over the years Preston has learned to temper the always-optimistic estimates made by Otto and Sally with a touch of reality, so he created his own pessimistic pro rata income statement. This income statement reflects what he called the "worst case scenario." Again, Preston needed only to change the three forecast variables to get the results of Figure Z5–3. As Preston observed, "the estimated P-E ratio is very sensitive to the estimates for sales and expenses. There's a lot of difference between a P-E of 5.87 and a P-E of 17.94!"

Of course, the possibilities of what Monroe and Preston can do with

```
A2: 'ZIMCO INCOME STATEMENT ($1000)
```

	A	B	C	D
1	==================================	==========	==========	==========
2	ZIMCO INCOME STATEMENT ($1000)	Next Year	This year	Last Year
3	----------------------------------			
4	Net sales	$157,590	$153,000	$144,780
5	Cost of sales & op. expenses			
6	Cost of goods sold	117,565	115,260	117,345
7	Depreciation	4,125	4,125	1,500
8	Selling & admin. expenses	20,670	19,875	15,000
9				
10	Operating profit	$15,230	$13,740	$10,935
11	Other income			
12	Dividends and interest	405	405	300
13				
14	TOTAL INCOME	$15,635	$14,145	$11,235
15	Less: interest on bonds	2,025	2,025	2,025
16				
17	Income before tax	13,610	12,120	9,210
18	Provisions for income tax	6,148	5,475	4,160
19				
20	NET PROFIT FOR YEAR	$7,462	$6,645	$5,050

```
A34: 'FORECAST VARIABLES FOR NEXT YEAR'S PRO RATA INCOME STATEMENT
```

	A	B	C	D
21	==	==========	==========	==========
22				
23				
24	==	==========	==========	==========
25	Shares outstanding	6,300,000	6,000,000	6,000,000
26	Market price	$21.25	$14.00	$13.00
27	Earnings per share	$1.18	$1.11	$0.84
28				
29	Price-earnings ratio	17.94	12.64	15.45
30	==	==========	==========	==========
31				
32				
33	==	==========	==========	==========
34	FORECAST VARIABLES FOR NEXT YEAR'S PRO RATA INCOME STATEMENT			
35	--			
36	Projected change in sales		3.00%	
37	Projected change in cost of goods sold		2.00%	
38	Projected change in administrative expenses		4.00%	
39	==	==========	==========	==========
40				

FIGURE Z5–3

A Pessimistic Pro Rata Income Statement for Zimco

The same electronic spreadsheet template used to produce the printout of Figure Z5–2 was used to produce a pessimistic pro rata income statement. Again, the only entries needed to produce the pro rata income statement for the coming year are the three forecast variables.

electronic spreadsheet software and micros are endless. The special skills section in this book on "Microcomputer Productivity Software" includes details on the function, concepts, and uses of electronic spreadsheet software. This section also includes details on how the income statement spreadsheet template of Figure Z5–2 is developed.

MICROS IN THE PERSONNEL DIVISION

The Personnel Division receives announcements of position openings each day from several departments. They respond by preparing releases to local newspapers. These releases are usually, but not always, placed in the "classified ads" section.

Peggy Peoples, VP of Personnel, explained the problems associated with placing ads in the newspaper and a computer-based solution. "We are obligated by company policy," she said, "to make these positions available to existing employees before we solicit outside applicants." In the past, circulating position announcements internally took several days, and only one of eight position openings is filled from within. Managers complained that delaying a public release of the available positions meant that they had to operate shorthanded longer than necessary."

A manager in the personnel division at Zimco uses his micro and electronic spreadsheet software to ask "what if" questions regarding a proposal for a new benefits package.
(Sperry Corporation)

Conrad Innis suggested a solution: "Don't use hard copy to announce position openings. Use our **electronic bulletin board.**" That's just what Peggy did. Now, minutes after a position opening is received from a department, it is posted on the Zimco Bulletin Board System (ZBBS). The ZBBS is affectionately known to Zimco employees as "Z-Buzz."

To post an item to Z-Buzz or scan its contents, employees simply log-on to the nearest workstation. Z-Buzz includes typical bulletin board items such as softball scores, "for sale" items, messages of all kinds, and of course, position announcements. Workstations, most of which are micros, are everywhere at Zimco, even in the halls, the cafeterias, and the executive washroom. Those employees that would like to transfer to another job or another office routinely scan the position announcements on Z-Buzz.

The position announcements appear immediately in the company's electronic bulletin board and they appear the same or the next day in local newspapers. The Personnel Division runs want ads in five to 12 newspapers every day of the year. For 30 years, they mailed or called in the ads to newspapers. Conrad Innis suggested that they will "save a lot of time and money by using their micros to transmit the ads electroni-

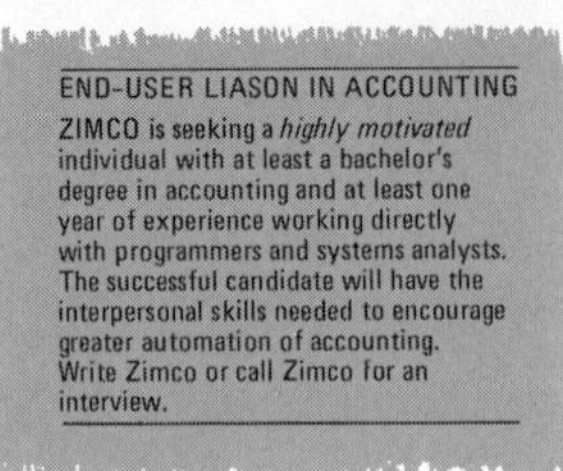

FIGURE Z5–4
The Text of a Position Announcement
The text of a position announcement is shown prior to its electronic distribution to area newspapers and as it appears in the classified ads section.

cally." Now people in the Personnel Division compose the text of the ads and insert standard electronic publishing symbols that designate size of print, centering of text, and so on. They then use their data communications software to automatically "dial up" the computers at the newspapers and transmit the ads electronically. Compositors at the various newspapers simply insert the ads in the appropriate section. No other keystrokes are required. Figure Z5–4 illustrates what is sent and how it appears in the "Want Ads." Because Zimco enters and formats their own ads, they pay substantially less than do other advertisers.

MICROS IN THE OPERATIONS DIVISION

Otto Manning, VP of Operations, said that "one of his division's biggest problems is planning and tracking projects." On numerous occasions in the past, he has requested help from CIS in implementing a mainframe-based project management system. The last system he proposed would cost $22,000 and require two person-months of programmer time to implement. His proposal, however, was a low-priority activity in the CIS backlog of user service requests.

Conrad Innis suggested to Otto that he consider a microcomputer-based project management system that cost $495. The system could be installed and used by the project managers in the Operations Division—without any assistance from CIS!

Otto took Conrad's advice. He even purchased a **site license** for $1600. The site license permits the duplication, distribution, and use of the software package within Zimco Enterprises. In contrast, the license agreement for the $495 version prohibited duplication; therefore, it could be used only by one manager at a time. The hardware needed to run the project management system, that is, the micros and associated peripheral devices, was already available. Today, all projects within the Operations Division are scheduled and monitored using the micro-based project management system.

The Research and Development Department is currently developing a second-generation Qwert, tentatively named the Qwert-Plus. Figure Z5–5 illustrates a bar chart that was produced for the Qwert-Plus development project. The project management system produces bar charts and a variety of reports: "Ahead/Behind Report," "Project Personpower Utilization Report," and the "Project Costs Report," to mention a few.

Otto Manning later remarked: "And to think that we implemented a computer-based project management system with $1600, our existing micros, and without assistance from CIS." This is the trend, not only at Zimco, but elsewhere. Users are finding that they can attend to many of

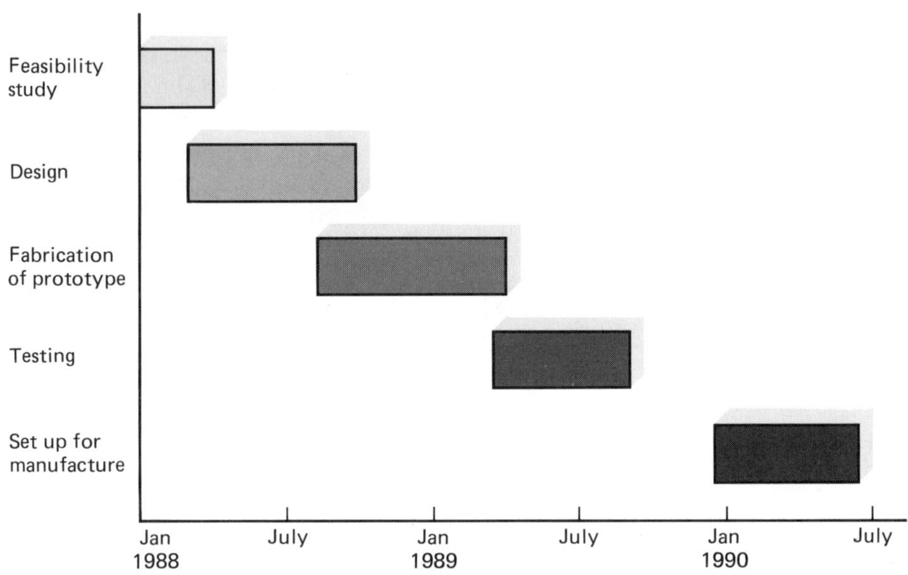

FIGURE Z5–5
Bar Chart for the Qwert-Plus Development Project
This bar chart is an output from a microcomputer-based project management system
that is used by the Research and Development Department to monitor and track
projects.

their computing needs by simply taking full advantage of their existing
micros and a plethora of user-friendly micro-based software packages.

DISCUSSION QUESTIONS

1. Why do you think Conrad Innis, the VP of CIS, felt it necessary to
   invite Zimco's top management to an out-of-the-way retreat to talk
   about "Computer Applications at Zimco"?

2. Zimco is in the top 10 percent of all manufacturing companies in
   the number of micros per white-collar worker. Does this reflect frivo-
   lous spending or a conscious effort to make effective use of available
   technology. Explain.

3. Customer service representatives spend almost 70 percent of their
   day interacting directly with customers. Approximately one hour each
   day is spent preparing courtesy follow-up letters, primarily to enhance
   goodwill between Zimco and its customers. Do you think the "personalized" letters are a worthwhile effort? Why or why not?

4. The case study describes how the Sales and Marketing Division takes advantage of the dual-purpose capabilities of micros in the Customer Service Department. Discuss how other departments in the same division can do the same.

5. A company policy requires that a warning label be affixed to the front of every microcomputer at Zimco. The label reads: "This computer is not to be used for the unlawful duplication of copyright software." What do you suppose prompted Zimco's top management to implement such a policy?

6. Describe an electronic spreadsheet template that would be helpful to all four regional sales managers.

7. Compare Monroe Green's and Preston Smith's electronic spreadsheet analysis of Zimco's pro rata income statement for the coming year (Figures Z5–2 and Z5–3). If they were to compare notes, what do you think would be their next step in the analysis? Explain.

8. Besides announcing internal position openings, identify other management uses of Z-Buzz, Zimco's electronic bulletin board system, that involve the enterprise-wide distribution of information.

CASE STUDY 6

Microcomputer Acquisition Policy and Procedures at Zimco

THE PC PROLIFERATION PROBLEM

At present, Zimco has 345 workstations throughout the enterprise, about 200 of which are microcomputers. All micros can serve as stand-alone systems or as workstations. The overwhelming majority of these micros are HAL PCs or HAL-compatible PCs, but it wasn't always that way. This movement in the direction of HAL PCs or HAL compatibles is by design. When Conrad Innis, the VP of Computer and Information Services, arrived on the scene in 1981, his focus was mainframe activities. But by early 1983, the "PC proliferation problem" had become acute and needed attention.

In early 1983, Zimco had 42 micros: 10 Oranges, 12 HALs, 15 RTS-88s, and 5 others, all from different vendors. Conrad was concerned because micro users were depending on his CIS people to provide technical support. In an executive meeting, Conrad said: "Our CIS programmers and analysts are spending an inordinate amount of their time supporting micros from eight different vendors."

Initially, users viewed the purchase price of the micros as the majority of the expense associated with buying a micro. Some found out later that the successful implementation of a micro may result in costs of several times the purchase price. Conrad circulated a blunt memo to all Zimco employees who had enough discretionary buying power to purchase a micro. In effect, the memo said to cease and desist buying micros

Over half of the workstations at Zimco are microcomputers. About half of those have a dedicated printer and the remainder share a printer with one or two other micros.
(Dataproducts Corporation)

until you know what you are doing. Managers were buying micros without any forethought as to what they wanted to do with them.

Being responsible for the effective use of computer resources at Zimco, Conrad decided to confront the "PC proliferation problem" and establish a policy regarding the acquisition of micros. He wanted to avoid the plight of those companies that did not set a standard. These companies ended up with a wide variety of micros, and more often than not, the programs and data were not **compatible;** that is, programs and data prepared for one micro could not be used on another. The policy and associated guidelines established at Zimco for the acquisition of micros are discussed in this case study.

ZIMCO'S MICROCOMPUTER REVIEW BOARD

The first action taken by Conrad to address PC proliferation at Zimco was to establish a *Microcomputer Review Board*. The board, which was

to meet on the first working Wednesday of each month, was given five
fundamental charges.

1. Establish guidelines for the acquisition of microcomputer hardware,
   specifying which micros and associated peripheral devices would
   be supported by CIS personnel.
2. Establish guidelines for the acquisition of microcomputer software,
   specifying which microcomputer productivity software tools (e.g.,
   electronic spreadsheet, word processing, database, graphics, communications, and idea processor) would be supported by CIS personnel.
3. Review and approve/disapprove all user requests to purchase microcomputer hardware or software.
4. Set up and monitor a volume microcomputer purchase program that
   enables departments and employees to purchase a micro hardware
   and software at substantial discounts.
5. Educate users in the purchase and acquisition of microcomputer hardware and software.

The Microcomputer Review Board is composed of five department heads,
one from each of the five divisions at Zimco. The chairperson is always
the manager of the Programming Department in CIS, currently Gram Mertz.

Selecting a "Standard" Micro for Zimco

As you can imagine, there was considerable debate as to which micro
or micros should become the standard at Zimco. Before making their
decision, the review board solicited input from throughout the enterprise.
Preston Smith, the president, was a proponent of HAL PCs. Conrad Innis
and Peggy Peoples, the VP of Personnel, were high on the Orange PCs.
Virtually everyone in manufacturing wanted the new T&T multiuser PCs
to be selected as the standard.

The board took the conservative route and selected a micro that had,
in effect, become the de facto standard for business microcomputers—
the HAL PC. They considered selecting another noncompatible micro
as an "alternative standard," but the members unanimously agreed that
having to provide technical support to two very different micros would
place too much of a burden on CIS personnel. The board's decision to
choose HAL PCs was based primarily on the availability of software.
Chairperson Gram Mertz justified the board's decision: "We felt that even
though several of the other top candidates were more user friendly, they
simply don't offer the scope of software that is available for the HAL
PC."

Because so much software was being written to run on the HAL PC,
a number of companies manufacture HAL "clones," or micros that run

the same software and accomplish the same functions as the HAL PC. The board designated one of these HAL PC-compatible micros, the Zap-100, as an acceptable alternative to the HAL PC. The Zap-100 was priced 30 percent lower than the HAL PC. This gave users a choice.

Selecting "Standard" Software

The Microcomputer Review Board's charge was to evaluate and select only software that fit into one of six "productivity tool" categories: electronic spreadsheet, word processor, database, graphics, communications, and idea processor. There are literally hundreds of software packages in one or several of these categories. The board selected 12 software packages, several of which were integrated packages; that is, they performed the functions of several software packages (e.g., electronic spreadsheet, database, and graphics).

The evaluation and selection of software that relates to a particular application, such as accounting or marketing, is done by the people in the affected departments.

The Microcomputer Purchase Request Form

Any micros purchased within Zimco must be approved by the Microcomputer Review Board. At first the idea of filling out a *Microcomputer Purchase Request Form* seemed a little silly, but when Conrad explained the logic behind the form, most agreed that it was necessary. In a general session for management personnel, Conrad explained the need for the form. "Look around you. Half of the micros at Zimco are either underutilized or they are just gathering dust. Too many people are buying micros without any plans as to how they will be used. It is our hope that the mandatory request form will encourage potential micro users to do a little up-front thinking. It's not our intention to discourage the purchase of micros; on the contrary, they're wonderful business tools, but Zimco can't afford the luxury of having a bunch of PCs around that are more cosmetic than functional."

The Volume Purchase Program

Zimco employees were made aware that microcomputers and personal computers can be purchased at retail chains, such as Computerland, EN-TRE Computer Center, 20/20, MicroAge, and other vendor product centers. However, Conrad wanted to offer Zimco employees a "computer perk." In cooperation with HAL and the HAL-compatible vendor, the Microcomputer Review Board makes volume purchases of PCs at discount rates, then resells "extras" to employees at substantial savings. This plan benefits

Some Zimco employees prefer to purchase their micros through a computer retail store rather than participate in the company program because they want a guarantee of immediate service if the system malfunctions. Salespersons at computer retail stores are usually happy to show customers what options are available for a particular microcomputer. (Courtesy of International Business Machines Corporation)

everybody (except local retailers) because Zimco obtains PCs at volume prices for internal use; the manufacturers sell their computers; and the employees get an inexpensive PC. But the real reason Conrad encouraged this computer perk is to promote "computer literacy." He knew that employees would inevitably begin to use and understand their computers and, in the long run, their computer savvy would be translated into improved productivity in their jobs.

Steps to Buying a Micro

The following is the actual text from Zimco's internal document entitled "Steps to Buying a Micro." The Microcomputer Review Board was aware that buying a computer can be a harrowing experience or it can be a thrilling and fulfilling one. As Gram Mertz said: "If you go about the acquisition of a micro methodically and with purpose, micros will add another dimension to your work. If not, you may curse the day that you decided to buy a micro." The following hints for the evaluation and selection of a microcomputer were compiled by the review board.

- *Step 1. Achieve computer literacy.* You don't buy an automobile before you learn how to drive, and you shouldn't buy a microcomputer without a good understanding of its capabilities and limitations. Zimco's CIS education coordinator offers a self-paced course that will give you the knowledge to make informed decisions when buying a micro. Several local colleges offer such courses as well.

■ *Step 2. Determine your information and computer usage needs.* There is an old adage: "If you don't know where you are going, any road will get you there." The statement is certainly true of choosing a PC. "Knowing where you are going" can be translated to mean "How do you plan to use the PC?" You must answer this question in the Microcomputer Purchase Request Form.

■ *Step 3. Investigate software options.* Determine what software is available to meet your prescribed information needs. When evaluating available software, consider these items: Does it provide the functionality you need; would it be difficult to learn; does the software make effective use of the hardware (e.g., function keys on keyboard, color monitor); is the documentation clear, concise, and well organized; and is it easy to use? Be sure to look over the documentation and spend some time working with a software package before making a commitment to purchase.

■ *Step 4. Investigate hardware options.* If you select a specific software product in Step 3, your selection may dictate the general computer system configuration requirements. In all likelihood, you will have several, if not a dozen, hardware alternatives available to you. Become familiar with the features, and options, of each alternative system.

■ *Step 5. Determine features desired.* You can go with a "minimum" configuration, or you can add a few "bells and whistles." Expect to pay for each feature in convenience, quality, and speed that you add to the minimum configuration. For example, people are usually willing to pay a little extra for the added convenience of a two-disk system, even though one disk will suffice. On the other hand, a color monitor may be an unnecessary luxury for some applications. The peripherals that you select depend very much on your specific needs and volume of usage. For example, the type of printer that you choose would depend on the volume of hard-copy output that you anticipate, whether you need graphics output, whether you need letter-quality print, and so on.

■ *Step 6. "Test drive" several alternatives.* Once you have selected several software and hardware alternatives, spend enough time to gain some familiarity with them. Do you prefer one keyboard over another? Does a word processing system fully use the features of the hardware? Is one system easier to understand and use than another? Use these sessions to answer any questions that you might have about the hardware or software. Salespeople at most retail stores are happy to give you a test drive; just ask.

■ *Step 7. Select and buy.* Apply your criteria, select, then buy your hardware and software.

Zimco employees are encouraged to familiarize themselves with the capabilities of a particular software package before making the decision to buy.
(Western Union Corporations)

FACTORS TO CONSIDER WHEN BUYING A MICRO

During the fourth meeting of the Microcomputer Review Board, Gram Mertz discussed one of his many observations. He said: "Users still need more direction. They're still buying first and asking questions later. I think we should give them something to think about before buying." The result of Gram's comments is a pamphlet entitled, "Factors to Consider when Buying a Micro." The pamphlet, which is distributed along with each Microcomputer Purchase Request Form, enumerates the following considerations.

1. *Future computing needs.* What will your computer and information processing needs be in the future? Most micros provide room for growth; that is, you can add more memory and other peripheral devices as you need them. Make sure that the system you select can grow with your needs.

2. *Who will use the system?* Plan not only for yourself but for others in your home or office who will also use the system. Get their input and consider their needs along with yours.

3. *Availability of software.* Software is developed for one or several microcomputers, but not for all microcomputers. As you might expect, a more extensive array of software is available for the more popular

micros. Make sure that the micro you select has an array of available software that will support your short- and long-term information and processing needs.

4. *Service.* Computing hardware is very reliable. Even so, the possibility exists that one or several of the components will eventually malfunction and have to be repaired. Before purchasing a micro, identify a reliable source of hardware maintenance. Most retailers service what they sell. If a retailer says that the hardware must be returned to the manufacturer for repair, choose another retailer or another system.

5. *Obsolescence.* "I'm going to buy one as soon as the price goes down a little more." If you adopt this strategy, you may never purchase a computer. If you wait another six months, you will probably be able to get a more powerful micro for less money. But what about the lost opportunity?

6. *Other costs.* The cost of the actual microcomputer system is the major expense, but there are numerous incidental expenses that can mount up and may influence your selection of a micro. If you have a spending limit, consider these costs when purchasing the hardware (the cost ranges are for the business user at Zimco): software, $100 to $1500; instructional literature, $0 to $100; maintenance $0 to $500 per year; diskettes, $50 to $200; furniture, $0 to $350; insurance, $0 to $20; and printer cartridges, paper, and other supplies, $40 to $200.

DISCUSSION QUESTIONS

1. Zimco standardized on the HAL PC and a HAL PC compatible, the Zap-100. Since the compatible costs 30 percent less than the actual HAL PC, why didn't Zimco just standardize on the compatible?

2. What was meant when people at Zimco referred to the "PC proliferation problem"?

3. Should a company specify what microcomputer hardware and software users can buy, or should users be permitted the flexibility to choose whatever they want? Justify your position.

4. Zimco encourages their micro users to be "computer literate" (Step 1 in the suggested steps to buying a micro) by providing an in-house education program for computer literacy. Should users study computers on company time or on their own time? Explain.

5. Zimco's Microcomputer Review Board now requires any employee desiring to purchase micro hardware or software to complete a Microcomputer Purchase Request Form. Why do you think the board implemented this requirement?

6. What would you look for when taking a word processing package for a "test drive"?

7. Identify the types of expenses that a product manager at Zimco can expect to incur during the first year if he or she purchases and uses a microcomputer system, primarily for word processing, spreadsheet applications, and as a workstation.

8. "I'm going to wait a few more months for the price to go down." How would you respond to a Zimco manager who, year after year, used this excuse for not buying a micro?

CASE STUDY 7

Information Systems at Zimco:
Finance and Accounting

FACS: FINANCE AND ACCOUNTING CONTROL SYSTEM

Zeke Zimmers, Jr., then the president of Zimco Enterprises, walked into the accounting office just after a visibly tired group of accountants had completed the year-end closing for 1933. He announced very bluntly: "I've hired an automation expert and I want all of you to cooperate with him. Let's bring our accounting procedures into the twentieth century. We should not have to work night and day for months just to close our books each year. Technology has provided us with machines to help us and we should be using them!"

It was apparent to Zeke that accounting was the obvious place to begin automating Zimco's administrative activities. Automation expenses were easy to justify with accounting applications. The tasks were repetitive, they involved numerous calculations, and they required the periodic storage and retrieval of data.

Zimco's administrative activities have continued to evolve with the technology. Fifty-plus years later, the Finance and Accounting Division has a sophisticated system they proudly call the Finance and Accounting Control System, or FACS. FACS, which was developed in-house by CIS in close cooperation with the Finance and Accounting Division, is the envy of a good many businesses in the Dallas–Ft. Worth area. Monroe Green, the VP of Finance and Accounting, is always willing to demonstrate "his" system to noncompetitive companies.

The beauty of FACS is that it is one of four functional components of Zimco's integrated Management Information System (MIS). It is no coincidence that the four systems correspond to the four functional divisions at Zimco (see Figure Z3-3 in Zimco Cast Study 3). Zimco's MIS is an on-line, interactive, menu-driven system that puts data processing and information gathering at the fingertips of end users. The functional components of Zimco's MIS are:

- *FACS*: Finance and Accounting Control System (Process 1 of MIS: Finance and Accounting)
- *PERES*: Personnel Resources System (Process 2 of MIS: Personnel)
- *PICS*: Production and Inventory Control System (Process 3 of MIS: Operations)
- *SAMIS*: Sales and Marketing Information System (Process 4 of MIS: Sales and Marketing)

All the MIS component systems share a common data base, thereby eliminating much of the data redundancy that plagues other nonintegrated companies. FACS, which is Process 1 (Finance and Accounting) of Zimco's MIS overview data flow diagram (see Figure Z3–3), is discussed in this case study. PERES, PICS, and SAMIS (processes 2, 3, and 4 of the Zimco MIS) are discussed in the Zimco Case Studies 9, 10, and 11, respectively.

Zimco, like just about every other company, created acronyms for their system to make everyday conversation among workers a little more efficient. Conrad Innis, the VP of CIS, explained the need for acronyms very succinctly: "It's a whole lot easier to say 'picks' (for PICS) than it is to say 'Production and Inventory Control System'."

THE FIVE SUBSYSTEMS OF FACS

During the early stages of the FACS development project, the project team spent a week mapping out the information and control flows that involve the Finance and Accounting Division. An overview result of that work is shown in Figure Z7-1. The systems analysts, accountants, and financial people on the team decided to divide the system into five logical subsystems (see Figure Z7-1). The subsystems are not necessarily aligned with particular departments because FACS is an integrated system that is designed to support the needs of the organization as a whole.

Notice that each of the four components of the Zimco MIS are numbered 1, 2, 3, and 4. The numbering scheme is used in data flow diagrams to identify subordinate processes. Since the Finance and Accounting process (FACS) is numbered "1," the first-level subordinate systems are identified as 1.1, 1.2, 1.3, and so on. The five subsystems are:

and salary administration. Prior to each pay period, the people in the Personnel Division verify pay and benefits data on the integrated data base. The mechanics of producing and distributing the payroll checks are handled by the Disbursement Control Subsystem in the Finance and Accounting Division. The two primary outputs of the payroll application are the payroll check and stub, which are distributed to the employees, and the payroll register, which is a summary report of payroll transactions. These transactions, of course, are logged automatically on the general ledger portion of the integrated data base.

The payroll application handles all calculations associated with gross pay, taxes, and user-defined deductions. The payroll application is capable of generating a variety of management reports, such as the federal tax summary report and the retirement contribution summary report.

Any disbursement, be it pay, dividends, or payment for goods or services, is noted in the appropriate record(s) in the integrated data base. Summary and detailed disbursement reports are input to the Financial Reporting Subsystem (1.5).

Financial Planning (1.4)

The Financial Planning Subsystem (see Figure Z7-1) operates in support of the budgeting process. Monroe Green, himself an active participant in the budgeting process, says that "each year our financial planners, in cooperation with management, must decide how the company's revenues can be allocated to over 400 accounts."

Zimco's accounting is done on a calendar-year basis, so the budgeting process begins during the late summer and, if all goes well, takes effect at the beginning of the new year. During a prescribed period, managers enter their budget requests, with line-item detail, into the Financial Planning Subsystem from their workstations. Concurrent with the preparation of budget requests, the Sales and Marketing Division prepares a forecast of sales for the coming year. The Financial Planning Subsystem helps translate these sales into projected revenues.

Managers often spend months preparing their departmental budgets for the coming year. To aid in this task, the *budget* application provides each manager with historical information on past line-item expenditures (e.g., salaries, office equipment, office supplies, and so on). Based on this information and projected budget requirements, each manager can make budget requests for the next fiscal year.

Financial planners and top management match requests for funds against projected revenues. "At Zimco," says Monroe Green, "managers invariably ask for more than they need, knowing full well that they will never get what they request." Eventually, a workable budget is established.

Managers at Zimco frequently use the Financial Planning Subsystem to monitor expenditures in their departments. For example, Figure Z7-2 illustrates the display that was generated when the manager of the Purchasing Department inquired about the status of her department's travel budget. She entered only the coded travel account number (30300) to obtain the budget status of her travel account. Other managers routinely make similar inquires. Inordinate budget variances, such as the one shown in Figure Z7-2, prompt managers to take immediate action to get certain budget items under control.

Financial Reporting (1.5)

The Financial Reporting Subsystem (see Figure Z7-1) includes the *general ledger* application—the glue that integrates all the other accounting applications. In the not-too-distant past, accountants manually posted debits and credits for each account in a ledger book, thus the name "general ledger" for today's electronic system. Other "account" applications (accounts receivable, accounts payable, payroll, and so on) are sources of financial transactions and feed data to the general ledger application.

The general ledger application records every monetary transaction that occurs within Zimco. Payment of a bill, an interdepartmental transfer of funds, receipt of payment for an order, a contribution to an employee's retirement fund—all are examples of monetary transactions. The general ledger system keeps track of these transactions and provides the input necessary to produce Zimco's financial statement.

For the purposes of accounting, Zimco is divided up into 14 general accounting categories, such as current assets, current liabilities, cost of goods sold, and so on. These, in turn, are subdivided into as many accounts

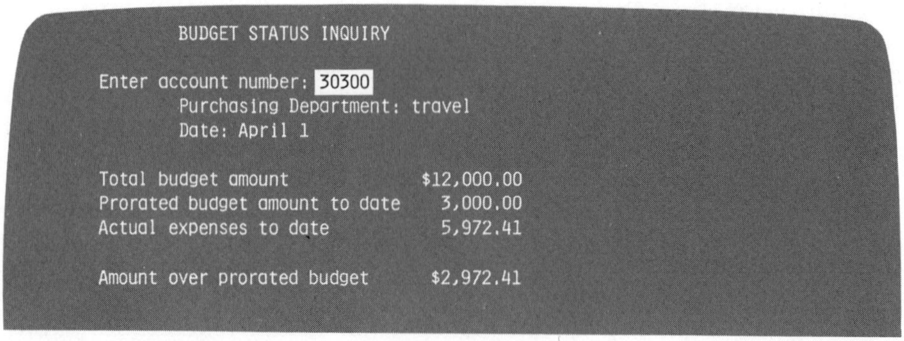

FIGURE Z7–2
Management Budget Inquiry
The Financial Planning Subsystem of FACS enables Zimco managers to make on-line budget inquiries regarding budgets.

as are needed to accurately reflect monetary flow within Zimco. Monetary transactions are recorded as a debit or a credit to a particular account. The *balance sheet*, one of two major components of Zimco's financial statement, reflects a summary of these accounts at the end of a particular day. The balance sheet is so named because the company's assets are equated with its liabilities. Since all monetary transactions are recorded on-line as they occur via FACS, managers can request a display of the balance sheet on any day of the year, not just at the end of each quarter.

The other major component of the financial statement is the *profit and loss statement*. Often called the "income statement," the profit and loss statement reflects how much Zimco makes or loses during a given period, usually a quarter or a year (see Figure Z5-2 for an example of an income statement).

The financial planners at Zimco routinely tap into the Financial Reporting Subsystem to ask "what if" questions. For example, they use decision support software to ask: "What if gross sales are increased by 10 percent and the cost of goods sold is decreased by 5 percent, how would net earnings be affected?" Managers also find prior- year comparisons helpful.

The Securities and Exchange Commission (SEC) requires publicly held companies such as Zimco to file quarterly financial statements. Every three months Zimco and thousands of other companies transmit these reports to the SEC electronically via data communications.

MAINTAINING FACS

All FACS subsystems are on-line 24 hours a day. Any authorized Zimco employee can tap into the interactive, menu-driven FACS system to make inquiries or to add, delete, or revise data. The Finance and Accounting Division is responsible for maintaining that portion of the integrated data base that deals with monetary accounting, even though much of the input comes from the other divisions. On occasion, this causes some problems. Monroe Green admits that "sometimes the Personnel Division has to be prodded to get the pay and benefits data in on time. However, you can always depend on the sales reps in the field to get their expense reports in on time."

DISCUSSION QUESTIONS

1. Explain why the expense of automating accounting applications is easy to justify. Give examples.

2. Why did the FACS project team decide to design the system around five logical subsystems rather than along organizational lines?

3. Do acronyms, such as FACS and PERES, foster cyberphobia, or do they serve to simplify interaction between users and computer professionals? Explain.

4. Draw a data flow diagram explosion of the Receipt Control Subsystem (1.2) showing the primary information flows between appropriate processes, the customer entity, and the integrated data base. Label subordinate processes 1.2.1, 1.2.2, and so on.

5. Explain the relationship between Zimco's accounts payable application and a supplier's accounts receivables application.

6. Draw a data flow diagram explosion of the Financial Reporting Subsystem (1.5) showing the primary information flows between appropriate processes, the managers and government entities, and the integrated data base. Label subordinate processes 1.5.1, 1.5.2, and so on.

7. Getting out the payroll at Zimco is a joint effort between the Personnel Division and the Finance and Accounting Division. Could the payroll application be made more efficient by consolidating it in one division or the other? Explain.

CASE STUDY 8

Zimco's Computer Network

THE DECENTRALIZATION OF INFORMATION PROCESSING

Centralization versus Decentralization. Through the mid-1970s, the prevailing thought at Zimco was to take advantage of the economies of scale and *centralize* all computer-based information processing in the Computer and Information Services Division. At the time, Zimco could get more computing capacity for its dollar by continuing to upgrade their centralized mainframe computer system. This is no longer true at Zimco or anywhere else.

Conrad Innis, VP of CIS, first talked about a new era in computer support during the annual executive retreat in 1984. He said: ''The computer center at Dallas has grown so big and complex that we have begun to lose our ability to be responsive to user information needs. It is this lack of responsiveness that has caused us to reevaluate our current centralized mode of operation. Otto Mann, our VP of Operations, has suggested that we *decentralize* by moving more in the direction of *distributed processing,* and we in CIS agree. We can get an outstanding price-performance ratio by networking micros and minis to our mainframe in Dallas.''

The Push to Distributed Processing. Distributed processing is both a technological and an organizational concept. Conrad Innis had convinced Zimco's management group that information processing can be more effective if computer *hardware* (usually micros and minis), *data, software,* and in some cases, *personnel* are moved physically closer to the people who use these resources. That is, if the people in the Operations Division need access to a computer and its information, these resources are made available to them in their work area. They don't need to go to the Computer and Information Services Division for every request. As Otto Mann says, "With distributed processing, users control their 'information' destiny."

At Zimco, computer systems are arranged in a computer network, with each system connected to one or more other systems. Distributed processing is usually designed around a combination of geographical and functional considerations. Figure Z8–1 illustrates the implementation of distributed processing at Zimco. At the headquarters location in Dallas,

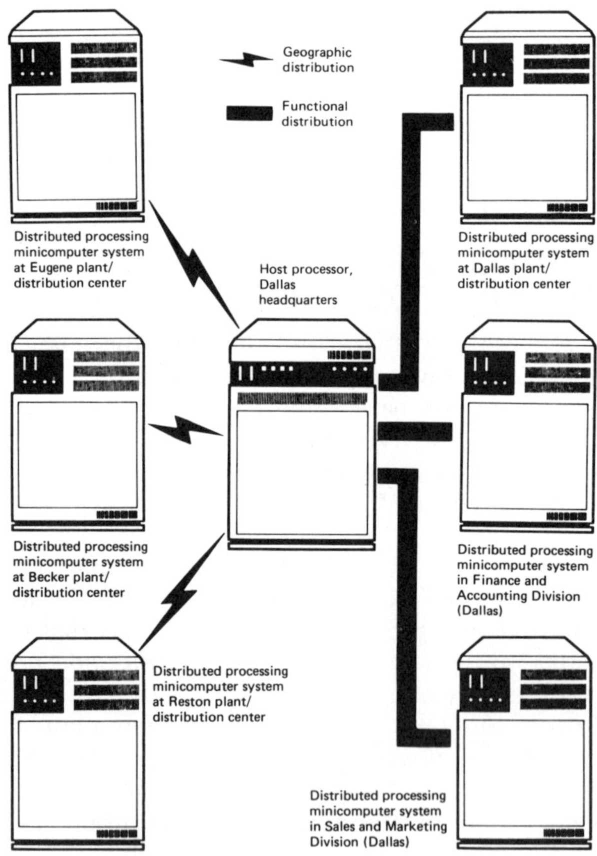

FIGURE Z8–1
A Distributed Processing Network
The distributed processing network of Zimco Enterprises demonstrates both geographic and functional distribution of processing.

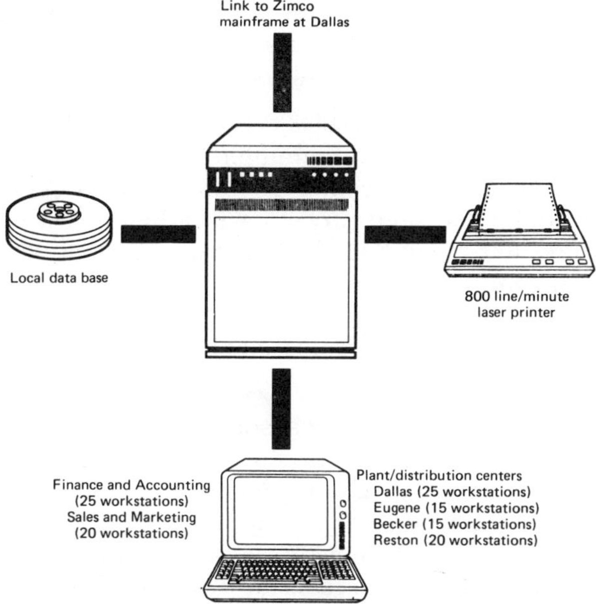

FIGURE Z8–2
Configuration of Minicomputer Systems in Zimco's Distributed Processing Network
The distributed minis at the plants and at the home office (see Figure Z8–1) have similar configurations. Each has a disk for a local data base, a laser printer, and from 15 to 25 workstations.

Zimco has *functionally* distributed processing systems in the Finance and Accounting Division, the Sales and Marketing Division, and the home office plant. These are supported by people in CIS. *Geographically* distributed processing systems are located at each of the three plant/distribution center sites in Eugene, Becker, and Reston. Each of the remote plant sites is supported by a small staff of computer professionals.

All six distributed systems are minicomputers with similar configurations. The basic configuration is shown in Figure Z8–2. Each has its own magnetic disk storage for a "local data base" and its own low-speed, letter-quality laser printer. Each distributed mini services the workstations in the local area.

THE COMPUTER NETWORK

The host computer system at Dallas serves as the hub of Zimco's computer network, maintains the integrated data base, and services all areas of

Zimco operation. The distributed processing systems can function as part of the Zimco computer network, or, since they are entirely self-contained, they also can operate as stand-alone systems.

The Mainframe Configuration at Dallas.   Conrad Innis likes to say: "What we have at Zimco is a host of computers." The mainframe computer system at the Dallas computer center has three processors: a host, a front-end processor, and a back-end processor (see Figure Z8–3). The central mainframe is the focal point of the star network that services the six distributed minicomputers.

Each of the special-function processors at Zimco is strategically located in the computer network to increase efficiency and **throughput,** or the rate at which work can be performed by a computer system.

The Need for Special-Function Processors.   Recently, Gram Mertz, the manager of the Programming Department, explained the need for special-function processors to a group of new programmers. He said: "A processor executes only one instruction at a time, even though it appears to be handling many tasks simultaneously. A **task** is the basic unit of work for a processor. At any given time, several tasks will compete for processor time. For example, one task might involve printing sales reports and another calculating finance charges."

Gram continued by discussing the limitations of a single-processor environment. "Since a single processor is capable of executing only one instruction at a time, one task will be given priority and the others will have to wait. The processor rotates between competing tasks so quickly, however, that it appears as if all are being executed at once. Even so, this rotation eventually takes its toll on processor efficiency. To improve the overall efficiency of a computer system, the processing load is dis-tributed among several other special-function processors."

The manager of the Programming Department explained to the new hires that the host processor in the computer center at Zimco's Dallas headquarters is responsible for overall control of the computer system and for the execution of certain applications programs. Other processors in the computer system are under the control of and subordinate to the host.

At Zimco, the front-end processor relieves the host processor of com-munications-related processing duties. All data being transmitted *to* the host processor *from* remote computers or workstations or *from* the host processor *to* remote computers or workstations are handled by the front-end processor.

The back-end processor, which is also called a *database machine* by some CIS personnel, handles tasks associated with the retrieval and manipulation of data stored on secondary storage devices (see Figure Z8–3). Gram Mertz explained the concept. "Suppose that a program execu-

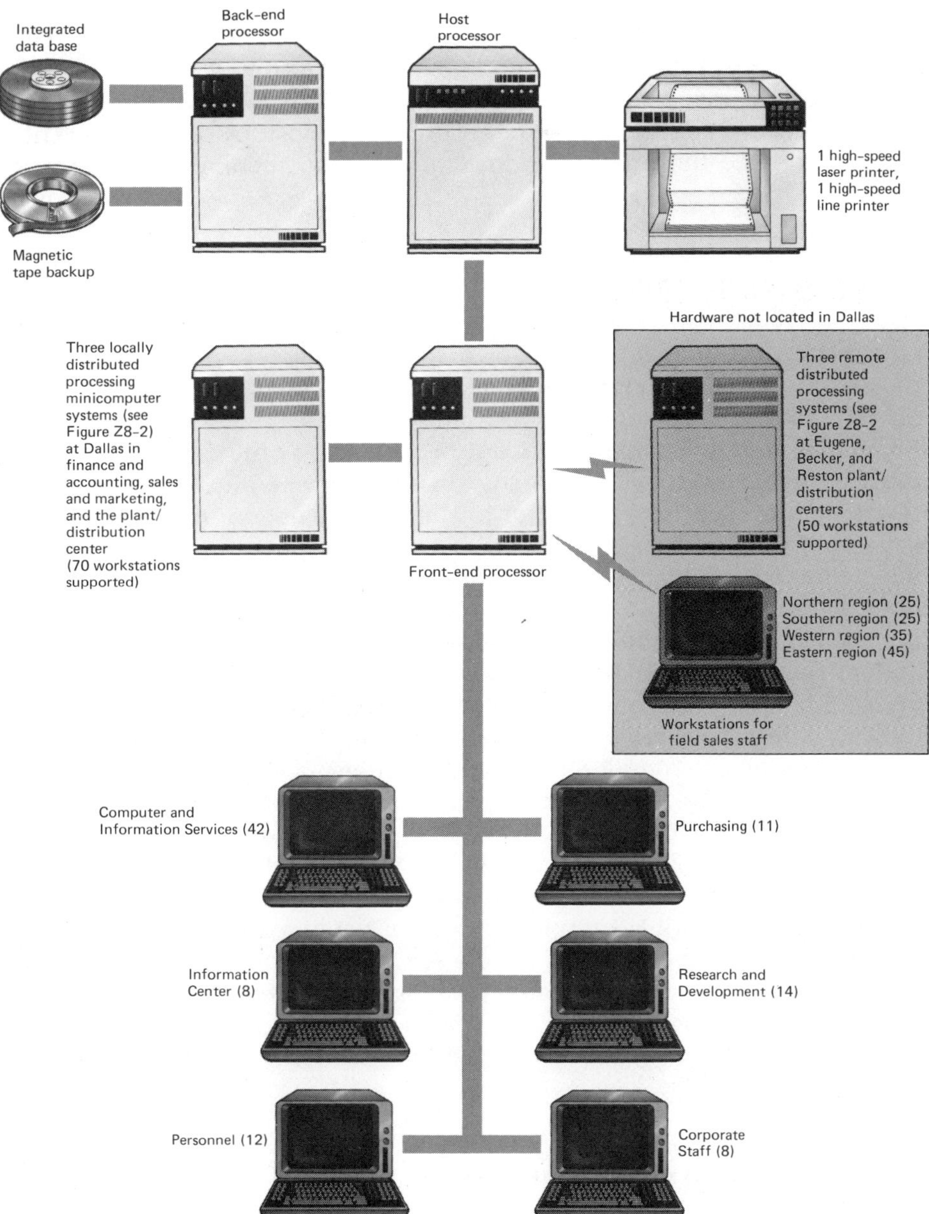

FIGURE Z8–3
The Computer Network at Zimco Enterprises
The host processor is the hub of a computer network that includes two special-function processors, six distributed minicomputers, and over 300 workstations. The configuration of the six distributed minis is shown in Figure Z8–2.

ting in the host needs Conrad Innis's record from the data base. The host issues a request to the back-end processor to retrieve Conrad's record. The back-end processor then issues the commands necessary to retrieve Conrad's record and transmits the record to the host for processing. This helps to reduce the processing load of the host, thereby increasing its efficiency."

THE DISTRIBUTED MINIS

Otto Mann is a real proponent of distributed processing. He said: "In the past, when the mainframe went down, our plants went down. Our manufacturing, inventory, and shipping activities are so dependent on PICS (Production and Inventory Control System) that the computer system must be up at all times for us to remain fully operational. Now, with distributed processing we can go to stand-alone operation in the plants if the Dallas mainframe goes down. If one of the plant minis goes down, the computer center at Dallas provides backup so we can continue operation."

Each of the distributed processors is essentially a "host" processor system that is "distributed" or physically located in a functional area or at a plant/distribution center site. These minicomputer systems have their own input/output (I/O), workstations, and storage capabilities, and can operate as a stand-alone (i.e., independent of the host) or as a distributed system (i.e., part of the Zimco computer network).

According to Otto Mann: "Most of the routine processing and data base activities are handled locally by the distributed systems in the four plants. For example, when I want information that deals strictly with the production of stibs, I tap into the local data base on the mini at the Dallas plant. However, when I need a summary of missed workdays due to illness, I tap into the integrated data base on the host at headquarters. When I make an inquiry about the Tegler inventory levels at the Reston Distribution Center, my request is routed to the local data base at Reston via the host in Dallas."

SERVICING REMOTE AND LOCAL PROCESSING

Figure Z8–3 graphically illustrates the scope of Zimco's computer network. Over 300 workstations, about 200 of which are micros, permit users to access the integrated data base supported on the host or to access one or more of the local data bases supported on the distributed minis. Zimco has a policy that limits data base access to employees with a "need to know." Conrad Innis explained: "Each employee at Zimco is assigned a password and an authorization code. The password gets them on to the system and the authorization code determines what data they can access."

Approximately half of the workstations are located outside Dallas and are therefore *remote* to the host computer system. Fifty workstations are serviced by the minis at the three remote plant sites (Eugene, Becker, and Reston). Each field sales representative has a portable personal computer that doubles as a workstation. While in a customer's office, the field reps establish a link with the Zimco computer network to enter orders, to make inquires about the status of orders, and to determine the delivery schedule for a particular product.

Almost 100 *local* workstations in Dallas are connected directly to the host. The bulk of these are in CIS and are used primarily for system development and maintenance work. Eight are located in the Information Center. The remainder are used by people in purchasing, research and development, personnel, and the corporate staff.

Conrad Innis explained: "Since our integrated MIS is part and parcel of just about everything we do, it is important that we make the system available to all who need it. Our goal is to provide every white-collar worker with a workstation by the end of this decade—and we're well on our way toward meeting that goal."

ON-LINE APPLICATIONS AT ZIMCO

Zimco's computer network puts its users on-line so that they can take advantage of a variety of data communications applications. Dale Connors, Manager of Data Communications, said: "Our computer network has made it possible for CIS to be even more responsive to end-user needs."

Dale continued discussing the "pluses" of Zimco's on-line, transaction-oriented environment. "Being on-line, our users can make a variety of inquiries from their workstations. For example, Peggy Peoples in Personnel can easily call up an employee's training record; or a field rep can inquire about a customer's credit limit. At Zimco, time is money, so we try to keep our response time to under 1 second." **Response time** is the elapsed time between when a message is sent and when a response is received.

Only 10 years ago, data entry was the responsibility of CIS, but now virtually all data are entered on-line, directly from the source location. For example, the sales staff enters the data for call-in orders directly into SAMIS (Sales and Marketing Information Systems) while they are talking with customers.

Scores of specialized programs are supported on the host computer system. Dale Connors says: "If a user requests a particular software package

and the cost of the software is within reason, we get it and put it on-line." These programs, which are available to all Zimco employees, are used for a variety of remote processing tasks on an as-needed basis. For example, the product managers in marketing are frequent users of the statistical packages. All programmers and many users, especially in research and development, write their programs interactively at workstations while in direct communication with the computer.

Conrad Innis points with pride to the fact that valuable information is as close as the nearest workstation. "Our full-scale support of an on-line, integrated MIS has made it possible for managers, administrative personnel, and programmers to work at home on their own workstations." Zimco encourages this "electronic cottage" concept by permitting employees the flexibility of "telecommuting" up to one day a week. Conrad said, "with the elimination of travel time, coffee breaks, idle conversations, and numerous office distractions, we have found that conscientious, self-motivated employees can be more productive at home when working on certain projects." Of course, there are differing opinions on the merits of the electronic cottage. Sally Marcio, VP of Sales and Marketing says: "I'm more productive working at the office, where household and family distractions fade into the distance."

DISCUSSION QUESTIONS

1. Discuss centralization and decentralization as they are applied to computers and information processing.

2. Elaborate on Zimco management's rationale for moving in the direction of distributed processing.

3. Discuss how special-function processors can enhance the throughput of Zimco's host computer system.

4. Would you classify Zimco's computer network as a star network or a hybrid network? Explain.

5. The trend at Zimco is to distributed processing. Besides processing, what else is distributed?

6. The only functional division at Zimco that does not have at least one distributed minicomputer system is the Personnel Division. Discuss possible reasons for not implementing a distributed system in the Personnel Division.

7. Conrad Innis would like to see a workstation on the desktop of every white-collar worker at Zimco. Some workers simply don't want a workstation. Should they be excluded from Conrad's plan? Explain.

8. Only 20 percent of the professional people at Zimco routinely take advantage of the opportunity to telecommute one day each week. If you worked at Zimco, would you telecommute? Why or why not?

CASE STUDY 9

Information Systems at Zimco: Personnel

PERES: PERSONNEL RESOURCES SYSTEM

PERES, which is pronounced like the French city, is an acronym for Zimco's Personnel Resource System. "PERES is one of the four major components of Zimco's corporate-wide MIS [see Figure Z3–3 in Zimco Case Study 3]," says Peggy Peoples, VP of Personnel. "PERES is essentially a personnel accounting system that maintains pertinent data on employees. Besides routine historical data, such as educational background, salary history, and so on, PERES includes data on performance reviews, skills, and professional development."

PERES is divided into three subsystems:

2.1 Recruiting

2.2 Pay and Benefits Administration

2.3 Training and Education

These subsystems are graphically illustrated in the data flow diagram of Figure Z9–1. Figure Z9–1 shows the explosion of the "personnel" component of the Zimco MIS. Each of these subsystems is described in the following sections.

THE THREE SUBSYSTEMS OF PERES

Recruiting Subsystem (2.1)

Peggy Peoples explained Zimco's recruiting policy. "It has long been a tradition at Zimco to hire quality people and promote from within. At the beginning of each quarter, the division VPs enter their work force requirements into PERES; it is our job to find candidates to fill these positions. Our Recruiting Subsystem (see Figure Z9–1) has proven to be a real help in landing the best people available.''

The Recruiting Subsystem (2.1) automatically distributes predefined job descriptions to selected colleges and to several personnel search agen-

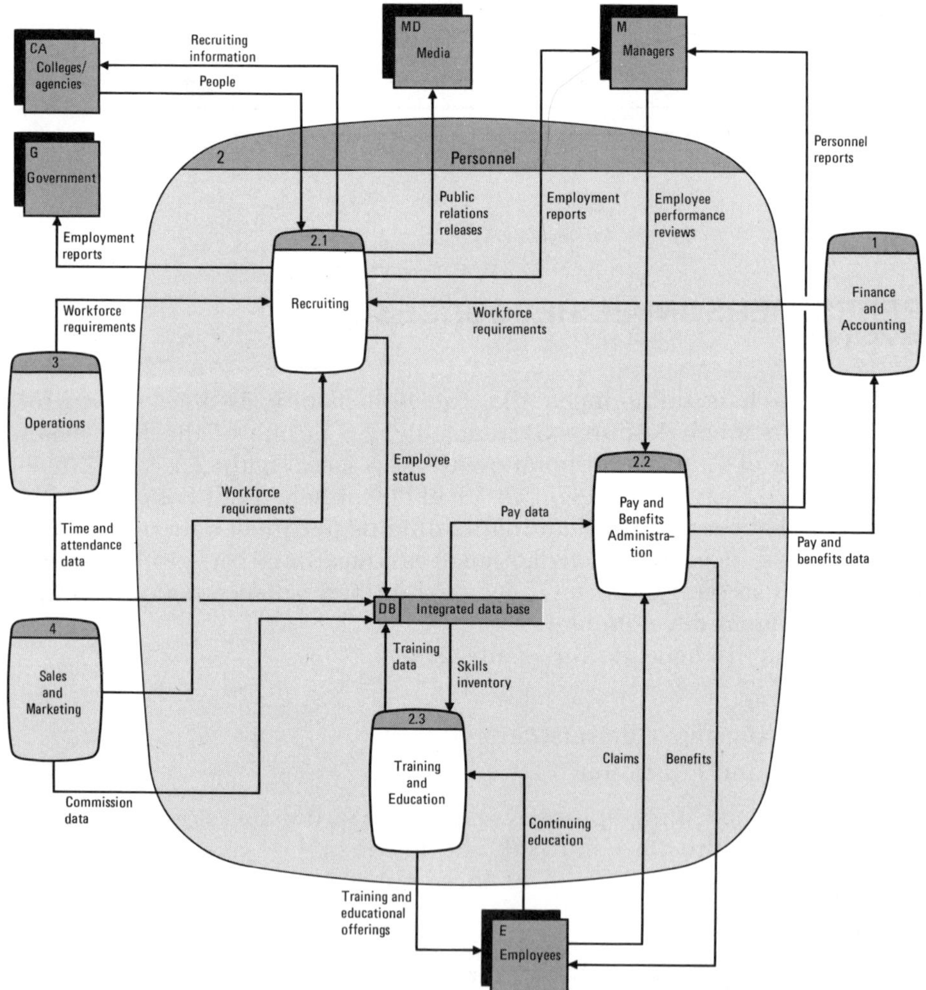

FIGURE Z9–1
Zimco's Personnel Resource System (PERES)
This data flow diagram is the explosion of the personnel (2) process of the MIS overview data flow diagram of Figure Z3–3.

cies. About 20 percent of these are distributed via electronic mail; the rest are generated in hard copy and sent via the postal service. The colleges and agencies suggest possible candidates; then the Recruiting Department conducts a preliminary interview. The results of the interview, which are entered into PERES, are on-line and readily accessible to management.

Managers can make on-line inquiries directly from their workstations. The following are examples of some of the on-line reports made available by the menu-driven Recruiting Subsystem.

- Work Force Summary: Current and Authorized
- Current Openings: By Division By Department
- Current Candidate Summary

Peggy says that "the first day a new hire comes to work, he or she reports to us. We give them a couple of minutes' instruction on the use of our workstations, then ask them to enter their personal data into PERES. This serves two purposes. We get the data into the system, but most important, the new hire realizes that computers are very much a part of how we conduct business at Zimco. This is the first activity of a two-day orientation that we give every new hire."

Classified ads, announcing Zimco job openings, are sent to local newspapers electronically in a format that needs no further editing by typesetters. This approach saves time and Zimco gets a discount for delivering machine-readable ad copy. This facet of the Recruiting Subsystem is explained in Zimco Case Study 5.

A variety of mandatory government reports, dealing primarily with equal opportunity employment, are generated from the Recruiting Subsystem.

Pay and Benefits Administration (2.2)

Maintenance and Preparation of Payroll Data. The *payroll application* is a joint effort between the Personnel Division and the Finance and Accounting Division (see Zimco Case Study on FACS, the Finance and Accounting Control System). Peggy Peoples once described the Pay and Benefits Administration Subsystems (see Figure Z9–1) as the "heart of the *wage and salary administration application*." She explained that "supervisors enter hours-worked data for hourly personnel directly into their workstations. We make any adjustments to pay, such as an optional purchase of Zimco stock, directly to an employee's record on the integrated data base. Then, prior to each pay period, we verify pay and benefits data on the integrated data base. Once the data are prepared, the actual preparation and distribution of the checks is handled by the Disbursement Control Subsystem (1.3) of FACS."

Many Zimco managers interact simultaneously with the Personnel Resources System (PERES) and their subordinates during a performance review.
(Photo courtesy of Hewlett-Packard Company)

Performance Reviews.   At Zimco, every employee has a semiannual performance review—even Preston Smith, the president. Each employee is evaluated by his or her immediate manager in six areas: ability to work with others, innovativeness, contribution through achievement of goals, potential for advancement, ability to communicate, and expertise in his or her area of specialty.

Many managers record their numeric evaluations, from 1 to 10, and add a verbal support statement while interacting directly with PERES. Opie Rader, the manager of the Operations Department in the CIS Division says: "I conduct performance reviews with my people while both of us are seated in front of the tube. When a subordinate comes in my office for the interview, I have already done the rating, usually on the low side. If, by virtue of other information, a subordinate can convince me that he or she should be rated higher, I change the rating on the spot. I feel that there should be some give and take between manager and subordinate. The PERES system gives me and other managers the flexibility to render a mutually agreeable performance review without unnecessarily causing hard feelings."

Management Reports.   Managers at Zimco use the company's fourth-generation query language to make ad hoc requests for information and reports. A manager obtains information by writing a short program that, in turn, "queries" the integrated data base. Such queries can be made to the data base for information in any functional area, not just personnel.

The *query language* used at Zimco is called INGEN (for Information Generator). INGEN, pronounced "engine," was developed by a Dallas entrepreneur. Ed Cool, the education coordinator in CIS, presents a four-hour training session on INGEN during the first week of each month. Ed says: "Seventy percent of the managers at Zimco, including top management, know, use, and love INGEN. INGEN is user friendly and managers can get the information they need without having to wait in line for a programmer."

A recent INGEN request by Monroe Green in the Finance and Accounting Division illustrates the use and applicability of fourth-generation languages. Monroe Green described what information he wanted: "There had been some rumblings about pay discrimination in two of my departments, so I used INGEN to find out for myself. I wrote a short INGEN program to print a list of the employees in each department along with other data, including last month's gross and net pay."

The six-instruction program that Monroe Green wrote (Figure Z9–2) is a good example of how a query language can be used to generate a management report. Monroe's 4GL (fourth-generation language) program is described below.

■ *Instruction 1* specifies that the payroll data are stored on a FILE called PAYROLL in the integrated data base. Although the data of only one file are needed in this example, requests requiring data from several files are no more difficult.

■ *Instruction 2* specifies that the information in the report is to be *sorted* (department 911 before 914) and LISTed BY DEPARTMENT. All "900"-level departments are in the Finance and Accounting Division. The codes "911" and "914" refer to the Financial Planning and Credit Departments. Instruction 2 also specifies which data elements within the file are to be included in the report of Figure Z9–3. If Monroe had written the instruction as LIST BY DEPARTMENT BY NAME, the employee names would be listed in alphabetical order for each department.

```
1.  FILE IS PAYROLL
2.  LIST BY DEPARTMENT NAME ID SEX NET GROSS
3.  SELECT DEPARTMENT = 911, 914
4.  SUBTOTALS BY DEPARTMENT
5.  TITLE: "PAYROLL FOR DEPARTMENTS 911, 914"
6.  COLUMN HEADINGS:   "DEPARTMENT", "EMPLOYEE, NAME";
    "EMPLOYEE, NUMBER"; "SEX"; "NET, PAY"; "GROSS, PAY"
```

FIGURE Z9–2
Query-Language Program to Produce Report of Figure Z9–3
Each instruction is discussed in detail in the case study.

PAYROLL FOR DEPARTMENTS 911, 914

DEPARTMENT	EMPLOYEE NAME	EMPLOYEE NUMBER	SEX	NET PAY	GROSS PAY
911	ARNOLD	01963	1	356.87	445.50
911	LARSON	11357	2	215.47	283.92
911	POWELL	11710	1	167.96	243.20
911	POST	00445	1	206.60	292.00
911	KRUSE	03571	2	182.09	242.40
911	SMOTH	01730	1	202.43	315.20
911	GREEN	12829	1	238.04	365.60
911	ISAAC	12641	1	219.91	313.60
911	STRIDE	03890	1	272.53	386.40
911	REYNOLDS	05805	2	134.03	174.15
911	YOUNG	04589	1	229.69	313.60
911	HAFER	09764	2	96.64	121.95
DEPARTMENT TOTAL				2,522.26	3,497.52
914	MANHART	11602	1	250.89	344.80
914	VETTER	01895	1	189.06	279.36
914	GRECO	07231	1	685.23	1,004.00
914	CROCI	08262	1	215.95	376.00
914	RYAN	10961	1	291.70	399.20
DEPARTMENT TOTAL				1,632.83	2,403.36
FINAL TOTAL				4,155.09	5,900.88

17 RECORDS TOTALED

FIGURE Z9–3
A Payroll Report
This payroll report is the result of the execution of the query-language program of Figure Z9–2.

■ *Instruction 3* specifies the criterion by which records are SELECTed. Monroe Green is interested only in those employees from DEPART-MENTs 911 and 914. Other criteria could be included for further record selections. For example, the criterion "GROSS > 400" could be added to select only those people (from departments 911 and 914) whose gross pay is greater than $400.00.

■ *Instruction 4* causes SUBTOTALS to be computed and displayed BY DEPARTMENT.

■ *Instructions 5 and 6* allow Monroe to enhance the appearance and readability of the report by including a title and labeling the columns. Instruction 5 produces the report title, and instruction 6 specifies descriptive column headings.

The COBOL equivalent of this request would require the efforts of a professional programmer from CIS and over 150 lines of code!

Monroe Green's authorization code permits him access to payroll data for those employees within his realm of responsibility—no one else. If he had requested the same report for a "600" department (Personnel Division), he would have received a message on his display screen denying him access to these data.

Query languages are effective tools for generating responses to a variety of requests for information. Short query-language programs, similar to the one in Figure Z9–2, are all that is needed to respond to the following typical Zimco management requests:

■ Which employees have accumulated over 20 sick days since January 1?

■ List departments that have exceeded their total budget allocation for the month of June in alphabetical order by department name.

Terri Suttor, manager of the Technical Support Department in CIS, is investigating the feasibility of implementing a natural language. She said: "It would be easier for managers to use (than INGEN), but they will be more limited in the kinds of requests they can make. State-of-the-art natural-language software can interpret no more than a one-sentence query at a time. A natural-language equivalent of the query-language program of Figure Z9–2 would be: "Show me a report of employee payroll data for departments 911 and 914." Department and overall summary data are automatically generated.

Training and Education (2.3)

The Training and Education Subsystem (2.3) monitors and tracks the ongoing career development of Zimco employees. Any external or internal training or education received by an employee is entered into his or her "skills inventory." Included in an employee's skills inventory are any special skills or knowledge. As a matter of policy, managers first conduct an internal search to fill openings. They do this by listing desired skills, knowledge, and so on, then initiating an automatic search of the skills inventory section of the integrated data base. Frequently, there is a match and an opportunity for promotion is extended to an existing employee.

The Personnel Division administers ongoing in-house training programs and evaluates employee requests for external educational support. The Training and Education Subsystem automatically informs employees of in-house offerings by posting a notice on Z-Buzz, the name employees have given to Zimco's electronic bulletin board.

DISCUSSION QUESTIONS

1. A proposal being seriously considered by Zimco's top management is to change all hourly employees to salaried employees. If adopted, what impact would this proposal have on the Pay and Benefits Administration Subsystem?

2. Monroe Green would like to produce a report that lists the employees in department 911 alphabetically by sex. He wants the name, employee number, department, net pay, and gross pay listed for each new employee. How would you modify the query-language program in Figure Z9–2 to generate this report?

3. Opie Rader and other Zimco managers conduct performance reviews with their subordinates while interacting with PERES. Discuss the pros and cons of this approach.

4. Zimco is one of the few companies that asks new hires to enter their own personal data into the corporate data base. Discuss the advantages of this approach.

5. Describe three management reports that you might expect to be generated by the Training and Education Subsystem.

6. Describe the information flow between PERES and FACS. Be specific.

7. What are the advantages of having an on-line skills inventory for all employees?

CASE STUDY 10

Information Systems at Zimco: Operations

PICS: PRODUCTION AND INVENTORY CONTROL SYSTEM

PICS, Zimco's Production and Inventory Control System, supports the Operations Division and is one of the four functional components of Zimco's integrated Management Information System (see Figure Z3–3 in Zimco Case Study 3). PICS is the central focus of this case study. FACS, the Finance and Accounting Control System, and PERES, the Personnel Resources System, are presented in Zimco Case Studies 7 and 9, respectively. SAMIS, the Sales and Marketing Information System, is featured in Zimco Case Study 11.

Figure Z10–1 graphically illustrates the scope of PICS by showing the explosion of Process 3, "Operations," of the Zimco MIS overview data flow diagram (Figure Z3–3). PICS is logically divided into five subsystems. These are:

3.1 Production

3.2 Research and Development

3.3 Schedule and Monitor Production

3.4 Acquire and Manage Materials

3.5 Shipping

The Operations Division's user liaison, Ursula Lain, is the interface between CIS people (programmers, systems analysts, and the data base

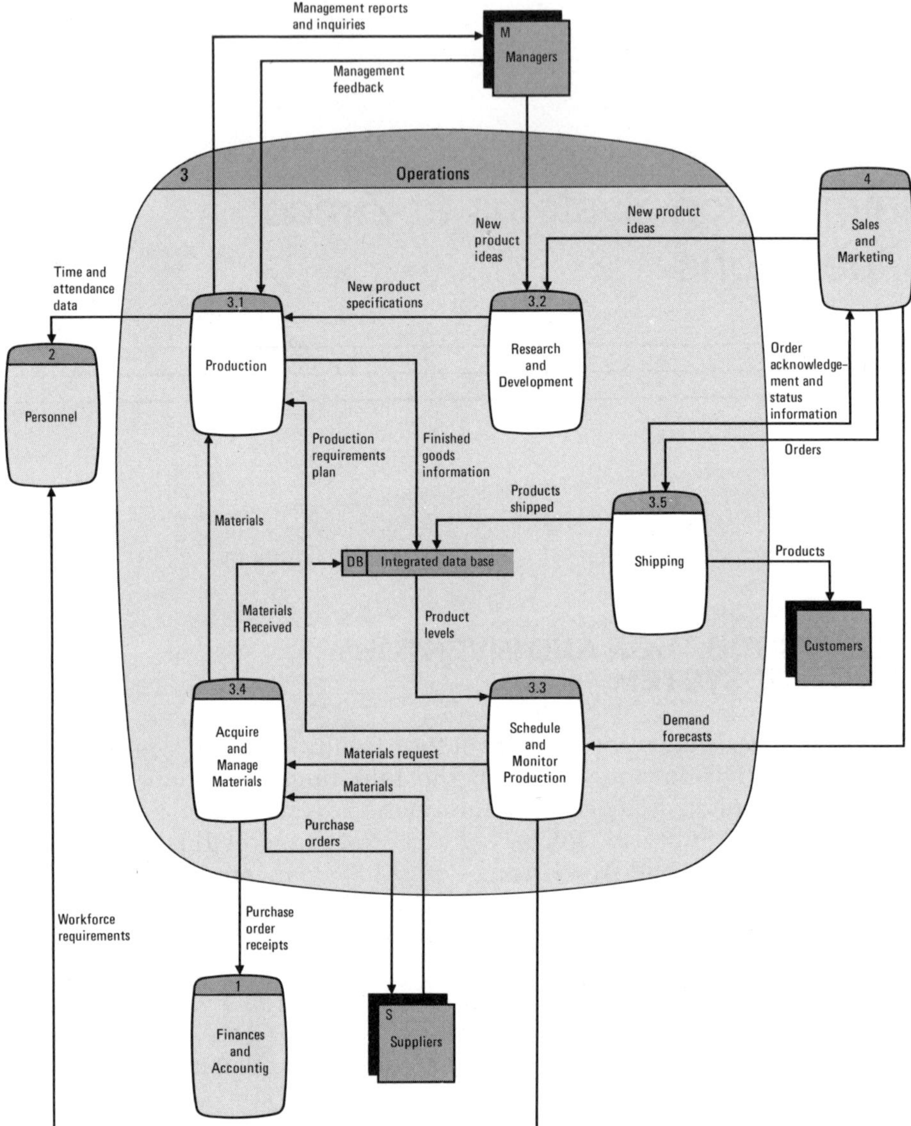

FIGURE Z10–1
Zimco's Production and Inventory Control System (PICS)
This data flow diagram is the explosion of the operations (3) process of the MIS
overview data flow diagram of Figure Z3–3.

administrator) and users. She made a valuable contribution to PICS during its design and implementation by facilitating and fostering verbal communication between CIS and user personnel. Ursula explained how the project team came up with the five subsystems. "The project team analyzed the Operations Division from an information processing perspective, not from a departmental perspective. Because the information and processing requirements of the various departments overlapped substantially, it seemed only logical that we design PICS as an integrated system. Although there is some correlation between the subsystems and departmental lines, this was not a criterion during the design phase. Our primary concern was to design a system that would best meet the needs of the Operations Division, while complementing Zimco's overall MIS."

TRANSITIONING TO A DATA BASE ENVIRONMENT

Otto Manning, the VP of Operations, was the real force behind the development and implementation of PICS and he was very much a proponent of designing it around an integrated data base. He said: "The Operations Division is very dynamic and hopelessly intertwined with everything we do here at Zimco. We get input from marketing, R&D, and accounting. Marketing tells us what products to make, how many to make, and when to have them in stock. R&D tells us how to make them and accounting tells us how much we can spend. All too often marketing wants the product before R&D is finished with the design, and accounting doesn't allocate enough money to cover the cost of production. These and other conflicts between divisions highlight the need for people throughout the company to be better informed. To help alleviate some of our misinformation problems, we decided that the nerve center of PICS should be an integrated data base."

Both users and CIS people knew that transitioning to an integrated data base from a traditional file environment would be a major undertaking. During the decision period in the early 1980s, Terri Suttor, the manager of the Technical Support Department in CIS, would often get on her soapbox to cite the tremendous advantages of having an integrated data base. According to Terri: "The traditional approach to data organization revolves around the file and our many sequential and direct access files are fraught with data redundancy." Terri liked to say: "We may be data rich but we are information poor. A DBMS can turn our wealth of data into a wealth of information."

Terri, who manages the data base administrators, would discuss the benefits of an integrated data base with anyone who would listen. "An integrated data base supported by a good database management system

Workstations strategically located throughout Zimco plants and warehouses make
production and shipping information readily available to authorized persons.
(Honeywell, Inc.)

(DBMS) will inevitably expand the scope of available information and
enable Zimco managers to make more informed and, therefore, better
decisions." Terri said that "by minimizing data redundancy, data collection and update procedures are simplified. We can have greater confidence
in the integrity of our data because we make the update in only one
place—the data base."

Terri was also quick to point out that having an integrated data base
would have a very positive impact on CIS. "The data base environment
opens new doors for programmers and systems analysts. It gives them
greater flexibility in the initial design of the system. And with a DBMS,
system maintenance is much easier and less expensive."

THE FIVE SUBSYSTEMS OF PICS

Production (3.1)

All activities in the Operations Division function to support the production
process, and so it is with PICS. All other subsystems support the Produc-

tion Subsystem (3.1). Plant managers get the specifications for new products and product enhancements from the Research and Development Subsystem (3.2). For example, the design of the new Qwert Plus is in an electronic format. When the prototypes of the new Qwert Plus pass acceptance testing, production will use the electronic form of the design to program the machine tools that will make the parts for the Qwert Plus.

Each day, plant managers at the four plant/distribution center sites tap into the Schedule and Monitor Production Subsystem (3.3) to monitor production levels. The Acquire and Manage Materials Subsystem (3.4) ensures that raw materials needed during production are at the right place at the right time. And, of course, the Shipping Subsystem (3.5) gets the products out the door to the customer.

Plant managers rely heavily on the linear programming and other mathematical models that are embodied in the Production Subsystem to help them make the most effective use of available resources. These models help schedule the arrival of raw materials and components, the use of machine tools and assembly stations, the use of the work force, and maintenance shutdowns.

An important aspect of the production process is quality control. Zimco uses sampling techniques to maintain a high level of quality control. Each plant has inspectors on the floor who examine both work-in-process and finished goods for defects. Inspectors enter defect data directly into the Production Subsystem. The subsystem then does the necessary statistical analysis and provides inspectors with immediate feedback as to whether a lot should be sampled further or deemed defective.

Research and Development (3.2)

Many data elements in the PICS data base are coded. Otto Manning says: "We try to code every data element we can, both to save data entry keystrokes and to save storage space." For example, the R&D "project code" data element (see Figure Z10–2) is coded. Engineers and supervisors need only enter a five-character code when making inquiries about a particular project. The code identifies whether the project is a development or applications project, whether it deals with a new product or an enhancement to an existing product, and if it is an enhancement, the code associates the project with one of the current Zimco products (e.g., Stib). The project code has a unique numerical identifier to distinguish between similar projects (e.g., multiple "DES" projects).

Otto says that "since many of our data elements are coded, they have special meaning and provide information to the user." For example, the project code DES03 describes a development project (#03) to enhance the Stib (see Figure Z10 2).

Position	A/N	Code	Description
1	Alpha	D A	Development Application
2	Alpha	N E	New product Enhancement
3	Alpha	S T Q F X	Stib Tegler Qwert Farkle Not application
4–5	Numeric	not applicable	Unique numerical project identifier

Examples:

DES03 — Development project #03 to enhance the Stib
AET01 — Application project #01 to improve production of the Tegler
DNX08 — New product development project #08

FIGURE Z10–2
Coded Data Elements
The figure illustrates the coding scheme for a five-position
R&D project code. Example coded data elements are shown
at the bottom.

Schedule and Monitor Production (3.3)

The Schedule and Monitor Production Subsystem receives the demand
forecast for the various Zimco products from the sales and marketing
component (4) of the overall Zimco MIS. These forecasts are what drive
the production process.

Mathematical models built into the Schedule and Monitor Production
Subsystem retrieve data from the integrated data base to generate a production requirements plan. This plan specifies week-by-week in-stock requirements for Stibs, Teglers, Farkles, and Qwerts. The plan tells the plant
manager what the rate of production for a particular product should be
over a period of time, usually six months. Plant managers take immediate
action if the information they get from this subsystem suggests that production levels may fall below production requirements.

The materials request, which is a by-product of the production requirements plan, is automatically generated and routed to the Acquire and
Manage Materials Subsystems (3.4).

Acquire and Manage Materials (3.4)

Materials Requirements Planning. Built into the overall Zimco MIS,
and specifically the Acquire and Manage Materials Subsystem, is the
philosophy of *material requirements planning*, often called *MRP*. MRP
is essentially a set of mathematical models that accepts data for production
requirements and translates these requirements into an optimal schedule

for the ordering and the delivery of the components and raw materials needed to manufacture Zimco's products.

Inventory Management and Control. The Acquire and Manage Materials Subsystem gets the materials request from the Schedule and Monitor Production Subsystem (3.3). The subsystem then generates purchase orders for the raw materials and components needed to meet production schedules. These purchase orders are sent to the suppliers, some via intercompany networking. An "electronic flag" is added to the integrated data base to notify the Finance and Accounting Division of the order.

Manufacturing companies such as Zimco must manage stock (components and raw materials) and finished-goods inventories. This subsystem (3.4) monitors the quantity on hand and the location of each inventory item. Figure Z10–3 illustrates the interactive, user-friendly nature of PICS with a few of the menus and input/output displays that are generated by the Acquire and Manage Materials Subsystem. The inventory inquiries in Figure Z10–3 are made by a user to Zimco's integrated data base, a CODASYL-based data base.

The data base subschema in Figure Z10–4 illustrates that portion of the integrated data base that relates specifically to the *inventory management and control application. The arrows indicate the one-to-many relationships between the five data base records; that is,* one record for a Zimco product will have cross-references to the *many* records of the stock items that make up that product.

The data base subschema in Figure Z10–4 is designed to minimize data redundancy. The *product* data base record contains a list of those items (e.g., components and raw materials) that are combined to produce a Zimco product. The two inventory records, *finished-goods* and *item,* maintain stock and order data. The *purchase* order record indicates what was ordered. The *supplier* record includes pertinent data about each supplier. The entire schema for Zimco's CODASYL-based integrated data base, which is not shown, includes relationships between these and other data base records.

Shipping (3.5)

In any manufacturing company, a product is conceived, designed, manufactured, sold, and ultimately shipped to the customer. The Shipping Subsystem (3.5) supports the last major activity in the manufacturing cycle. The orders are entered into SAMIS (Sales and Marketing Information System) by the field sales staff. Once an order is verified, a shipping notice is automatically sent to the Distribution Department via the Shipping Subsystem. Once the product is sent to the customer, acknowledgment is sent simultaneously to the Sales and Marketing Division and to

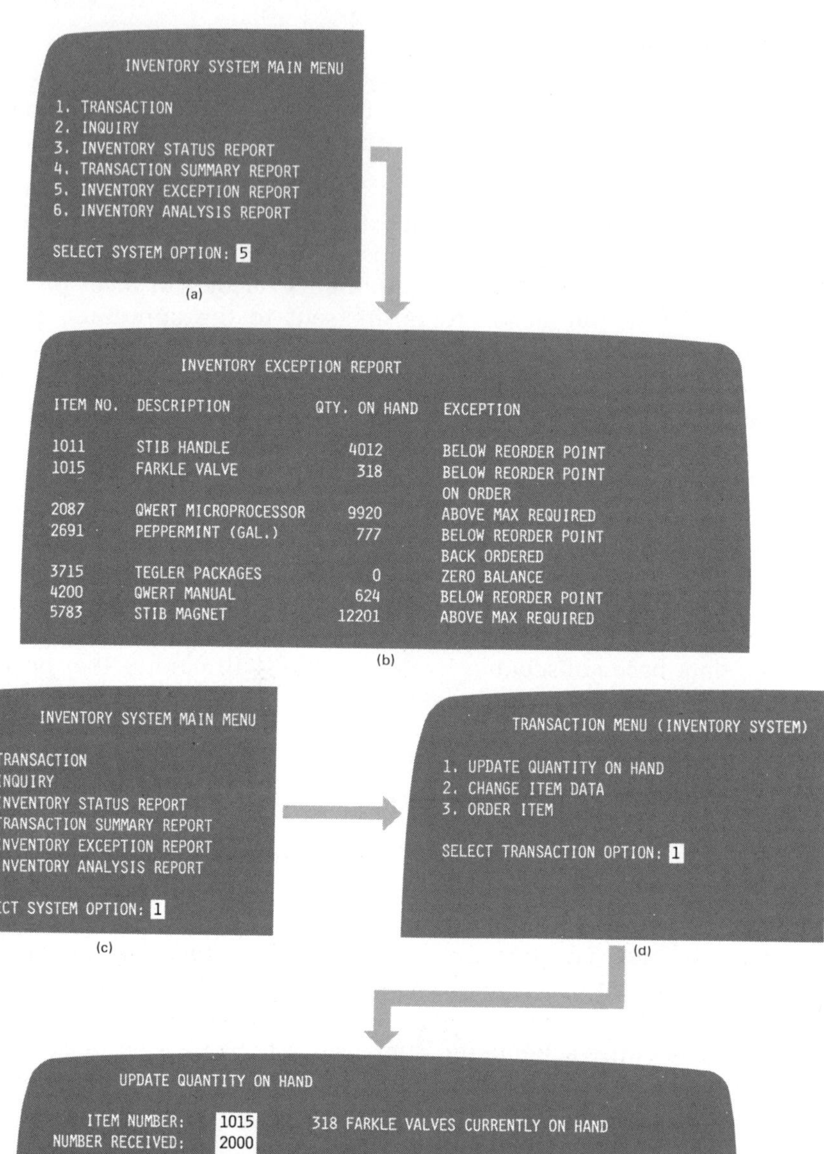

FIGURE Z10–3

Interactive Session with an On-Line Inventory System

(a) The main menu presents the user with six processing options. The user enters option "5" to obtain an inventory exception report. (b) This exception report is produced when main menu option "5" is selected. Only those inventory items whose quantity on hand is too high or too low are listed. (c) From the main menu, the user selected option "1" to get the transaction menu. (d) This screen is produced when main menu option "1" is selected. Desiring to update quantity on hand, the user selects transaction option "1." (e) From this transaction display screen, the user enters *item number* (1015), *number received* (2000), and *number used* (300) to update quantity on hand for Farkle valves.

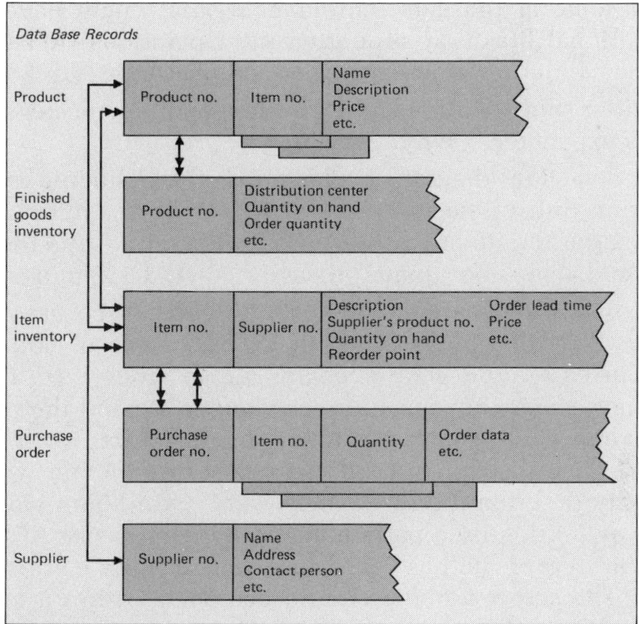

FIGURE Z10–4
**Data Base Subschema for the Inventory Management
and Control Application**
This data base subschema is that portion of Zimco's
integrated data base that deals directly with inventory
management and control. Links with these data base
records and other data base records in accounting and
finance are not shown.

the Finance and Accounting Division via the integrated data base. The
sales force monitors the progress of the order and accounting sends the
customer an invoice.

DISCUSSION QUESTIONS

1. Prior to implementing an integrated data base, Terri Suttor made
   the comment that Zimco may be data rich but it is information poor.
   Explain how Zimco can be data rich but information poor.
2. Ursula Lain, the Operations Division user liaison, was instrumental
   in the development and implementation of PICS. What can she do
   now to make PICS an even more effective tool for people in the Operations Division?

3. Identify some of the data redundancies that might have existed in the traditional files that supported the Operations Division prior to the implementation of an integrated data base.

4. Terri Suttor said: "With a DBMS, system maintenance is much easier and less expensive." Why?

5. Draw a data flow diagram explosion of the Schedule and Monitor Production Subsystem (3.3) showing the primary information flows between appropriate processes, the supplier entity, and the integrated data base. Label subordinate processes 3.3.1, 3.3.2, and so on.

6. A Zimco supplier manufactures screws and Zimco uses every type of screw that they make. They make all screws of both brass and steel. Currently, the screw lengths range from $\frac{1}{4}$ to 2 inches in $\frac{1}{4}$-inch increments, but the supplier plans to expand the product line to $3\frac{1}{2}$ inches. Each length of screw is manufactured with three types of heads—round, hex, and flat. Currently, production workers have to verbally describe the screw they want. Otto Mann would like an easier way to identify a particular screw.

   In that regard, he has asked that you set up a coding scheme to do this. The screw number should be coded within a minimum of positions to save disk storage. What coding scheme would you suggest?

CASE STUDY 11

Information Systems at Zimco: Sales and Marketing

MAKE VERSUS BUY

Zimco's original MIS Strategic Plan called for the in-house development of all four components of Zimco's MIS: FACS (finance and accounting), PERES (personnel), PICS (operations), and SAMIS (sales and marketing). Figure Z3–3 (in Zimco Case Study 3) contains an overview data flow diagram of Zimco's MIS. Limited resources dictated that the integrated MIS be developed and implemented in stages. The plan called for FACS to be implemented first, followed by PERES and PICS. SAMIS, the Sales and Marketing Information System, had the lowest priority, for two reasons. First, and perhaps most significant, Sally Marcio, VP of Sales and Marketing, was less vocal about the need for SAMIS than the other VPs were about their systems. Second, Sally was relatively satisfied with the information that she and her managers were receiving from an outside timesharing service.

The "Make" Alternative.   Several years ago during the early summer, Sally stormed into Conrad Innis's (VP of CIS) office and said: "The competition is getting the jump on us with better information. Also, that darned time-sharing service has doubled rates! We can't wait any longer; we've got to have SAMIS by the end of the year to stay competitive!"

At that time, work was not scheduled to begin on SAMIS for another 18 months. Conrad told Sally: "We simply don't have the resources to commit to a major new in-house development project. As an alternative, would you consider buying a commercial software package?"

The "Buy" Alternative. Zimco's Computer and Information Services (CIS) Division, like most centralized computer centers, suffers from a shortage of human resources. To help alleviate this problem, Zimco managers have occasionally opted to purchase and install commercially available software packages. The "package," sold by software vendors, consists of the programs (software) and their associated documentation. For larger, more complex packaged systems, vendors also provide training and consultation as part of the package.

Sally Marcio did not believe that the Sales and Marketing Division could wait a couple of years for CIS to develop an in-house (the "make" alternative) information system. She decided to take Conrad's advice and began looking for a packaged sales and marketing system (the "buy" alternative). After evaluating seven such systems, a search team recommended a package developed by a firm in Cleveland. Sally said: "With a few minor modifications, this system will fit our needs to a tee." Since the packaged system was compatible with Zimco's database management system, the modifications were relatively minor.

Because of the immediacy of the need and the availability of a product, Zimco management decided to "buy" rather than "make" the fourth component of the Zimco MIS. SAMIS went on-line in November, five months after Sally first related her sense of desperation to Conrad.

SAMIS: SALES AND MARKETING INFORMATION SYSTEM

SAMIS is that component of the integrated MIS that services the Sales and Marketing Division. The system interacts frequently with the other three MIS components: FACS, PERES, and PICS. Sally Marcio calls SAMIS the "wizard of Zimco" because of the way it helps to coordinate all activities within the Sales and Marketing Division. The five subsystems of SAMIS match up perfectly with the functions of the five departments in the Sales and Marketing Division. If you will remember, this is in contrast to the subsystems of FACS, PERES, and PICS which are not aligned with the organizational structures of their respective divisions. The five subsystems of SAMIS are:

4.1 Market Research Subsystem

4.2 Advertising and Promotion Subsystem

4.3 Customer Services Subsystem

4.4 Sales and Order Processing Subsystem

4.5 Sales Forecasting and Analysis Subsystem

The second-level data flow diagram of Figure Z11–1 is the explosion

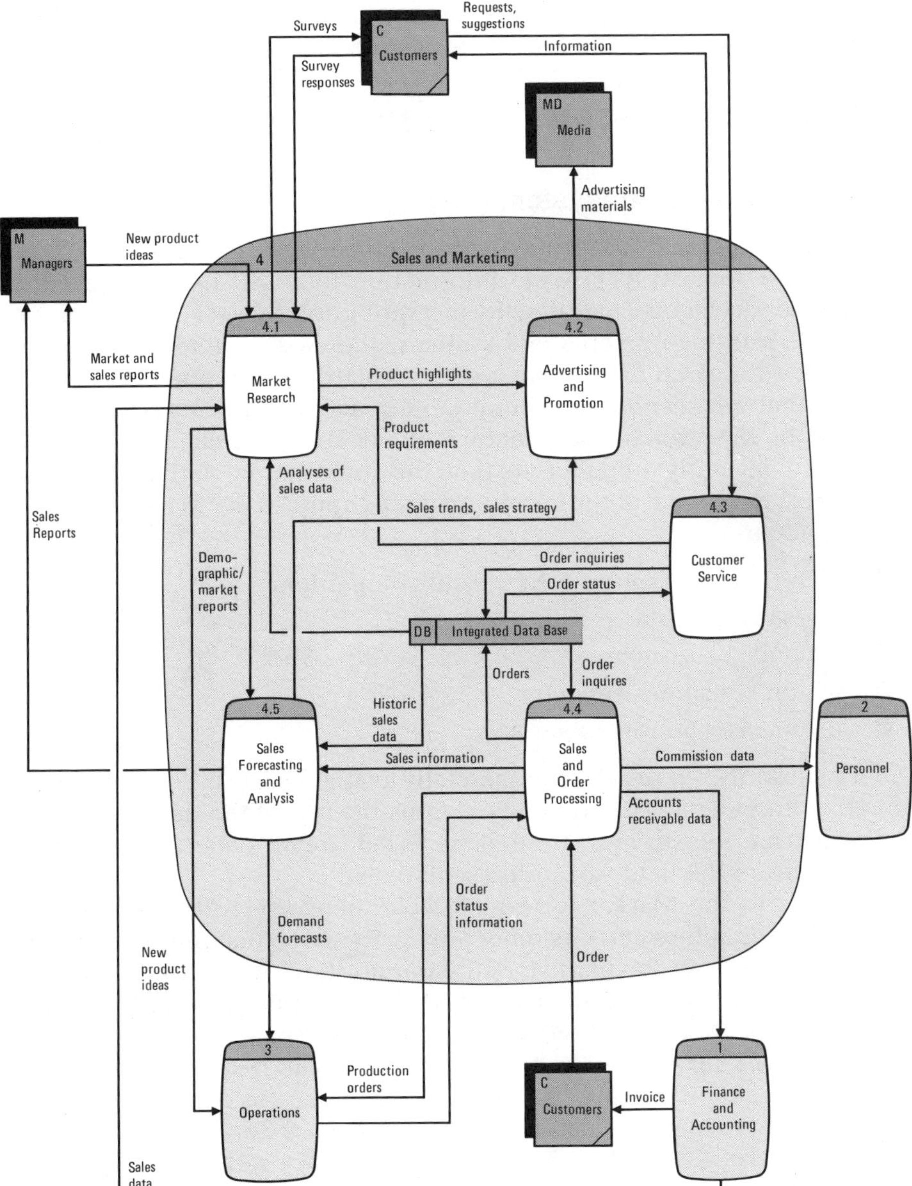

FIGURE Z11–1
Zimco's Sales and Marketing Information System (SAMIS)
This data flow diagram is the explosion of the sales and marketing (4) process of
the MIS overview data flow diagram of Figure Z3–3.

of the "sales and marketing" component of the Zimco MIS (see Figure Z3–3). Each of the five subsystems is described in the following sections.

THE FIVE SUBSYSTEMS OF SAMIS

Market Research Subsystem (4.1)

The Market Research Department systematically gathers all kinds of data that may in some way provide information that will help managers to make better decisions regarding the marketing and sale of Zimco products. Unlike accounting or personnel systems, the data gathered for input to the Market Research Subsystem are very volatile (see Figure Z11–1); that is, data that are seemingly accurate today may be erroneous tomorrow. Because of the everchanging nature of market research data, the data must be constantly updated so that the information derived from the data is representative of the current market. Inputs to the Market Research Subsystem are:

- Data on the marketing activities of competitors
- Demographic data
- Economic indicators
- Data on consumer behavior
- Customer responses to surveys

Zimco subscribes to several commercially available data bases that provide much of these data. The company obtains the rest of the data by periodically distributing surveys, from Zimco's integrated data base, and from feedback from the field sales representatives.

People in the Market Research Department use SAMIS to keep an eye on demographics and customer buying trends so that they can identify untapped niches in the market. Sally Marcio says: "Without SAMIS, certain segments of the marketplace would forever remain hidden. For example, for years we aimed the Farkles (inflatable cushions) sales pitch at commuters. A survey conducted by market research surfaced numerous domestic uses for Farkles. By broadening the scope of our advertising we were able to increase Farkle sales by 18 percent during the next year."

The Market Research Subsystem automatically gathers ideas for new products and enhancements to existing products from Zimco managers and from the Customer Service Subsystem. Last year one of Zimco's distributors reported that several women complained about the "unattractive" color of the Farkle. In response, the Market Research Department worked closely with the Operations Division to produce Farkles in pastel colors. Before releasing the pastel Farkles, Zimco test marketed them in Cincinnati and used SAMIS to monitor sales on a daily basis. The new brightly colored Farkles test marketed very well and are now a part of the product line.

The Market Research Subsystem includes a number of models that help researchers analyze and interpret the data. For example, each week the system determines if there is any statistically significant correlation between sales trends for the various Zimco products and other trends. For example, statistical techniques are used to correlate product sales to the consumer price index, unemployment level, furniture sales, and numerous other factors that might in some way influence the sale of a Zimco product. If a correlation exists, market researchers can identify trends early and give management some time to react, perhaps with an unscheduled price adjustment.

Advertising and Promotion Subsystem (4.2)

Zimco promotes their products through personal selling (exclusively to retailers and wholesalers), advertising, and promotional campaigns. The latter two are supported by the Advertising and Promotion Subsystem (see Figure Z11–1). The catalyst for the advertising and promotion activity is the information on sales trends and strategies provided by the Sales Forecasting and Analysis Subsystem.

Zimco routinely advertises in newspapers and magazines. The copy and graphics for these ads are generated on-line and routed directly to the print media via electronic mail. Occasionally, they advertise on television and radio. About three times a year, Zimco has promotional campaigns for each of their products. These campaigns usually involve price reductions or rebates. SAMIS has made it possible for the people at Zimco to analyze the effectiveness of their ads and promotional campaigns on a day-to-day basis. Sally Marcio is proud of SAMIS's contribution to her division's bottom line: "By identifying the most effective advertising medium, SAMIS helps Zimco managers to maximize the value of their advertising dollars."

The purchase price of SAMIS included the software and hardware for a computerized dialing system for *telemarketing*. The system, which is part of the Advertising and Promotion Subsystem, automatically dials a telephone number, then plays a prerecorded message. Sally Marcio decided to use this component of the subsystem to kick off a new promotional campaign. The telephone numbers of Zimco customers were entered into the system, then dialed automatically, one after another. Sally Marcio said: "Telemarketing sounded like a good idea, but it wasn't. Customer feedback was all negative. They let us know immediately that they didn't appreciate these 'computer' calls, so we turned the machine off the next day and haven't turned it on since." This incident reminds us that not all applications of computer technology are worthwhile.

Customer Services Subsystem (4.3)

The function of customer service representatives is to respond to any type of customer inquiry or complaint. Sally Marcio says: "Because of SAMIS, our customer service reps have on-line access to the integrated data base and just about any information that the customer would want to know."

For the more routine inquiries, many of Zimco's customers prefer the "Zimco Connection." Zimco customers are given a telephone number, a password, and an authorization code that will allow them to tap directly into SAMIS from their own workstations. Customers routinely establish an on-line link with the Customer Service Subsystem (see Figure Z11–1) to track orders and shipments and to get the latest pricing information. Of course, security precautions limit what customers can access and they can't change anything. According to Sally: "The Customer Service Subsystem has helped to build customer loyalty and has made relations with our customers much smoother. They know that if they have a question they can ask us or they can query our data base directly."

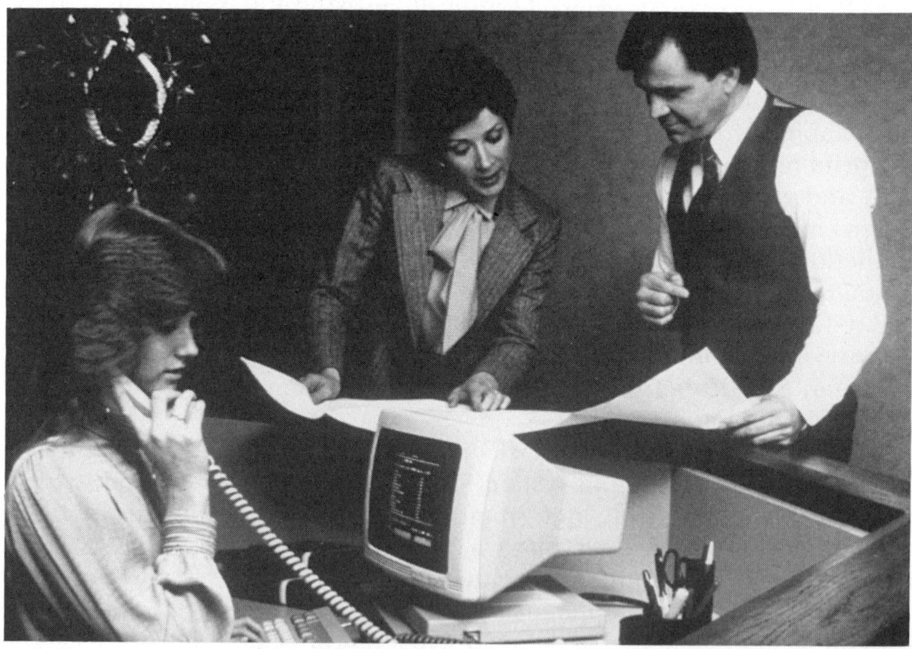

The Sales and Marketing Information System (SAMIS) provides Zimco customers with two methods for making inquiries about the status of an order. They can make their inquiry by telephone or they can use data communications to tap directly into customer-accessible portions of Zimco's integrated data base.

(Computer Consoles, Inc.)

One of the activities of the Customer Service Department is discussed in Zimco Case Study 5. That case study explains how customer service representatives use the integrated data base to send courtesy follow-up letters to customers with whom they have interactions during the day.

Sales and Order Processing Subsystem (4.4)

The Sales and Order Processing Subsystem (see Figure Z11–1) provides the facility for Zimco's field sales reps and Zimco's customers to enter orders directly into SAMIS and the integrated data base. Every field sales rep has a portable workstation. The rep can enter an order, make an inquiry, or send a message while in a customer's office. To do this, the rep simply dials the number of the Dallas mainframe on a telephone. Upon hearing the computer's high whistle "greeting," the rep inserts the telephone handset into the workstation's built-in modem. This makes the connection between the workstation and Zimco's mainframe computer.

Sally says that "the use of portables in the field has resulted in faster delivery to the customer, far less paperwork, and a better cash flow to Zimco. More often than not a sales rep can guarantee the customer that his order will be shipped within twenty-four hours. The customer appreciates that."

Just having the portable workstations gives the field reps a psychological boost. They know that they have a direct link to literally everyone in the company, even though they work out of their homes. All of them routinely send and receive electronic mail. Since the portable workstations double as microcomputers, the sales reps use them in stand-alone mode to do spreadsheet analysis and word processing.

The Sales and Order Processing Subsystem also provides support for *intercompany networking*. Some customers prefer to enter their orders directly from their mainframe computers into Zimco's mainframe at Dallas. Customers send the order data in a standard format and the order is confirmed with a return message from Zimco's mainframe computer. Sally reports: "Intercompany networking benefits our customer and us. Zimco customers are able to cut their inventories since they get quicker delivery. It cuts our paperwork substantially, thereby reducing the overall cost of sales."

Sales Forecasting and Analysis Subsystem (4.5)

The Sales Forecasting and Analysis Subsystem (see Figure Z11–1) uses mathematical models to combine the historical sales data, sales forecasts, and other predictive data to extrapolate sales trends for Zimco products. The production levels at each of the plants are based on the sales forecasts.

```
                      6-Month Demand Schedule (Stibs)
                Anticipated Unit Demand by Warehouse (1000s of units)

         Dallas % Chg.   Eugene  % Chg.   Benton  % Chg.   Reston  % Chg.   Total  % Chg
March     101    1.0%     210     1.5%     192     3.0%     222     0.5%     725    1.5%
April      97   -1.2%     215     4.0%     182    -2.0%     219    -1.0%     713    0.2%
May       105    5.0%     213     3.0%     183    -1.5%     225     2.0%     726    1.8%
June      109    8.0%     221     7.0%     197     6.0%     239     8.0%     766    7.2%
July       99    1.0%     206    -0.5%     184    -1.0%     230     4.0%     719    1.0%
August    110   -0.5%     205    -1.0%     187     0.5%     223     1.0%     725    0.1%
```

FIGURE Z11–2
6-Month Demand Schedule
This report is generated each month to help plant managers set production and finished-goods inventory levels. The "% Chg." columns indicate the percent change in the product demand estimate from the previous month's (February) "6-Month Demand Report."

Each month, the Sales Forecasting and Analysis Subsystem generates a 6-Month Demand Schedule for each of Zimco's products. Figure Z11–2 illustrates the March–August 6-Month Demand Schedule for Stibs.

The Operations Division uses these demand reports to schedule pro-

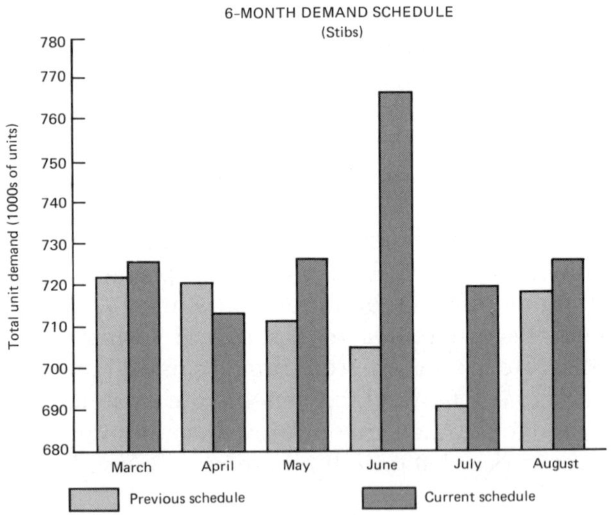

FIGURE Z11–3
Bar Chart for 6-Month Demand Schedule
This bar chart graphically highlights any major changes in the total product demand forecast (e.g., June) by comparing the demand estimates for the current "6-Month Demand Schedule" with the estimates on the previous month's schedule.

duction levels at the plants and to set minimum finished-goods inventory levels at each of the warehouses. Each month the "6-Month Demand Schedule" is updated to reflect current information. Notice the "% Chg." columns in Figure Z11–2. These figures indicate the percent change in the product demand estimate from the previous month's (February) "6-Month Demand Schedule." For example, the March Stibs demand for the Dallas warehouse is forecast to be 1 percent greater than it was a month ago. The bar chart in Figure Z11–3 graphically highlights any major changes in the monthly total demand estimates. From the figure, it is obvious that there will be a far greater demand for Stibs in June than was earlier expected.

SAMIS Summary

The examples presented in this case study represent only a small fraction of the capabilities of SAMIS. Sales managers can request a sales summary of the top 10 accounts in their regions. Orders can be received, processed, and billed without human intervention. When sales fall below the historical norm in a particular sales territory, the appropriate regional sales manager is automatically notified via electronic mail. Sally Marcio summed up her impressions of SAMIS very succinctly. "Before SAMIS, we had too much data and not enough information. Now we use information as a competitive weapon."

DISCUSSION QUESTIONS

1. Zimco management is routinely confronted with a "make versus buy" decision regarding software. Discuss the advantages and disadvantages of each alternative.

2. The Sales and Order Processing Subsystem permits field sales reps to make inquiries to the integrated data base from their portable workstations while in a customer's office. Discuss the types of inquiries that a sales rep might make.

3. Describe the benefits of intercompany networking for both Zimco and for Zimco's customers.

4. Zimco follows the five-phase system development methodology, from prototyping to post-implementation evaluation. Only part of the methodology was applied to SAMIS, since it is a software package. Identify these activities.

5. A search team, made up of people from both the CIS and Sales and Marketing Divisions, was formed to evaluate commercially available sales and marketing software packages. Discuss the criteria they might have used to select SAMIS.

6. What observations can you make about the information presented in the "6-Month Demand Schedule for Stibs" in Figures Z11–2 and Z11–3?

7. Currently, Zimco's computerized dialing system is unused. Suggest applications for this system that would benefit Zimco.

CASE STUDY 12

Productivity Improvement at Zimco

THE PRODUCTIVITY IMPROVEMENT PROGRAM

Three years ago, Preston Smith, Zimco's president, initiated a "Productivity Improvement Program" and challenged his management team to "do more work with less by increasing productivity." When he kicked off the program, he said: "The opportunities to increase productivity are staring us in the face. It's up to us to make a concerted effort to take advantage of them."

Preston was well aware of the fact that the "Productivity Improvement Program" (PIP to Zimco insiders) would be met with some resistance. People tend to resist change. In a half-encouraging and a half-threatening way, he told managers "to stop thinking status quo management and to get ready to make some bold decisions. If we plan to compete in a world economy, we can't rest on our laurels. We must agressively pursue every opportunity to make a better product at a lower cost."

This case study discusses some of the steps that Conrad Innis and his managers took to meet Preston Smith's challenge to improve productivity in the Computer and Information Services Division.

INCREASING PRODUCTIVITY IN CIS

During the first three months of the PIP program, Conrad Innis held weekly roundtable meetings with his managers for the express purpose of exchanging ideas on how the CIS Division could improve productivity. Literally hundreds of ideas were discussed, but the management group decided to focus on implementing only those that showed the most promise. Several of the more effective approaches are discussed in the following sections.

Adopting a Standardized Systems Development Methodology.   Besides providing a framework for coordinating the many activities during system development, a systems development methodology encourages project teams to do it right the first time. An oversight (perhaps an error in system logic) left undetected becomes more and more difficult to correct as the project progresses. A logic error that would take one hour to correct in Phase II would take nine days to correct in Phase V (see Figure Z12–1)!

With the systems development methodology now in place (see Chapter 11, "The Systems Development Process"), rigorous attention to detail causes errors to surface in the early stages of development.

Starting a Comprehensive In-House Education Program.   Conrad knew that there is a direct correlation between productivity and education, so he hired an education coordinator and provided funding for up to one month of education, for all technical professionals in CIS. In his argument to get funding for the education program, Conrad told Preston Smith:

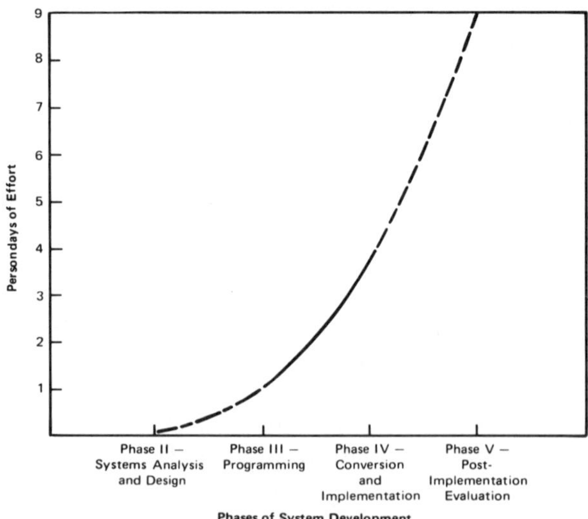

FIGURE Z12–1
The Cost of an Error
This chart depicts the relative personnel time required to correct a logic error when first detected in the different phases of development.

Through Zimco's in-house education program, users and computer specialists learn
new and better ways to use computer technology to improve their productivity.
(Cromemco, Inc.)

"Before we can realize the full potential of the division's productivity
efforts, the people in CIS must learn to exploit the latest technology."
Today, the education program is credited with making programmers, analysts, and other specialists much more productive because they are constantly learning new and better ways to apply the tools of their trade.

Establishing an Information Center.   Three years ago, three out of every
four user service requests were for one-time, ad hoc reports. And as Conrad
is often fond of saying: "The users always want these reports yesterday."
Today, Zimco users, from clerks to top management, routinely go to an
information center to get the information they need, usually in less time
than it would take to explain their need to a CIS programmer. The information centers, which are simply rooms with micros, workstations, and
user-oriented software, are located at the headquarters office and at each
of the plants. The availability of information centers has reduced time-
consuming one-time requests by 80 percent. Programmers and analysts
now have more time to devote to ongoing development projects.

Capturing Data Closer to the Source.   Three years ago, CIS still had 18
data entry operators; today, only two remain. Methodically, data entry

Throughout Zimco, data are captured as close
to the source as possible. Instead of filling out
a hard-copy source document that must be
transcribed into machine-readable format,
workers enter data directly to the integrated data
base from their workstations.
(Mohawk Data Sciences Corporation)

is being moved as close to the source as possible. For example, field
sales reps use their portable computers to enter orders directly into the
mainframe computer at Dallas. In the past, data entry operators had to
transcribe the data from the order form, usually from one to five days
after the field sales rep filled out the form. Also in the order processing
area, customers sometimes send in their orders via intercompany networking (data are sent computer to computer).

Implementing a Project Management System. When Conrad arrived at
Zimco in 1981, he observed that when a project got behind schedule,
the tendency was to "throw people at the project in an attempt to meet
an unrealistic deadline." Inevitably, the extra people caused more problems than they did good. This prompted Conrad to order a computer-
based project management system that would permit managers to monitor
and control project progress. Gram Mertz, the manager of the Programming

Department, said: "With the project management system, we are better able to isolate problems and make adjustments before things get out of hand."

Initiating Mandatory Periodic System Reviews.   Opie Rader, the manager of the Operations Department, was convinced that much of the computer capability and information that CIS was providing was not used. Opie said: "Over time, some of the services we provide became useless to our users, but nobody bothered to tell us. Now, each year we conduct a system review on all major systems. Each review usually results in our discontinuing certain marginal services."

Implementing a Chargeback System.   Before implementation of a charge-back system, the CIS Division was an information "candy store" and the candy was free. Users didn't appreciate the scope of their requests. Today, users are charged for all services provided by CIS. Conrad explained: "We implemented a chargeback system to encourage the judicious use of Zimco's computer and information resources. People, by nature, are more deliberate about what they ask for when they are spending their own money."

Encouraging Technology Transfer.   "Why reinvent the wheel?" asked Conrad Innis. "We should be applying existing technology whenever possible." Zimco has adopted a policy that requires systems analysts and programmers to evaluate the possibility of using commercially available proprietary software as an alternative to developing original software in house. Gram Mertz, manager of Programming, said: "It's a lot less expensive to buy a software package that the user likes than it is to make one ourselves from scratch."

Using Fourth- and Fifth-Generation Languages.   "Since we decided to use fourth- and fifth-generation languages, our programming productivity has increased at least 75 percent," says Gram Mertz. "We still do about half of our program development work in COBOL and Pascal (third-generation languages), but all of our quick-and-dirty reports are done with INGEN, our query language, and much of our production code is generated with our application generator."

Inviting Advice from Consultants.   Only recently did CIS begin using outside consultants. Old-timer Sybil Allen, manager of the Systems Analysis Department, said: "For years, if we got in a technical bind, we would drop everything and spend endless amounts of time fighting through the learning curve. Now if we have an occasional problem, we call in an expert consultant rather than disrupt operations." Zimco found out that by using consultants wisely, they could save money and time. Conrad retained a consultant to help CIS personnel create and implement their current systems development methodology.

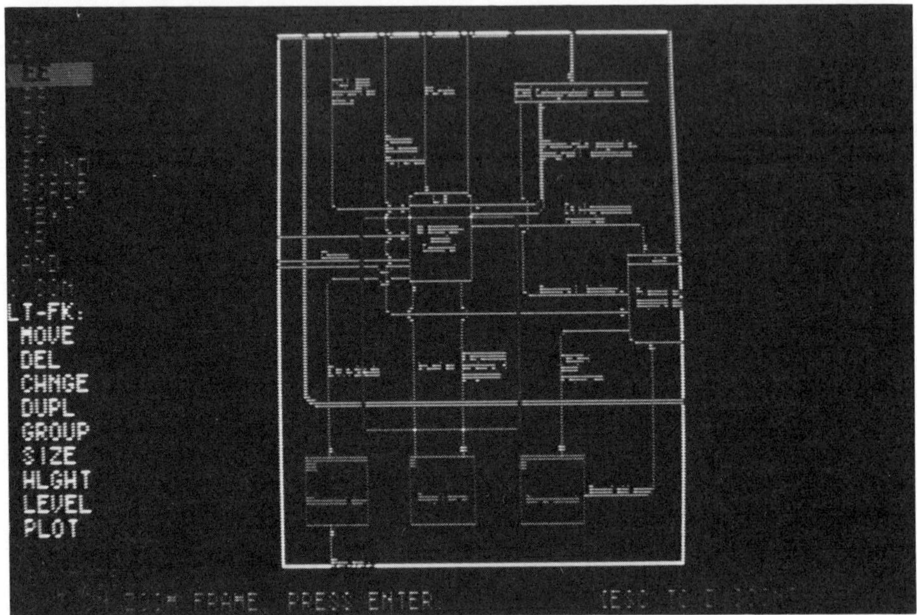

Software packages are available that enable programmers to design programs
interactively at their workstations. Zimco programmers and systems analysts have
made significant strides in productivity improvement since they began using an
automated package, called DFDraw, to create data flow diagrams.
(Long and Associates)

Promoting Better Keyboarding Skills. Every professional in the CIS division spends an average of four hours per day at a workstation. Ironically,
only one out of three had any formal keyboard skills training—most used
the "hunt-and-peck" method. Conrad said: "If we can improve the keyboarding skills of the people in CIS, we could improve productivity substantially." Those with marginal keyboarding skills were asked to spend
30 minutes a day for a month working with a self-paced microcomputer-
based keyboarding tutorial. By learning better keyboarding skills, programmers and analysts have improved their interactive effectiveness to the
point that they save from 30 minutes to one hour a day!

Using Automated Design Tools. Just two years ago, programmers and
analysts at Zimco were spending untold hours meticulously drafting and
revising flowcharts and data flow diagrams. Now, they design programs
and information systems using automated design tools. Instead of using
pencils, paper, templates, and erasures, they use computers and graphics
software. For example, analysts create data flow diagrams interactively
on a display screen by designating the type of symbol, where it is to go,
and its caption. Once all the symbols and flow lines are on the screen,

they can be moved, added, deleted, and revised to test out various solutions to a problem. Sybil Allen claims that "by using these on-line interactive design tools my analysts effectively work an extra hour a day."

More Ways to Improve CIS Productivity.   CIS took steps, other than those discussed in previous sections, to improve productivity. Other efforts included: reorganizing CIS to be more responsive to user needs; implementing a database management system to minimize data redundancy; rearranging the work areas for more efficient person/person and person/ machine interactions; and soliciting ongoing worker feedback through quality circles.

"THERE IS A BETTER WAY"

Conrad Innis often made the point, "there is a better way." He encouraged everyone in CIS to search for this better way, apply it, then tell others about it. Just three years after the initiation of Zimco's Productivity Improvement Program, CIS is claiming an overall increase in productivity of almost 100 percent. By religiously seeking a "better way," CIS has been able to keep pace with Zimco's ever-increasing demand for information and data processing services.

DISCUSSION QUESTIONS

1. Certainly, one of the advantages of a chargeback system is that user managers tend to be more judicious about the kinds of service that they request from CIS. What are the disadvantages of a chargeback system?
2. Figure Z12–1 illustrates how it is increasingly time consuming to correct a logic error in a system design as the project progresses. Explain why this is the case.
3. Conrad Innis said: "Before we can realize the full potential of the division's productivity efforts, the people in CIS must learn to exploit the latest technology." Give a couple of examples in support of Conrad's comment.
4. Why is the use of fourth- and fifth-generation languages considered a means to improve productivity?
5. How does having a systems development methodology help a project team to "do it right the first time"?
6. Sally Marcio, VP of Sales and Marketing, encouraged her division's participation in the PIP program. Do you think the Sales and Marketing

Division would be dependent on the CIS Division to help implement some of their productivity improvement measures? Explain.

7. Rather than take advantage of an information center to make their own ad hoc inquiries, a few Zimco users still rely on CIS personnel. What arguments would you make to convince these people that Zimco's information centers can benefit them, the company, and CIS?

CASE STUDY 13

Zimco's MIS Strategic Plan

MIS PLANNING AT ZIMCO ENTERPRISES

Three years ago Preston Smith, Zimco's president, made a rather profound statement during the annual meeting. He said: "At Zimco, our Computer and Information Services Division is no longer simply a data processing support function. With the capability to provide managers with valuable information on a timely basis, CIS is emerging as one of Zimco's most valuable strategic tools." This statement by Preston Smith set the stage for the development of Zimco's first *MIS Strategic Plan*. The first comprehensive plan was created in 1985 and it has been updated annually to reflect new directions in the area of computers and information processing.

The MIS Strategic Plan is compiled at two levels: the *strategic level* and the *operational level*. The more general strategic level contains the strategic objectives for the Computer and Information Services Division and is aimed primarily at top management. The operational portion of the plan identifies the specific activities that must be accomplished in order to achieve the strategic objectives, and it serves as a working document for CIS managers.

MIS Strategic Planning

The Need for Planning.   The MIS strategic planning effort evolved at Zimco because of a desperate need for corporate coordination of the development of the data base and in information dissemination. The MIS Strategic

Plan is subordinate to, and supportive of, Zimco's corporate *Five-Year Long-Range Plan*. The Five-Year Long-Range Plan focuses on the company's products and the MIS Strategic Plan focuses on the company's information and data processing needs. Conrad Innis, the VP of CIS, knew that it is easier to coordinate plans with the same planning horizon, so he chose a five-year planning horizon for the MIS Strategic Plan.

Even after Preston Smith made his statement at the annual meeting, the concept of MIS strategic planning had to be sold to management. Conrad Innis knew that if the plan was to be successful, he had to have the full cooperation of all managers at Zimco. To develop a viable plan, CIS planners need direction from top management and from user managers throughout the enterprise. Conrad used another one of his maxims to solicit their cooperation. He told them: "The time and money that you spend on helping us plan your information future is easily justified when you consider the potential cost of not planning."

Focus and Scope of the MIS Strategic Plan.   Conrad Innis says: "At Zimco, the compilation of the MIS Strategic Plan is viewed as an opportunity to recognize the shortcomings of the past and to lay the groundwork for a more responsive information services function in the future." The *focus* of the MIS Strategic Plan is on the *strategic objectives* and the *one-time and ongoing activities* that will enable CIS to provide the computer/information services support necessary to accommodate the growth and flexibility requirements of Zimco. The *scope* of the plan includes the *events and activities that are affected by or under the control of CIS*. Applications of computer technology are so pervasive at Zimco that the scope of the plan includes just about every area of corporate activity.

THE INFORMATION SYSTEMS POLICY COMMITTEE

CIS resources are not adequate to handle all user requests for service. Therefore, these requests must be prioritized for the overall good of the company. Conrad says: "I am not in a position to choose an accounting project over a manufacturing project. Wisely, Preston Smith decided that the best approach is to let those who are affected make these critical decisions. To do this, he created the Information Systems Policy Committee. We call it the ISPC for short." The members of the ISPC, Zimco's five vice-presidents, are charged with the following duties:

- Approve or reject requests for major MIS services.
- Set priorities among approved major information systems projects.
- Monitor the progress of major information systems development projects.

- Monitor the performance of ongoing information systems (e.g., PICS and PERES).
- Arbitrate differences between departments and/or divisions arising from CIS operations.
- Set policy that relates to computers and information processing.

The ISPC meets on the second Wednesday of each month. Inevitably, there are serious problems and priorities to be resolved. Conrad says: "If I made all the decisions regarding computer applications at Zimco, I wouldn't have very many friends. We have many heated debates during ISPC meetings, but ultimately, the cumulative thinking of top management determines what is best for Zimco."

THE CIS SITUATION ASSESSMENT

Zimco's MIS Strategic Plan is updated annually to reflect more current information and changing circumstances. The first planning activity, which is always conducted during the month of January, is the *situation assessment*. The situation assessment is an in-depth investigation of CIS by CIS managers. The end product of the situation assessment is a status report on the CIS Division. The investigation has three primary objectives:

1. To provide a candid assessment of where Zimco Enterprises stands with respect to the computer/information services technology as compared to other similar companies and the state of the art of the technology
2. To highlight areas for improvement within CIS and within the enterprise
3. To provide a foundation for the initiation of the annual CIS strategic and operational planning efforts

"The situation assessment is our report card," says Conrad Innis. "It tells what we've done right and it points out areas in which we need improvement." Some of the areas investigated during the situation assessment include: staffing, morale, operations and controls, standards, priorities, quality and effectiveness of information systems, hardware capacity, security, and relations with users.

STRATEGIC OBJECTIVES FOR CIS

Zimco's strategic objectives, which are listed in the following sections for each of 13 planning areas (see Figure Z13–1), are complementary to one another and to the focus of the overall plan. The strategic objectives

<table>
<tr><td>

Service
Policy
Information systems
Hardware
Systems software
Communications
Organization
Personnel
Management
Operations
Standards and procedures
Facilities
Office automation

</td><td>

FIGURE Z13–1
Strategic Planning Areas

</td></tr>
</table>

(the bulleted items) are followed by a brief discussion of several of the activities that would need to be accomplished to achieve these strategic objectives. These activities would be prioritized and scheduled in the operational portion of the MIS Strategic Plan.

Service

■ To support the information requirements of all levels of business activity in a timely, responsive, and cost-effective manner

One of the objectives outlined in Zimco's MIS Strategic Plan is to support the information requirements of all levels of business activity in a timely, responsive, and cost-effective manner.
(Photo courtesy of Hewlett-Packard Company)

Policy

- To establish policy for computer and information resources that provides guidelines for common situations and a framework by which CIS, corporate, and user management can cope with exceptional situations

Information Systems

- To integrate existing and proposed information systems in a data base environment
- To provide on-line inquiry capability in appropriate proposed and existing systems
- To emphasize user friendliness and distributed processing in systems design
- To make judicious use of proprietary software packages
- To conduct periodic system reviews

One of the objectives outlined in Zimco's MIS Strategic Plan is to provide greater user accessibility to the computer and information services through distributed processing. The Sales and Marketing Division has a distributed minicomputer for local processing. Division personnel can access the mini or Zimco's mainframe computer.
(Courtesy of Wang Laboratories, Inc.)

Hardware

- ■ To continue to upgrade and expand existing hardware to accommodate the growing data processing and information needs of the corporation
- ■ To provide greater user accessibility to the computer and information services through distributed processing
- ■ To integrate state-of-the-art hardware technology into the design of existing and proposed systems

Systems Software

- ■ To provide systems software support for distributed processing
- ■ To support user-oriented query languages

Communications

- ■ To emphasize data communications in the design of future information systems
- ■ To implement more effective approaches to verbal and written communication

Organization

- ■ To structure the organization within CIS to meet operational commitments and be responsive to Zimco's information services needs

One of the objectives outlined in Zimco's MIS Strategic Plan is to implement more effective approaches to verbal and written communication. The plant manager at Eugene, Oregon feels that the presentation of summary data in graphic format is more effective than a tabular presentation of the same data. (Photo courtesy of Hewlett-Packard Company)

Personnel

- To recruit and retain outstanding individuals with management potential
- To improve the quality of existing CIS personnel through career development
- To provide career alternatives for personnel who are not inclined to management
- To maintain a high level of CIS morale

Management

- To recognize the importance of good management
- To improve management's ability to manage through the effective use of proven management approaches and techniques

Operations

- To provide sufficient operational capability to achieve acceptable response times and turnaround times during peak periods

Standards and Procedures

- To develop and implement the standards and standardized procedures necessary to create the proper framework for information systems development and maintenance, and for effective interaction with users

Facilities

- To provide ergonomically sound working space for CIS personnel
- To work with corporate facility planners to ensure consideration of future communications, hardware, and security requirements
- To establish and maintain information centers at headquarters and at all plant sites

Office Automation

- To coordinate the integration of office automation equipment and applications into the Zimco computer network and into future information systems designs
- To encourage office automation in support of increased productivity for office personnel

THE OPERATIONAL PORTION
OF THE PLAN

The details for achieving the strategic objectives are explained and illustrated in the operational portion of the MIS Strategic Plan. In this part of the plan, the anticipated start and completion dates and the commitment of resources (e.g., person-months) for all activities within CIS are identified. A few of the many activities listed on the current plan include: the hiring of three new programmers and seven new analysts, a mainframe upgrade in the Dallas computer center, an enhancement to PICS, updating the programming standards manual, the presentation of four bimonthly user seminars on presentation graphics, and 55 other major activities to be accomplished over the next five years.

Identifying Specific Activities.   Since CIS resources are scheduled and allocated by activity, specific activities necessary to carry out the strategic objectives are identified. At Zimco, management identifies two types of activities: *project-oriented* (one-time) and *ongoing* activities.

Examples of project-oriented activities that were scheduled as a result of a previous Zimco MIS Strategic Plan include:

- The development of a prototype system for FACS
- An MIS security audit
- An enhancement to the Customer Service Subsystem of SAMIS
- The presentation of three in-house seminars on "The Effective Use of Business Graphics"
- A mainframe upgrade

Examples of ongoing activities that were scheduled as a result of a previous Zimco MIS Strategic Plan include:

- Operational support, control, and maintenance of PERES
- MIS strategic planning
- Compilation and distribution of "Compu-Talk," the monthly CIS newsletter

Setting Priorities and Scheduling.   Once the specific activities needed to carry out the strategic objectives have been identified, the ISPC (Information Systems Policy Committee) determines the priorities for major activities and CIS management prioritizes minor activities. The activities are now ready to be scheduled by CIS planners. The scheduling process requires that preliminary estimates of cost and personnel be made for each activity proposed.

The scheduling of CIS activities is essentially a trade-off between

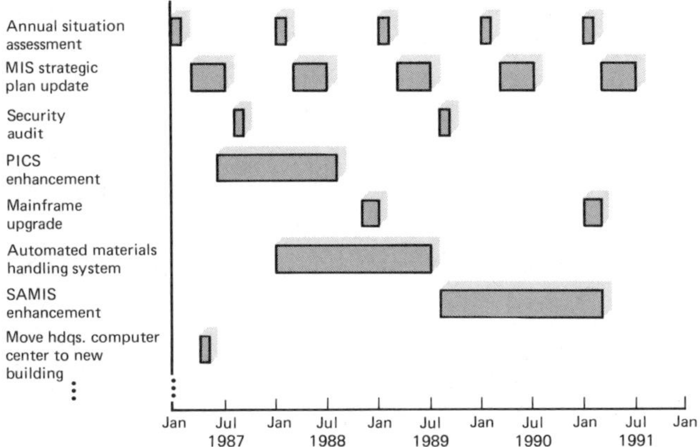

FIGURE Z13–2
CIS Project Schedule Chart (Partial)
The CIS Project Schedule Chart is a by-product of the
operational portion of the MIS Strategic Plan. It graphically
illustrates the scheduled start and end dates for all approved
projects.

maintaining the priorities set by the ISPC and CIS management and minimizing the fluctuation in personnel requirements (i.e., *work-load leveling*).
At any given time, CIS has 50 to 70 approved activities that are ready
to be scheduled. A portion of the CIS Project Schedule Chart is shown
in Figure Z13–2. The complete chart graphically illustrates the scheduled
start and end dates for all approved projects.

Summary.   Conrad Innis is very outspoken in his praise for the benefits
of MIS strategic planning. "MIS planning will never be easy. It requires
a commitment of support and cooperation from CIS managers, users managers, and top management. But in the long run, all of us would be
hard pressed to find a more cost-effective investment opportunity than
MIS strategic planning."

DISCUSSION QUESTIONS

1. Both the MIS Strategic Plan and the corporate Five-Year Long-Range
   Plan deal with all facets of Zimco operation. Why not combine them
   into a single plan?
2. What did Conrad Innis mean when he told Zimco managers to "consider the potential cost of not planning"?
3. The scope of the MIS Strategic Plan includes the events and activities

that are affected by or under the control of CIS. Describe areas within the Operations Division and within the Sales and Marketing Division that would be within the scope of the MIS Strategic Plan. What areas in these two divisions would not be considered within the scope of the MIS Strategic Plan?

4. Discuss the relationship between the strategic portion and the operational portion of the MIS Strategic Plan.

5. One of the charges of the Information Systems Policy Committee (ISPC) is to set priorities among major information systems projects that have been approved for development. Prior to the formation of the ISPC, Conrad Innis set all MIS priorities. Discuss the advantages of having the ISPC set the priorities.

6. Discuss the criteria that the Information Systems Policy Committee might use to set priorities for major information systems development projects.

7. Several of the CIS managers were very outspoken against conducting an annual situation assessment. Why?

8. Besides the MIS Strategic Plan, CIS also maintains a contingency plan that details what to do if some extraordinary event (e.g., fire in the machine room) drastically disrupts the operation of the headquarters computer center in Dallas. What kinds of information do you think would be included in the contingency plan?

Part II

Microcomputer Productivity Software

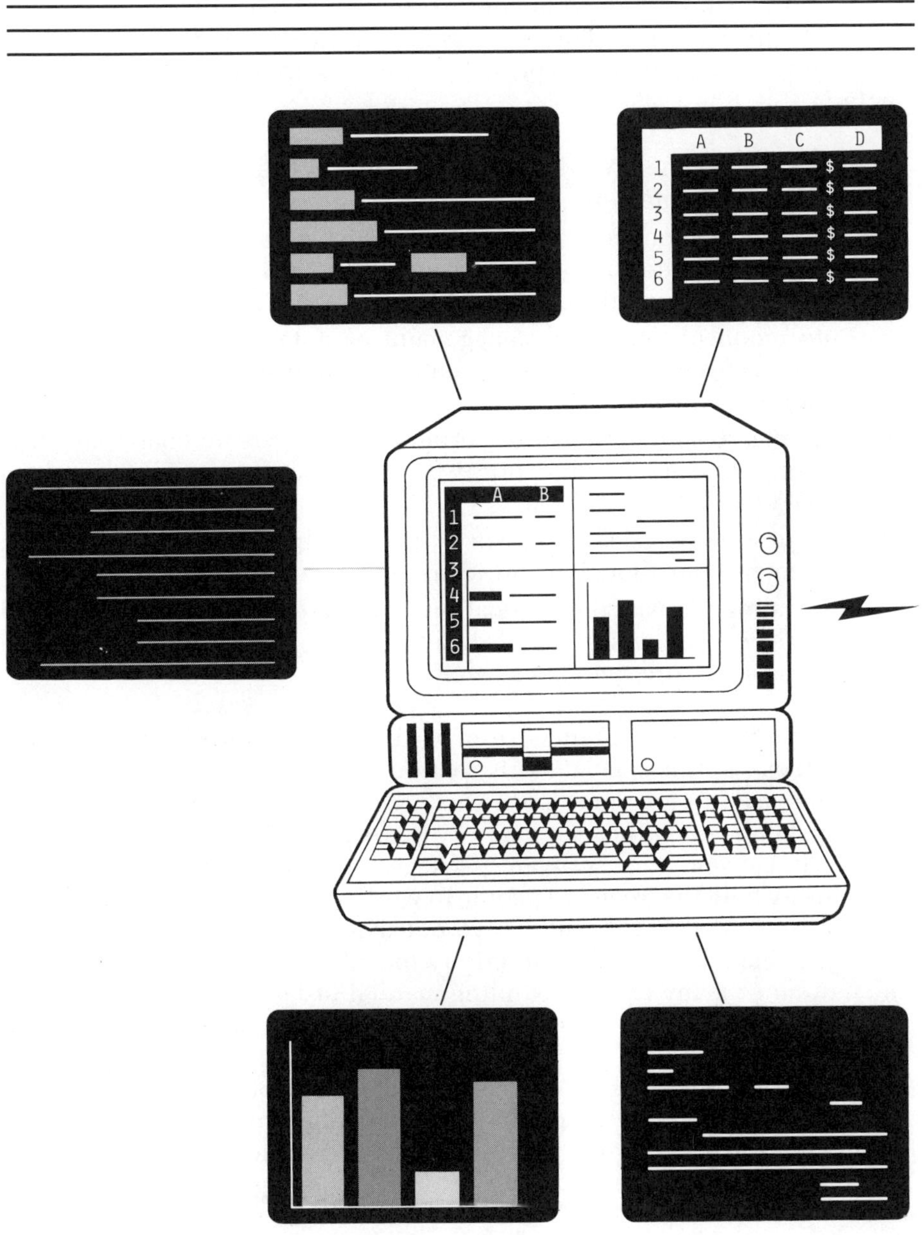

S-1   THE MICROCOMPUTER FAMILY OF PRODUCTIVITY SOFTWARE

Thousands of commercially available software packages run on microcomputers, but the most popular business software is the family of "productivity" software packages. These programs are the foundation of personal computing in the business world. The microcomputer productivity tools include:

- *Word processing.* Word processing software permits users to enter, store, manipulate, and print text.
- *Electronic spreadsheet.* Electronic spreadsheet software permits users to work with the rows and columns of a matrix (or spreadsheet) of data. Several spreadsheets can be contained in a single worksheet.
- *Data management.* Data management or **database** software permits users to create and maintain a data base and to extract information from the data base.
- *Graphics.* Graphics software permits users to create charts and line drawings that graphically portray the data in an electronic spreadsheet or data base.
- *Idea processors.* Idea processor software helps users to organize and document their thoughts and ideas.
- *Communications.* Communications software permits users to send and receive transmissions of data to/from remote computers, and to process and store the data as well.

The *function, concepts,* and *use* of each of these micro software tools are the focus of this special skills section.

"This used to take me over a week, and now I do it in 30 minutes!" Similar statements have been made by thousands of business micro users. These six categories of software packages are now proven productivity tools in any field that requires people to work with text, numbers, graphics, or ideas (and that list doesn't leave out many people!). These packages are often characterized as productivity tools because they help to relieve the tedium of many time-consuming manual tasks.

No more retyping—thanks to word processing software. Electronic spreadsheets permit us to perform certain arithmetic and logic operations without writing programs. With data management software we can format and create a data base in minutes. Say goodbye to grid paper, plastic templates, and the manual plotting of data: graphics software prepares bar, pie, and line charts without our drawing a single line. When brainstorming with idea processors, the result is a logical outline of conclusions, not indecipherable notes on a yellow pad. And communications software helps to minimize redundant data entry by permitting the transfer of files between computers.

In each productivity tool category, there are dozens of commercially available software packages from which to choose. The software packages in each category accomplish essentially the same functions. They differ primarily in the scope and variety of the special features they have to offer and in their "user friendliness."

S-2 INTERACTING WITH THE SYSTEM

User Friendly.   Software is said to be **user friendly** when someone with relatively little computer experience has little difficulty using the system. User-friendly systems communicate easily understood words and phrases to the end user, thus simplifying the user's interaction with the computer system. A central focus of the design of micro productivity software is user friendliness.

There are, of course, degrees of user friendliness. At the first level, it is assumed that the user has little or no experience and that the user's interaction with the software will be tentative and deliberate. At this level, the system offers some welcome "hand holding." For example, some software packages use **icons** or pictographs, rather than words or phrases, to communicate with the end user. When you wish to issue a file handling command, for example, you position the cursor near the icon representing files (perhaps a file cabinet or a diskette). When you select a particular icon, you are then presented with a menu of file handling choices. Your choices might be to save, retrieve, or delete a file.

The first level of user friendliness may be too friendly, and even cumbersome, for the seasoned user. Too much hand holding forces experienced users to work more slowly than they would like; therefore, micro software provides alternatives. As you become familiar with the software, you can learn and use techniques that offer more efficient interaction with the system.

A handy feature available on most software packages is the **help command.** When you find yourself in a corner, you can press the "help" key, and more explanation or instruction is displayed on the screen. When you are finished reading the help information, the system returns you to your work at the same point that you left it.

Input and Control.   A microcomputer's *keyboard* is normally the primary input and control device. You enter data and issue commands via the keyboard. It has, besides the standard typewriter keyboard, *function keys,* also called *soft keys*. When pressed, these function keys trigger the execution of software, thus the name "soft" key. For example, pressing a particular function key might call up a menu of possible activities that can be performed. Another function key might rearrange the words in a paragraph for right and left justification. Some keyboards are equipped with a *10-key pad* (numbers for rapid numeric data entry).

A keyboard also has *cursor control keys*. These "arrow" keys allow you to move the cursor up, down, left, and right. Pressing the *HOME* key results in different actions for different packages, but often, the cursor is moved to the beginning of a work area (e.g., the start of the document in word processing).

Other important keys common to most keyboards are the *backspace* (*BKSP*), *escape* (*ESC*), *control* (*CTRL*), and *alternate* (*ALT*) keys.

Press the BKSP key to move the cursor one position to the left and delete the character in that position. The ESC key may have many functions, depending on the software package, but in most situations you can press the ESC key to negate the current command. The CTRL and ALT keys are used in conjunction with another key. You hold down a CTRL or ALT key to give another key new meaning. For example, on some word processing systems you press HOME to move the cursor to the top left corner of the screen. When you press CTRL and HOME together, the cursor is positioned at the beginning of the document.

Another device used for input and control is the *mouse*. The hand-held mouse is connected to the computer by an electrical cable (the mouse's tail) and rolled over a desktop to move the cursor. Buttons on the mouse are activated to select a menu item or to perform certain tasks, such as moving blocks of data from one part of the screen to another.

Menus.   When using these productivity tools, you issue commands and initiate operations by selecting activities to be performed from a *hierarchy of menus*. These hierarchies are sometimes called "menu trees." When you select an item in the *main menu*, you are normally presented with another menu of activities, and so on—thus the "tree." Depending on the items you select, you may progress through as many as eight levels of menus before processing is initiated. The menus appear in a *control panel* or a *pull-down menu*. The control panel is usually, but not always, located at the bottom or top of the screen. The pull-down menus are superimposed in a **window** over whatever is currently on the screen. You select a particular menu item by positioning the cursor over or next to the desired menu item with the cursor control keys or a mouse.

The main menu of a graphics software package might give you the choice of what type of chart you want produced: *bar chart*, *pie chart*, or *line chart*. If you select *bar chart*, then another menu gives you more choices: Do you wish to *create* a new one or *revise* an existing one? If you select *create*, then more menus are presented that permit you to describe the appearance of the chart (e.g., labels) and to identify what data are to be charted.

At some point in the menu hierarchy, the user is asked to enter the specifications for data to be charted (graphics software) or the size of the output paper (word processing software), and so on. As a convenience to the user, many of the specification options (size of output paper) are already filled in to reflect common situations (e.g., document size is set at $8\frac{1}{2}$ by 11 inches). If the user is satisfied with these **default options,** no further specifications are required. The user can easily revise the default options to accommodate the less common situations. For example, to print a document on legal-size paper, the default paper length of 11 inches would need to be revised to 14 inches.

The Operating System.   The nucleus of a microcomputer system is its **operating system.** All hardware and software, including micro productivity software, are under the control of the operating system. It is to the advantage of the users of micro software to learn something about the operating system for their particular micro. Beside being "the boss" program, the operating system enables users to run application programs such as word processing and it provides users with a variety of file handling capabilities. Unfortunately, the logic, structure, and nomenclature of the different operating systems vary considerably, so we'll not present operating system specifics in this section. Your instructor will tell you what you need to know to run a particular software package.

Micro Operating Systems.   The operating system is usually, though not always, supplied by the micro vendor. Some of the more popular micro operating systems are MS DOS, developed by Microsoft Corporation, CP/M, developed by Digital Research Corporation, and UNIX, developed by AT&T. You may encounter spin-offs of these operating systems. For example, PC DOS for the IBM PC is based on Microsoft's MS DOS, and XENIX is a spin-off of UNIX.

Booting the System.   Before you can use a microcomputer, you must "**boot** the system." The procedure for booting the system on most micros is simply to load the operating system from disk storage into main memory. For most micros, this is no more difficult than inserting an operating system diskette (floppy disk) in a disk drive and flipping the "on" switch. On some systems all you have to do is turn the system on. A few seconds later, with the operating system in memory, you are ready to begin processing. Some operating systems give you the option to enter date and time data before displaying the **system prompt.**

Running a Software Package.   The system prompt is the operating system's message to you, the user, so that you can now enter a *system com-*

mand (e.g., to copy files from one diskette to another) or the name of the program (e.g., if you wish to run an applications program such as an electronic spreadsheet). The form of the system prompt varies among operating systems. A common prompt is the "greater than" symbol prefaced by a disk drive specification (e.g., A> is the prompt when the disk drive "A" is the active or default drive). Other common system prompts are the "$" (dollar sign) and the "]" (close bracket).

Once you have loaded the operating system to memory and the system prompt is displayed on the screen, you are ready to run a graphics package, a word processing package, or any other software package. To run a software package, you simply insert the diskette containing the software in the appropriate disk drive (if needed), then enter the name of the file that contains the applications software. For example, to run a particular word processing package on an MS DOS-based micro, you would load the software diskette to drive A, then key in "wp" (the name of the program file) after the system prompt. The command would look like this:

    A> wp

The next thing you would see would be the opening screen and eventually the main menu for the word processing package. All micro productivity tools are run in the same manner, unless they are made to be *self-booting* (i.e., the operating system and the applications software are on the same diskette). By making a software package self-booting, you can bypass the step that requires you to enter the name of the program file after the prompt.

Utility Programs.   The operating system contains certain utility programs that allow you to perform such activities as:

- Formatting (preparing) a diskette for processing
- Copying the contents of one diskette to another diskette
- Renaming, copying, or deleting a file
- Listing the files on a particular **directory**

A directory is a named area on disk in which files are stored. Hard disks can be divided into several logical directories. All files on a particular diskette take on the directory designation for the disk drive into which the diskette is loaded (e.g., the directory for drive A).

Learning to Use Micro Productivity Tools.   The fundamental operation of the various word processing software packages is essentially the same. The same is true of the other productivity tools. Their differences are primarily in the way the software interacts with the user (e.g., menus options, presentation of output). The software tutorials in this special skills section are designed to give you a strong conceptual understanding of the features and use of these micro productivity tools.

SuperSoftware, one of the software supplements to this text, contains generic hands-on tutorials that demonstrate the features and operation of these tools. Between the textual material, hands-on experience with SuperSoftware, and in-class lectures, you should develop skills that can easily be translated to using any of the software packages that you might encounter at your college or place of business.

When you purchase a software package, you will receive at least one manual, the software on diskettes, and a *tutorial disk*. It is a good idea to go over the tutorial disk to get a feeling for the menu options and how the software interacts with the user. When you load the tutorial disk on the micro, an instructional program interactively walks you through a simulation (demonstration) of the features and use of the software. Once you have an overview understanding of the features and how the components fit together, it is easy to go to the manual for specific operational questions.

REVIEW EXERCISES (S-1 and S-2)

1. Name and briefly describe the six microcomputer productivity tools.
2. What is the function of soft keys? Of cursor control keys?
3. Name microcomputer input devices other than the keyboard.
4. Describe the attributes of user-friendly software.
5. Contrast a control panel and a pull-down menu.
6. Most word processing packages have a default document size. What other defaults would a word processing package have?
7. What is meant by "booting the system"?

S-3 WORD PROCESSING

Function

Word processing, the "glamor" software of the 1970s, has become the mainstay application of computers in virtually every office. Word processing is using the computer to enter, store, manipulate, and print text in letters, reports, books, and so on. Once you have used word processing, you will probably wonder (like a million others before you) how in the world you ever survived without it!

Word processing has virtually eliminated the need for opaque correction fluid and the need to re-key revised letters and reports. Revising a hard copy is time consuming and cumbersome, but revising the same text in electronic format is quick and easy. You simply make corrections and revisions to the text on the computer before the document is displayed or printed in final form.

Concepts

Formatting a Document.   When you *format* a document, you are describing the size of the print page and how you want the document to look when it is printed. As with the typewriter, you must set the left and right margins, the tab settings, line spacing (e.g., lines/inch), and character spacing (e.g., characters/inch). Depending on the software package, some or all of these specifications are made in a *layout line*. You can have as many layout lines as you want in a single document. Text is printed according to specifications in the most recent layout line until another layout line is defined. You must also specify the size of the output document, then set margins for the top and bottom of the text. The default document size is almost always $8\frac{1}{2}$ by 11 inches.

As an option, you can even *justify* (line up) both the left and the right margins, like the print in newspapers and this book. Word processing software is able to produce "clean" margins on both sides by adding small spaces between characters and words in a line.

Entering Text.   To begin preparation of a document, all you have to do is begin typing. Text is entered in **replace mode** or **insert mode.** When in replace mode, the character that you enter *overstrikes* the character at the cursor position. For instance, suppose that you typed the word "the," but you wanted to type "and." To make the correction in replace mode, you would position the cursor at the "t" and type a-n-d, thereby replacing the "the" with "and."

On most word processing systems, you "toggle" or switch between replace and insert mode by pressing a key. When in insert mode, you can enter *additional* text. Let's use a memo written by George Brooks, the Northern Regional Sales Manager for Zimco Enterprises to illustrate the effects of insert mode data entry. George often uses word processing to generate memos to his staff. The first draft of one of George's memos is shown in Figure S-1. George wanted to emphasize that an upcoming meeting was to be on Thursday, so he decided to insert "See you Thursday! " just before the last sentence. To do this, he selected the insert mode, placed the cursor on the "W" in "We'll," and entered "See you Thursday! " (see Figure S-2).

Word processing permits *full-screen editing*. That is, you can move the cursor to any position in the document to insert or replace text. You can browse through a multiscreen document by *scrolling* a line at

```
To:      Field Sales Staff
From:    G. Brooks, Northern Sales Manager
Re:      Weekly Briefing Session

     The Sales Department's weekly briefing session will be
held at 9:00 a.m. this Thursday.  Last month's sales figures
and new sales strategies for the Tegler and Qwert will be
discussed.  We'll meet in the second floor conference room.
```

FIGURE S-1
Word Processing: Memorandum
This first-draft memo is revised for illustrative purposes in Figures S-2 through S-6.

a time or a "page" (a screen) at a time. You can edit any part of any screen.

When you enter text, you press the carriage return key only when you wish to begin a new line of text. As you enter text in replace mode, the computer automatically moves the cursor to the next line. In insert mode, the computer manipulates the text such that it *wraps around*, sending words that are pushed past the right margin into the next line, and so on, to the end of the paragraph. In Figures S-1 and S-2, notice how the words "conference room." (in the last sentence) are wrapped around to the next line when "See you Thursday! " is inserted.

Block Operation.   Features common to most word processing software packages are mentioned and discussed briefly in this section. The *block* operations are among the handiest of word processing features. They

```
To:      Field Sales Staff
From:    G. Brooks, Northern Sales Manager
Re:      Weekly Briefing Session

     The Sales Department's weekly briefing session will be
held at 9:00 a.m. this Thursday.  Last month's sales figures
and new sales strategies for the Tegler and Qwert will be
discussed.  See you Thursday!  We'll meet in the second floor
conference room.
```

FIGURE S-2
Word Processing: Insert Mode
This memo is the result of the sentence "See you Thursday!   " being inserted before the last sentence of the memo of Figure S-1. Notice how the text wraps around to make room for the addition of a sentence.

are the block *move*, the block *copy*, and the block *delete* commands. Let's discuss the move command first. These commands are the electronic equivalent of a "cut and paste" job. With the move feature, you can select a block of text (e.g., a word, a sentence, a paragraph, a section of a report, or as much contiguous text as you desire) and move it to another portion of the document. To do this, follow these steps:

1. Issue the move command (a main menu option or a function key).
2. Indicate the start and ending positions of the block of text to be moved (*mark* the text).
3. Move the cursor to the beginning of the designation location (where you wish the text to be moved).
4. Press the carriage return (or the appropriate function key) to complete the move operation.

At the end of the move procedure, the entire block of text that you select is moved to the location that you designate and the original is deleted. The sequence of the text is adjusted accordingly.

The following example demonstrates the procedure for marking and moving a block of text. After reading over the memo (of Figure S-2), George decided to edit his memo to the field staff to make it more readable. He did this by "moving" the last sentence from the end of the memo to just after the first sentence. To perform this operation, he first selected the move option (a function key on his word processing system) and designated the beginning ("W" in "We'll") and end ("." at end of paragraph) of the block. On most word processing systems, the portions of text that are marked for a block operation are usually display in *reverse video* (see Figure S-3). After marking the block, George then positioned the cursor at the designation location (just after the first sentence) and pressed the appropriate key (a function key) to complete the operation (see Figure S-4).

```
To:     Field Sales Staff
From:   G. Brooks, Northern Sales Manager
Re:     Weekly Briefing Session

     The Sales Department's weekly briefing session will be
held at 9:00 a.m. this Thursday.  Last month's sales figures
and new sales strategies for the Tegler and Qwert will be
discussed.  See you Thursday! We'll meet in the second floor
conference room.
```

FIGURE S-3
Word Processing: Marking Text for a Block Operation
The last sentence of the memo of Figure S-2 is marked to be moved.

```
To:     Field Sales Staff
From:   G. Brooks, Northern Sales Manager
Re:     Weekly Briefing Session

     The Sales Department's weekly briefing session will be
held at 9:00 a.m. this Thursday. We'll meet in the second
floor conference room. Last month's sales figures and new
sales strategies for the Tegler and Qwert will be discussed.
See you Thursday!
```

FIGURE S-4
Word Processing: Move Text
This memo is the result of the marked block in Figure S-3 being moved to a position following the first sentence.

The copy command works in a similar manner, except that the text block you select is copied to the location that you designate. At the completion of the operation, two exact copies of the text are present in the document. To delete a block of text, mark the block in the same manner, then select the delete block option.

The "Search" Features.   Just as George Brooks was about to print his memo (Figure S-4), he learned that an important client was coming to town on Thursday, so he decided to switch the meeting from Thursday to Friday. He can make the necessary revisions to the memo by using any of several word processing features. One option is to use the *search* or *find* feature. This feature permits George to search through the entire document and identify all occurrences of a particular character string. For example, if George wanted to search for all occurrences of "Thursday" in his memo of Figure S-4, he would simply initiate the search command and type in the desired *search string*, "Thursday" in this example. The cursor is immediately positioned at the first occurrence of the character string "Thursday" so he can easily edit the text to reflect the new meeting day. From there, he can "find" other occurrences of "Thursday" by pressing the appropriate key.

As an alternative approach to making the Thursday-to-Friday change, George could use the *search and replace* feature. This feature enables George to selectively replace occurrences of "Thursday" in his memo with "Friday." Since he knew that he wanted *all* occurrences of "Thursday" to be replaced by "Friday," he performed a *global search and replace* (see Figure S-5).

Features That Enhance Appearance and Readability.   George used several other valuable word processing features to enhance the appearance and readability of his memo before distributing it to his staff. First, he decided

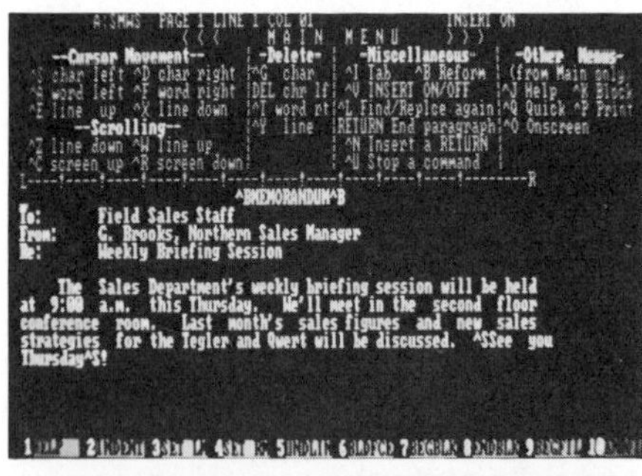

FIGURE S-5
Word Processing: Search and Replace
With the search and replace command, the two occurrences of "Thursday" in Figure S-4 are located and replaced automatically (option "A") with "Friday."

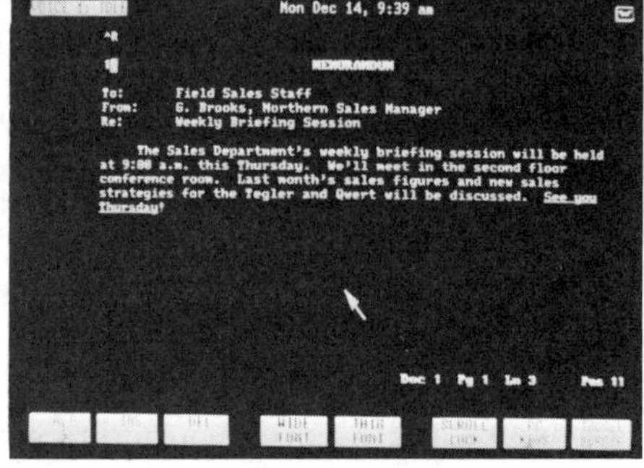

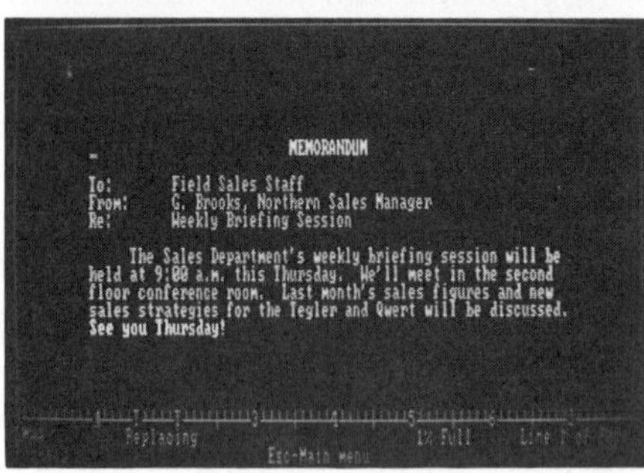

The memo of Figure S-6 was prepared and printed with three popular word processing packages. The first photo illustrates how the memo would be displayed using WordStar (WordStar is a trademark of MicroPro International Corporation). The second photo illustrates how the memo would be displayed using WordPerfect (WordPerfect is a trademark of Satellite Software International). The third photo illustrates how the memo would be displayed using Writing Assistant (Writing Assistant is a trademark of IBM Corporation).

(Long and Associates)

to enter the word "MEMORANDUM" at the top of his memo and use the automatic *centering* feature to position it in the middle of the page. On his word processing system, all he has to do to center whatever is on a particular line is to move the cursor to that line and press the "center" function key. The rest is automatic (see Figure S-6).

```
                    bMEMORANDUMb

To:-    Field Sales Staff
From:   G. Brooks, Northern Sales Manager
Re:     Weekly Briefing Session


    The Sales Department's weekly briefing session will be
held at 9:00 a.m. this Thursday.  We'll meet in the second
floor conference room.  Last month's sales figures and new
sales strategies for the Tegler and Qwert will be discussed.
uSee you Thursdayu!
```

```
                  MEMORANDUM

To:     Field Sales Staff
From:   G. Brooks, Northern Sales Manager
Re:     Weekly Briefing Session


    The Sales Department's weekly briefing session will be
held at 9:00 a.m. this Thursday.  We'll meet in the second
floor conference room.  Last month's sales figures and new
sales strategies for the Tegler and Qwert will be discussed.
See you Thursday!
```

```
                  MEMORANDUM

To:     Field Sales Staff
From:   G. Brooks, Northern Sales Manager
Re:     Weekly Briefing Session


    The Sales Department's weekly briefing session will be
held at 9:00 a.m. this Thursday.  We'll meet in the second
floor conference room.  Last month's sales figures and new
sales strategies for the Tegler and Qwert will be discussed.
See you Thursday!
```

FIGURE S-6
Word Processing: Boldface and Underline
Text to be in boldface type or underlined is displayed differently, depending on the word processing system and the color or resolution of the monitor.

Word processing provides the facility to *boldface* and/or *underline* parts of the text for emphasis. In the memo of Figure S-6a, the reverse video "b" before and after the word "MEMORANDUM" causes it to appear in boldface print on output (see Figure S-7). The reverse video "u" before and after the sentence "See you Thursday!" (see Figure S-6a) causes it to be underlined on output (see Figure S-7). Some word processing systems display text that is to be in boldface type or underlined on output in reverse video. On a color monitor, the distinction can be made by displaying the text in different colors (see Figure S-6b). Systems with high-resolution monitors permit text to be displayed in boldface and underlined directly on the display screen (see Figure S-6c).

In creating the memo of Figure S-7, George Brooks used many, but not all of the features commonly used to enhance appearance and readability. He did not need the feature that allows him to *indent* a block of text. Also, his word processing software automatically prints *header* and *trailer labels*. The *pagination* feature automatically numbers the pages. On long reports, George usually repeats the report title at the top of each page (header label) and numbers each page at the bottom (pagination). These and other word processing features are illustrated in Figure S-8.

Printing a Document.   To print a document, all you have to do is ready the printer (turn it on and align the paper) and select the print option on the main menu. Some word processing systems present you with a few final options. For example, you can choose to print the document as single or double spaced, or you are given the option to print specific pages or the whole document. Depending on the type of software and printer you have, you may even be able to mix the size and style of type fonts in a single document. For example, George could print the word "MEMORANDUM" in 48-point (about $\frac{1}{2}$ inch high) old English print if he wanted to.

For some word processing packages, what you see is what you get. That is, what is displayed on the screen is what the document will look

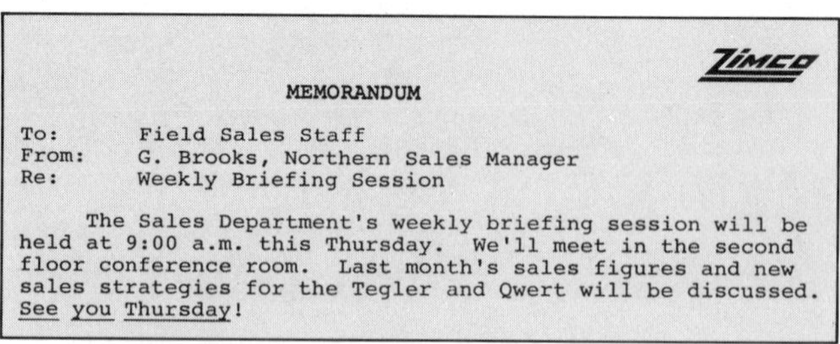

FIGURE S-7
Word Processing: Printing Text
The memo of Figure S-6 is printed on letterhead paper.

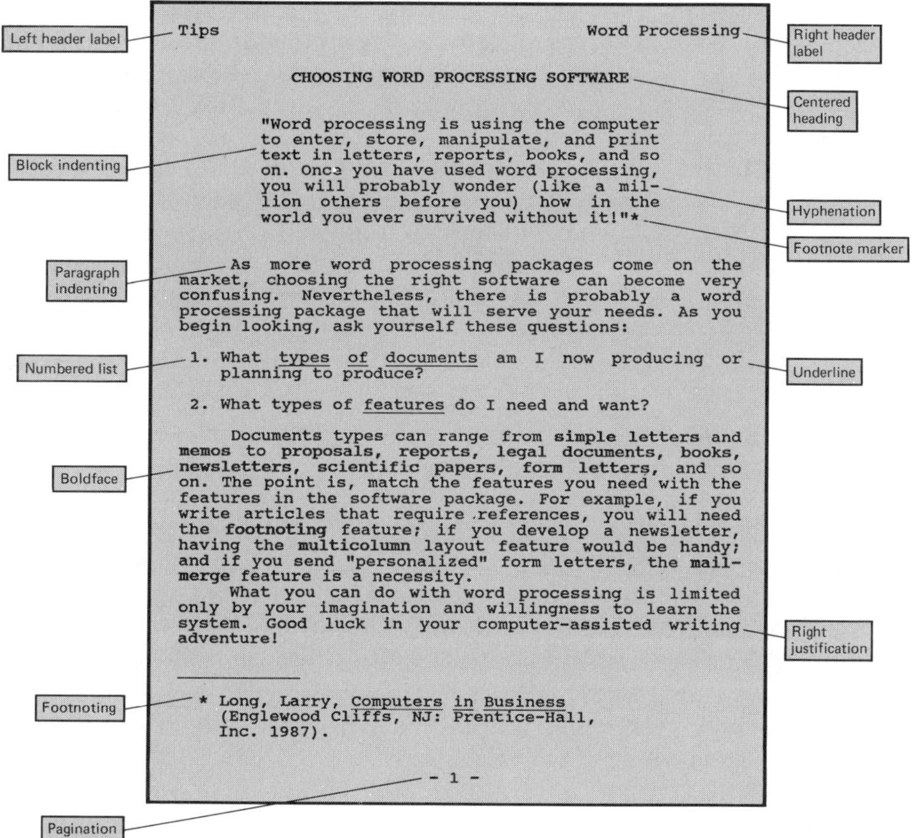

FIGURE S-8
Word Processing: Features Overview
Many of the more common capabilities of word processing software are illustrated in this example printout of a text file.

like when it is printed. Other word processing packages use embedded commands (e.g., a reverse video "b" to indicate the start and end of boldface text). These packages usually have a *preview* feature that permits you to "format" and display the document as it would appear when printed.

File Features.   Certainly, one of the most important features of a word processing package is the ability to store a document on disk storage for later recall. The stored version of a document is referred to as a *text file*. The *file* feature permits you to save, retrieve, and *delete* a text file. To perform a file operation, select the "file" option on the main menu, then select "save," "retrieve," or "delete." No matter which option you choose, you are asked by the system to identify the file (document). You would then enter an arbitrary name that in some way identifies the document (e.g., "MEMO"). Enter the file name of an existing file to retrieve or delete a file.

George Brooks "saved" his memo (stored it on disk) under the file name "MEMO." He stored it on disk because he knew that he was planning a similar meeting next week at the same time and place to discuss sales and strategies for Farkles and Stibs. Since he had already prepared the memo of Figure S-6, all that he would have to do to prepare a memo to announce next week's meeting would be to retrieve the "MEMO" file and change the phrase "Tegler and Qwert" to "Farkle and Stib."

Advanced Features.   The features discussed in this section are available with the more sophisticated word processing packages. For example, some word processing software has sophisticated features for writers. A simple command creates a *table of contents* with page references for the first-level headings. An alphabetical *index of key words* can be created that lists the page numbers for each occurrence of designated words. One of the most tedious typing chores, *footnoting*, is done automatically (see Figure S-8). Footnote spacing is resolved electronically before anything is printed. Another feature permits a *multicolumn* output (e.g., one or more columns of text on a single page). The *hyphenation* feature automatically breaks and hyphenates words that fall at the end of the line on output (see Figure S-8).

Have you ever been writing along and been unable to put your finger on the right word? Well, some word processing packages have a built-in *thesaurus*! Suppose that you have just written: "The Grand Canyon certainly is beautiful." But "beautiful" is not quite the right word. Your electronic thesaurus is always ready with suggestions: pretty, elegant, exquisite, angelic, pulchritudinous, ravishing, ... Pulchritudinous? Oh, well.

If spelling is a problem, then word processing is the answer. Once you have entered the text and formatted the document the way you want it, you can call on the *spell* feature. The spell feature checks every word in the text against an electronic dictionary (usually from 75,000 to 150,000 words), then alerts you if a word is not in the dictionary. Upon finding an unidentified word, the spell function will normally give you several options.

1. You can correct the spelling.
2. You can ignore the word and continue scanning the text. Normally, you do this when a word is spelled correctly but is not in the dictionary (e.g., a company name such as Zimco).

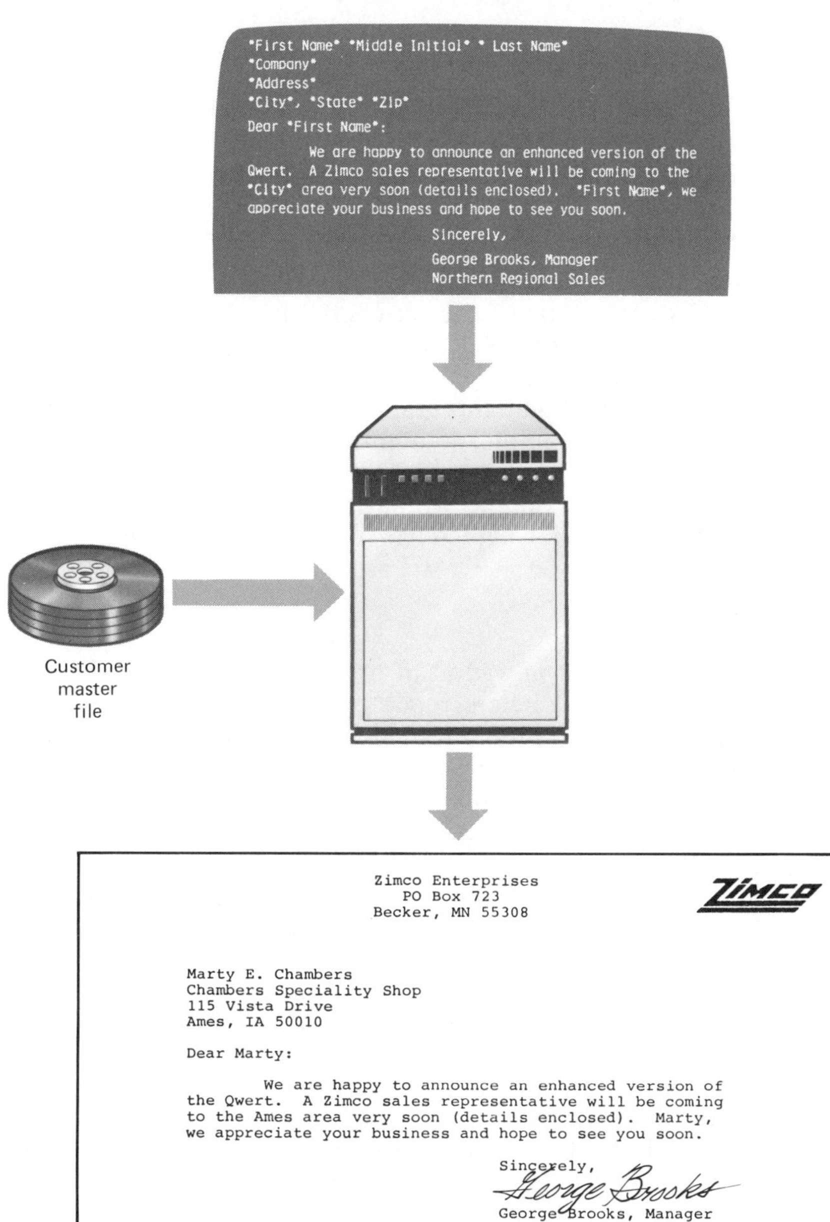

FIGURE S-9
Merging Data with Word Processing

The names and addresses from a customer master file are retrieved from secondary storage and merged with the text of a letter. In the actual letter, the appropriate data items are inserted for *First Name*, *Company*, *Address*, *City*, and so on. In this way, a "personalized" letter can be sent to each customer.

3. You can ask for possible spellings. The spell function then gives you a list of words of similar spelling from which to choose. For example, upon finding the nonword "persors," the spell function might suggest: person, persona, persons, personal, and personnel.

4. Or you can add the word to the dictionary and continue scanning.

Another advanced feature—*numbered lists*—is illustrated in the list above and in Figure S-8. When using the numbered list feature, all you have to do is enter the items in the list. The spacing and the addition of the numbers are automatic.

The *grammar* feature highlights grammatical concerns and deviations from conventions. For example, it highlights split infinitives, phrases with redundant words (e.g., "very highest"), misuse of caps (e.g., JOhn or MarY), sexist phrases, double words (e.g., and and), and sentences that are written in the passive voice (versus the active voice).

Use

You can create just about any kind of text-based document with word processing (see Figure S-8): letters, reports, books, articles, forms, memos, tables, and so on. The features of some word processing packages go beyond the generation of text documents. For example, some word processing systems provide the capability to merge parts of the data base with the text of the document. For example, a common application of word processing is to merge the names and addresses in a data base with the text of a letter to create "personalized" letters. An example of this merge application is illustrated in Figure S-9 and discussed in detail in the Zimco case study, "Office Automation at Zimco."

When working with word processing software, you are likely to enter long, continuous strings of text, as opposed to commands and data for the other types of micro software. Therefore, if you expect to use word processing capabilities frequently, you might consider acquiring a solid foundation in keyboarding skills, if you have not already done so. Super-Software, one of the software supplements that accompanies this text, includes a comprehensive keyboarding tutorial.

REVIEW EXERCISES (S-3)

1. What is the function of word processing software?

2. What must be specified when formatting a document?

3. What is meant when a document is formatted to be right and left justified?

4. Text is entered in either of what two modes? What mode would you select to change "the table" to "the long table"? What mode would you select to change "pick the choose" to "pick and choose"?

5. What causes text to wrap around?

6. Give an example of when you might issue a global search and replace command.

7. When running the "spell" function, what options does the system present to you upon encountering an unidentified word?

HANDS-ON EXERCISES

1. Enter the following text into your word processing system:

Too Much Paper!

Last year, the Public Relations Department's paper budget was overrun by $350. Therefore, Public Relations personnel are requested to learn word processing. It is apparent that Public Relations has not taken full advantage of the word processing capabilities of its microcomputers.

Use the default layout line options (normally $8\frac{1}{2}$- by 11-inch document size, 1-inch right and left margins, 6 lines per inch, and so on). Justify on the right margin. Print the document.

In the exercises that follow, make the changes cumulative; that is, revise whatever text is left after the previous revision. Each exercise builds on the results of the previous exercise.

2. In insert mode, insert the word "all" before "Public" in the second sentence. In replace mode, replace the lowercase letters in the title with capital letters. Print the document.

3. Center the title. Print the document.

4. At the end of the second sentence, add "by the end of the month." Observe how words at the end of the line wrap around to the next line. Print the document.

5. Use the move command to move the second sentence to the end of the document. Print the document.

6. Designate the word "all" to be underlined and the title to be in boldface when printed. Print the document.

7. Place the "page" (new page) marker at the end of the document and use the copy command to produce another copy of the entire document just below the original. Print the documents.

8. Use the search and replace command to replace all occurrences of

"Public Relations" in the second document with "Research and Development." Revise $350 in the second document to be $525. Print the documents.

9. Run the spell function. Print the document. If you performed all the hands-on exercises, your printed output should be similar to examples that follow. Since the default margins vary among word processing systems, the lines in your printouts may break differently than those of the following example outputs.

TOO MUCH PAPER!

Last year, the Public Relations Department's paper budget was overrun by $350. It is apparent that Public Relations has not taken full advantage of the word processing capabilities of its microcomputers. Therefore, *all* Public Relations personnel are requested to learn word processing by the end of the month.

TOO MUCH PAPER!

Last year, the Research and Development Department's paper budget was overrun by $525. It is apparent that Research and Development has not taken full advantage of the word processing capabilities of its microcomputers. Therefore, *all* Research and Development personnel are requested to learn word processing by the end of the month.

S-4 THE ELECTRONIC SPREADSHEET

Function

In 1978, a Harvard student convinced a couple of recent MIT graduates to rewrite their new business software to run on a personal computer. The software, called VisiCalc, became the first electronic spreadsheet. The 1979 introduction of VisiCalc revolutionized the way people perceived microcomputers. Suddenly, microcomputers were no longer just for games or education; they could also be a valuable asset for business.

The name "electronic spreadsheet" describes the software's fundamental application. The spreadsheet has been a common business tool for centuries. Before computers, the ledger (a spreadsheet) was the accountant's primary tool for keeping the books. Professors' grade books are set up in spreadsheet format.

Electronic spreadsheets are simply an electronic alternative to thousands of traditionally manual tasks. No longer are we confined to using pencils, erasers, and hand calculators for applications that deal with rows and columns of data. Think of anything that has rows and columns of data and you have identified an application for spreadsheet software. For example, how about income (profit and loss) statements (see Figure S-10), personnel profiles, demographic data, and budget summaries—to mention a few? Because electronic spreadsheets so closely resemble many of our manual tasks, they are enjoying widespread acceptance.

All commercially available electronic spreadsheet packages provide the facility to manipulate rows and columns of data. However, the *user interface*, or the manner in which the user enters data and commands, differs from one package to the next. The conceptual coverage that follows is generic and is applicable to all electronic spreadsheets. The examples, however, are oriented to Lotus 1–2–3 and symphony, products of Lotus Development Corporation.

Concepts

The example that we will use to illustrate and demonstrate electronic spreadsheet concepts is the Zimco income statement that was first presented in Zimco Case Study 5, "Micros at Zimco" (Figures Z5-2 and Z5-3). Monroe Green, the VP of Finance and Accounting at Zimco, often uses an electronic spreadsheet **template** of Zimco's income statements for the past two years to do financial planning. The template, which is simply a spreadsheet model, contains a column that allows him to produce a pro rata income statement for next year (see Figure S-10). In Figure S-10, the actual income statement is shown on the first screen. The second screen contains the calculations for the price-earnings ratio and the display of the variables used to produce the pro rata income statement for next year. Since only 20 lines of the spreadsheet can be displayed at once, Monroe Green must "page up" or "page down" to see all of this spreadsheet.

Organization.   Electronic spreadsheets are organized in a *tabular structure* with **rows** and **columns.** The intersection of a particular row and column designates a **cell.** As you can see in Figure S-10, the rows are *numbered* and the columns are *lettered.* Single letters identify the first 26 columns and double letters are used thereafter (A, B, . . . , Z, AA, AB, . . . , AZ, BA, BB, . . . , BZ). The number of rows or columns available to you depends on the size of your micro's RAM (random-access memory). Most spreadsheets permit hundreds of columns and thousands of rows.

Data are entered and stored in a cell, at the intersection of a column and a row. During operations, data are referenced by their **cell address.** A cell address identifies the location of a cell in the spreadsheet by its

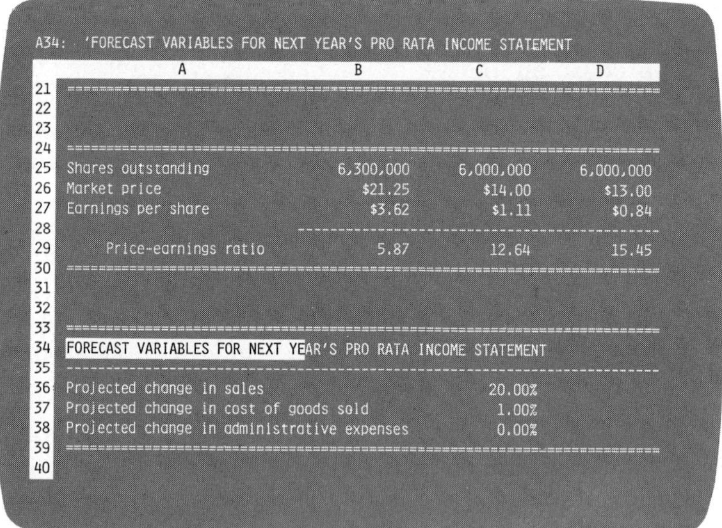

FIGURE S-10

Electronic Spreadsheet: An Income Statement Template

This electronic spreadsheet template (both screens) is the basis for
the explanation and demonstration of spreadsheet concepts. The "Next
Year" pro rata income statement is extrapolated from the data in
the "This Year" income statement and the values of forecast variables.
The price-earnings ratio is calculated for each year.

column and row, with the column designator first. For example, in the income statement example of Figure S-10, C2 is the address of the column heading "This Year," and C4 is the address of net sales amount for this year ($153,000).

A movable highlighted area "points" to the *current cell*. This highlighted area, which is appropriately called the **pointer,** can be moved around the spreadsheet with the cursor control keys to any cell address. To add, delete, or edit an entry at a particular cell, the pointer must be located at the desired cell. The address and content of the current cell (location of the pointer) are displayed in the *control panel* (C4 and A4 in Figure S-10) and the content or resultant value (from a formula) of

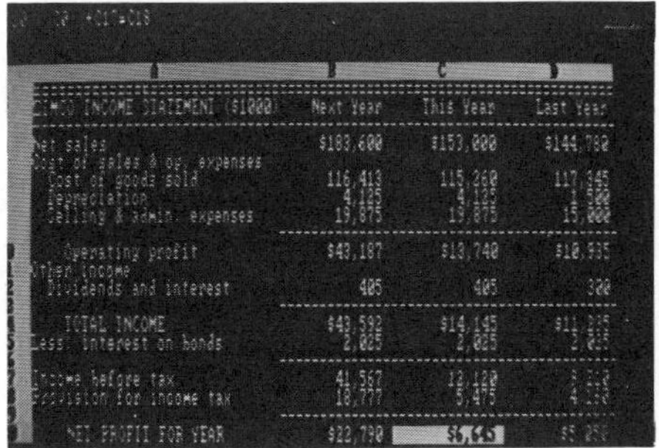
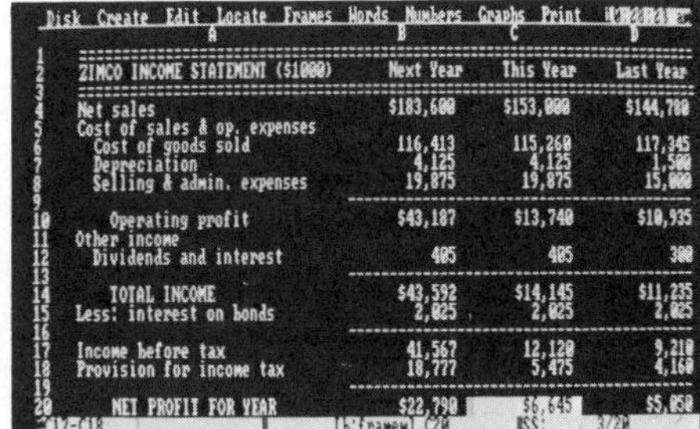
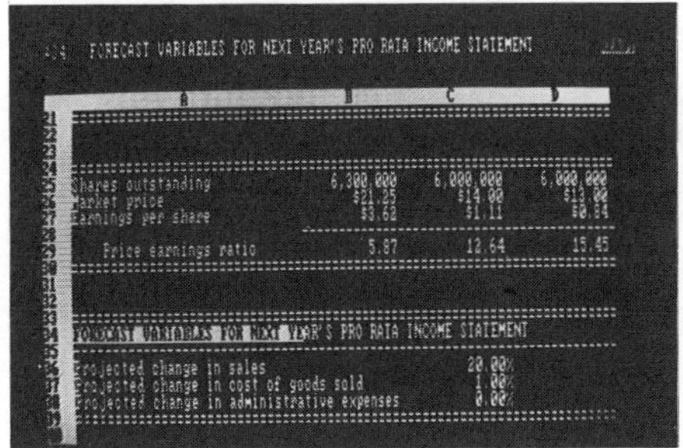
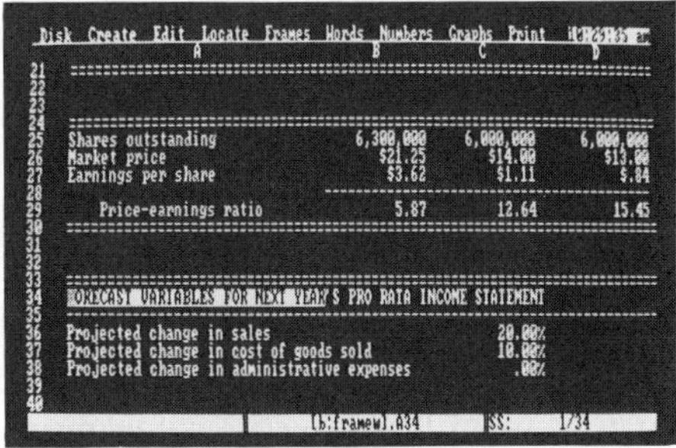

The income statement template of Figure S-10 was prepared using two popular electronic spreadsheet packages: The first two photos (shown vertically) illustrate how the template would be displayed using Lotus 1–2–3 (1–2–3 is a trademark of Lotus Development Corporation). The second two photos illustrate how the template would be displayed using Framework, an integrated package (Framework is a trademark of Ashton-Tate).
(Long and Associates)

the current cell is displayed in reverse video (e.g., black on white with monochrome monitors) in the spreadsheet display.

Cell Entries.   To make an entry in the spreadsheet, simply move the pointer with the cursor control keys to the appropriate cell and key in the data. To *edit* or replace an existing entry, you also move the pointer to the appropriate cell. The new or revised entry appears first in the control panel beside the cell address (see Figure S-10). Once you have completed work on a particular entry, press the carriage return or a cursor control key to make the entry in the actual spreadsheet. For example, let's say that "Net sales" in A4 was incorrectly entered initially as "New sales." To make the correction, the user would move the pointer to A4, indicate that the cell value is to be edited (usually an edit key), then delete the "w," insert a "t," and press the carriage return.

Numeric, Label, and Formula Entries.   The value that you enter in a cell is either *numeric*, a *label*, or a *formula*. In Figure S-10, the values in C4 and D4 are numeric. A label is a word, phrase, or any string of alphanumeric text (spaces included) that occupies a particular cell. In the example of Figure S-10, "This Year" in cell C2 is a label value, as is "Net Sales" in A4 and "FORECAST VARIABLES FOR NEXT YEAR'S PRO RATA INCOME STATEMENT" in A34. Notice that the label in A34 extends across columns B and C. If an entry were made in B34, only the first 30 positions, or the width of column A, would be visible on the spreadsheet (e.g., "FORECAST VARIABLES FOR NEXT YE"). Spreadsheet packages permit the user to vary the column width to improve readability. The column width for columns B, C, and D is set at 15 positions.

Unless otherwise specified, numeric entries are right justified (lined up on the right) and label entries are left justified. However, you can specify that entries be left or right justified, or centered in the column. Note that the column heading in A2 is left justified and that the column headings in B2, C2, and D2 are right justified to improve the appearance of the spreadsheet.

Cells C10 and C14 contain formulas, but it is the numeric results (e.g., $13,740 and $14,145) that are displayed in the spreadsheet. The formula value of C10 (see Figure S-11) computes the operating profit (e.g., net sales less the cost of sales and operating expenses or +C4−C6−C7−C8). With the pointer at C10, the formula appears in the control panel and the actual numeric value appears in the spreadsheet. When the pointer is moved six rows up to C4, the actual numeric value (153000) is displayed in the control panel and an optional *edited* version (with $ and comma) is displayed in cell C4 (see Figure S-11).

Spreadsheet formulas use standard notation for **arithmetic operators:** + (add), − (subtract), ∗ (multiply), / (divide), ˆ (raising to a power, or

```
C10: +C4-C6-C7-C8
```

	A	B	C	D
1	==		
2	ZIMCO INCOME STATEMENT ($1000)	Next Year	This Year	Last Year
3	--		
4	Net sales	$183,600	$153,000	$144,780
5	Cost of sales & op. expenses			
6	Cost of goods sold	116,413	115,260	117,345
7	Depreciation	4,125	4,125	1,500
8	Selling & admin. expenses	19,875	19,875	15,000
9				
10	Operating profit	$43,187	$13,740	$10,935

FIGURE S-11
Electronic Spreadsheet: Formulas
The actual content of C10 is the formula in the control panel in the upper left-hand part of the screen. The result of the formula appears in the spreadsheet at C10.

exponentiation). The formula contained in C10 (top of Figure S-11) computes the operating profit for "This Year." Compare this formula:

+C4−C6−C7−C8

to the formula in cell D10 (below):

+D4−D6−D7−D8

The formulas are similar, but the first formula references those amounts in column C and the second formula references those amounts in column D.

Relative and Absolute Cell Addressing. Monroe Green, Zimco's VP of Finance and Accounting, uses the income statement spreadsheet template of Figure S-10 to create "what if" scenarios. For example, the VP of the Operations Division has told him that he is implementing a number of cost-cutting measures. He anticipates that the Operations Division can hold the "cost of goods sold" to a 1 percent increase, even though more products will be built and shipped. The VP of Sales and Marketing has predicted that next year will be a "great year" and net sales will increase by 20 percent. The president of Zimco has asked all managers to "hold the line" on all selling and administrative expenses; therefore, these expenses are expected to remain about the same.

    With spreadsheet software, Monroe was able to answer the question: "What if the cost-of-goods-sold increased by 1 percent, sales increased by 20 percent, and everything else remained the same for the coming year?" Monroe entered only the three forecast variables in C36, C37, and C38 (see Figure S-10) to get the pro rata income statement (the "Next Year" column of Figure S-10). All calculations (e.g., sales with a 20 percent increase, net profit, earnings per share, taxes) are performed automatically because the appropriate formulas are built into the spreadsheet template. The formulas that compute the "Next Year" values for net sales (B4), cost of goods sold (B6), and selling and administrative expenses (B8) are:

B4:   +C4*(1+C36)
B6:   +C6*(1+C37)
B8:   +C8*(1+C38)

Some entries are unchanged (e.g., depreciation, dividends, and interest); however, if Monroe wanted to reflect a change in depreciation, he would simply change the value of the "depreciation" entry in the "Next Year" column. The "provision for income tax" entry is extrapolated from the "This Year" column data by a formula that assumes the taxes will be paid at the same rate as the previous year [e.g., B18: (C18/C17)*B17]. The distinction between the way the dollar amounts and the forecast variables are represented in the formulas highlights a very important concept of electronic spreadsheets, that of **relative cell addressing** and **absolute cell addressing.**

In creating the spreadsheet template for the income statement of Figure S-10, Monroe Green entered the operating profit formula only once: in C10 (see Figure S-11). Then spreadsheet commands were selected that *copied* or *replicated* the formula into cell D10. You can see from the results in Figure S-10 that the exact formula was not copied. Instead, the formula in D10 (+D4-D6-D7-D8) manipulates the data in the cells for "Last Year," not "This Year" (as in the formula in C10: +C4−C6−C7−C8). The same is true of other formulas that were copied from the "This Year" column to the "Last Year" column.

The formula in C10 references cells that have a "relative" position to C10, the location of the formula. When the formula in C10 is copied to D10, the electronic spreadsheet software revises these *relative cell addresses* so they apply to a formula that is located in D10. As you can see, the formula in D10 references cells that contain the data for "Last Year."

Each of the three forecast variables (C36 . . C38) is assigned an *absolute cell address.* The absolute cell address does not change when a formula in which it appears is copied from row to row or from column to column. The formula in B4 will always reference the forecast variable in cell C36, even if copied to any other location in the spreadsheet. In a formula, an absolute cell address is denoted by a dollar sign ($) prefix before the column and before the row (e.g., $C$36).

The relative cell address is based on its position relative to the cell containing the formula. When you copy or replicate a formula to another cell, the relative cell addresses are revised to reflect their new position relative to the new location of the formula. The absolute cell addresses remain unchanged. The two types of cell addressing are illustrated in the spreadsheet in Figure S-12. Suppose that the formula B3*$E$1 is in cell A1. B3 is a relative cell address that is one column to the right of and two rows down from A1. If this formula is copied to C2, the formula in C2 is D4*$E$1. Notice that D4 has the same relative position to the formula in cell C2: one column to the right and two rows down. The absolute cell address remains the same in both formulas.

You might ask: "Why beat around the bush? Why not just enter the value of the forecast variables directly in the formula?" Well, you could, but then Monroe would have to revise the formulas to do "what if" analysis.

Ranges.   Many electronic spreadsheet operations ask you to designate a **range.** The four types of ranges are highlighted in Figure S-13:

1. A single cell (example range is B12)
2. All or part of a column of adjacent cells (example range is A17 . . A20)
3. All or part of a row of adjacent cells (example range is B2 . . D2)
4. A rectangular block of cells (example range is B6 . . D8)

A particular range is depicted by the addresses of the endpoint cells and separated by two periods (some packages use only one period, e.g., C6.D8). Any cell can comprise a single cell range. The range for the total income amounts in Figure S-13 is B14 . . D14 and the range for the row labels is A4 . . A20. The range of the dollar amounts in the three income statements for "Next Year," "This Year," and "Last Year" data is depicted by any two opposite corner cell addresses (e.g., B4 . . D20 or D4 . . B20).

Many spreadsheet operations require users to designate one or several

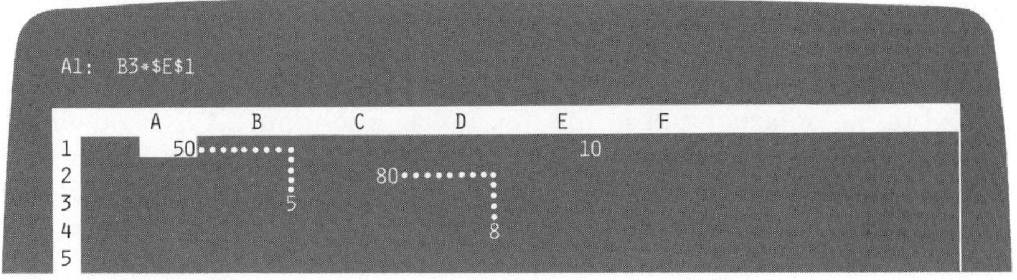

FIGURE S-12
Electronic Spreadsheet: Relative and Absolute Cell Addressing
When the formula in A1 is copied to C2, the formula in C2 becomes D4*$E$1.

	A	B	C	D
1	================================	=========	=========	=========
2	ZIMCO INCOME STATEMENT ($1000)	Next Year	This Year	Last Year
3	--------------------------------	---------	---------	---------
4	Net sales	$183,600	$153,000	$144,780
5	Cost of sales & op. expenses			
6	Cost of goods sold	116,413	115,260	117,345
7	Depreciation	4,125	4,125	1,500
8	Selling & admin. expenses	19,875	19,875	15,000
9				
10	Operating profit	$43,187	$13,740	$10,935
11	Other income			
12	Dividends and interest	405	405	300
13				
14	TOTAL INCOME	$43,492	$14,145	$11,235
15	Less: interest on bonds	2,025	2,025	2,025
16				
17	Income before tax	41,567	12,120	9,210
18	Provision for income tax	18,777	5,475	4,160
19				
20	NET PROFIT FOR YEAR	$22,790	$6,645	$5,050

FIGURE S-13
Electronic Spreadsheet: Ranges
The four types of ranges are highlighted: cell (B12), column (A17..A20), row (B2..D2), and block (B6..D8).

ranges. Do this by moving the pointer to an endpoint cell. Then you *anchor* the pointer by pressing a particular key, often a tab or a period. Once you have set the anchor (e.g., C6), move the pointer to the other endpoint (e.g., D8), press return, and you have defined the range (C6 . . D8). Ranges can also be defined by simply keying in the addresses of the endpoint cells.

The copy operation requires users to define a "copy from" range and a "copy to" range. When the operating profit formula in C10 was copied to the adjacent cell in the "Last Year" column, C10 was defined as the "copy from" range, and D10 was the "copy to" range. When you want to erase a portion of the spreadsheet, you first define the range that you wish to erase. For example, if you wish to erase the line of ='s on row 1, you define the range to be A1 . . D1, then issue the erase command.

Formatting Data for Readability.   The appearance of data in a spreadsheet can be modified to enhance readability. For example, the value .2 was entered as the projected change in sales in C36 (Figure S-10), but it appears in the spreadsheet display as a percent (20 percent). This is because the range C36 . . C38 was *formatted* so that the values are automatically displayed as percents rather than fractions (i.e., 0.2 becomes 20 percent). The methods of formatting data vary considerably between spreadsheet software packages.

Currency amounts can be formatted so that commas and a dollar sign are inserted. For example, in Figure S-10 the value for net sales for "This Year" is entered as 153000 in C4, which is formatted for currency. Notice that it is displayed as $153,000.

Numeric data can be defined so that they are displayed with a fixed number of places to the right of the decimal point. In Figure S-10, the format of the net sales data in the range B4 . . D4 is currency with the number of decimal places fixed at zero. The format of the market price data in the range B26 . . D26 is currency with the numbers of decimal positions fixed at two. Numbers with more decimal digits than specified in the format are rounded when displayed.

Creating Spreadsheet Formulas.   The three types of cell entries are numbers, labels, and formulas. This section expands on the use and application of formulas—the essence of spreadsheet operations.

A formula causes the spreadsheet software to perform numeric and/or string calculations and/or logic operations that result in a numeric value (e.g., 13740) or an alphanumeric character string (e.g., "ABOVE 25% LIMIT"). A formula may include one or all of the following: *arithmetic operations, functions,* and *logic operations.* Each is discussed below in more detail. The *string operations* (e.g., joining or concatenating character strings) capabilities are beyond the scope of this presentation.

When you design the spreadsheet, keep in mind where you want to place the formulas and what you want them to accomplish. Since formulas are based on relative position, you will need a knowledge of the layout and organization of the data in the spreadsheet. When you define a formula, you must first determine what you wish to achieve (e.g., calculate net profit). Then select a cell location for the formula (e.g., C20) and create the formula by connecting relative and absolute cell addresses with operators, as appropriate. In many instances, you will copy the formula to other locations (e.g., C20 was copied to D20) in Figure S-10.

Spreadsheet applications begin with a blank screen and an idea. The spreadsheet that you create is a product of skill and imagination. What you get out of a spreadsheet is very dependent on how effectively you use formulas.

Arithmetic Operations.   Formulas containing arithmetic operators are resolved according to a hierarchy of operations. That is, when more than one operator is included in a single formula, the spreadsheet software

The Hierarchy of Operations	
OPERATION	**OPERATOR**
Exponentiation	$\wedge$
Multiplication-Division	* /
Addition-Subtraction	+ –

FIGURE S-14
Hierarchy of Operations

uses a set of rules to determine which operation to do first, second, and so on. In the hierarchy of operations, illustrated in Figure S-14, exponentiation has the highest priority, followed by multiplication-division and addition-subtraction. In the case of a tie (e.g., * and /, or + and −), the formula is evaluated from *left to right. Parentheses,* however, override the priority rules. Expressions placed in parentheses have priority and are evaluated innermost first, and left to right.

The formula that results in the value in B4 (183600) of Figure S-10 is shown below:

+C4*(1+$C$36)

The parentheses in the cell B4 formula cause the expression inside the parentheses to be evaluated first; then the value of the expression is multiplied times the value in cell C4. All of the formulas in the spreadsheet of Figure S-10 are listed in Figure S-15.

Remember, once entered, these formulas can be copied such that they apply to a different set of data. For example, the earnings-per-share formula was entered in B27 and copied to the range C27 . . D27. Compare these three formulas in Figure S-15.

Functions. Electronic spreadsheets offer users a wide variety of predefined operations called **functions.** These functions can be used to create formulas that perform mathematical, logical, statistical, financial, and character-string operations on spreadsheet data. To use a function, simply preface the desired function name (e.g., AVG for average) with a prefix symbol (e.g., "@"; the symbol may vary between software packages), and enter the **argument.** The argument, which is placed in parentheses, identifies the data to be operated on. The argument can be one or several numbers, character strings, or ranges that represent data.

In the spreadsheet example of Figure S-10, the operating profit (C10) can be calculated (see the formula in Figure S-15) by subtracting the individual cell values under the "cost of sales and operating expenses" heading (C6, C7, and C8) from the net sales (C4).

	A	B	C	D
1	==
2	ZIMCO INCOME STATEMENT ($1000)	Next Year	This Year	Last Year
3	--
4	Net sales	+C4*(1+$C$36)	153000	144780
5	Cost of sales & op. expenses			
6	Cost of goods sold	+C6*(1+$C$37)	115260	117345
7	Depreciation	+C7	4125	1500
8	Selling and admin. expenses	+C8*(1+$C$38)	19875	15000
9	---
10	Operating profit	+B4-B6-B7-B8	+C4-C6-C7-C8	+D4-D6-D7-D8
11	Other income			
12	Dividends and interest	+C12	405	300
13	---
14	TOTAL INCOME	+B10+B12	+C10+C12	+D10+D12
15	Less: interest on bonds	+C15	2025	2025
16	---
17	Income before tax	+B14-B15	+C14-C15	+D14-D15
18	Provision for income tax	(C18/C17)*B17	5475	4160
19	---
20	NET PROFIT FOR YEAR	+B17-B18	+C17-C18	+D17-D18
21	==
22				
23				
24	==
25	Shares outstanding	6300000	6000000	5000000
26	Market price	21.25	14	13
27	Earnings per share	(B20*1000)/B25	(C20*1000)/C25	(D20*1000)/D25
28	---
29	Price-earnings ratio	+B26/B27	+C26/C27	+D26/D27
30	==
31				
32				
33	==
34	FORECAST VARIABLES FOR NEXT YEAR'S PRO RATA INCOME STATEMENT			
35	---
36	Projected change in sales	0.2		
37	Projected change in cost of goods sold	0.01		
38	Projected change in administrative expenses	0		
39	==

FIGURE S-15

Electronic Spreadsheet: Actual Content of Spreadsheet Cells

This figure illustrates the actual content of all cells in Figure S-10. In an actual spreadsheet display, the formulas would be resolved when displayed (e.g., C10 would appear as $13,740) and the values would be displayed according to a preset format (e.g., C36 would appear as 20%).

```
C10: +C4-C6-C7-C8
```

Or the total of the "cost of sales and operating expenses" items can be computed with a function and its argument:

```
C10: +C4-@SUM(C6 . . C8)
```

The use of predefined functions can save a lot of time. What if the range to be summed was C6 . . C600?

In the same spreadsheet template, Monroe Green created a "THREE-YEAR SUMMARY DATA" section in the range A121 . . D127. He did this by copying the range A1 . . D20 (see Figure S-10) to the range A121 . . D140. He then edited the heading information to be as shown in row 122 of Figure S-16. Monroe then deleted unneeded rows of data to end up with the spreadsheet section in Figure S-16. In this section of the spreadsheet, Monroe used functions to calculate the overall average

```
B124: @AVG(B4..D4)

            A                      B            C            D
121 ================================================================
122 THREE-YEAR SUMMARY DATA    Average      Minimum      Maximum
123 ----------------------------------------------------------------
124 Net sales                 $160,460     $144,780     $183,600
125    Operating profit        $22,621      $10,935      $43,187
126    TOTAL INCOME            $22,991      $11,235      $43,592
127    NET PROFIT FOR YEAR     $11,495       $5,050      $22,790
```

FIGURE S-16
Electronic Spreadsheet: Functions
The average, maximum, and minimum spreadsheet functions are used to compute summary data in the range B124..D127.

and to determine the minimum and maximum values for selected entries in the three-year income statement. To do this, he entered the following functions in B124, C124, and D124, respectively:

    B124: @AVG(B4 . . D4)
    C124: @MIN(B4 . . D4)
    D124: @MAX(B4 . . D4)

The argument for each of these functions is the range of cells that represents the net sales for each of the three income statements. To complete the segment of the spreadsheet shown in Figure S-16, Monroe copied the contents of B4 [@AVG(B4 . . D4)] to the range B125 . . B127 (the "average" column), thereby making every entry in this column an average of the three years. He performed the same type of operation for the other two columns. These copy operations are possible because the formulas are automatically revised "relative" to their new position.

Other spreadsheet functions include: trigonometric functions, square root, comparisons of values, manipulations of strings of data, computation of Julian dates, computation of net present value and internal rate of return, and a variety of techniques for statistical analysis. Vendors of spreadsheet software create slightly different names for their functions.

Logic Operations.   Logical operations involve the use of **relational operators** and **logical operators** (see Figure S-17) to compare numeric and string values. The result of a logical operation is that an expression is either *true* or *false*.

Logical operations are used primarily in defining conditions for record selection (discussed in data management section) and in formulas containing an IF function. The format of the IF function is

    IF(*condition, result* [*condition true*], *result* [*condition false*])

Relational Operators

COMPARISON	OPERATOR
Equal to	=
Less than	<
Greater than	>
Less than or equal to	<=
Greater than or equal to	>=
Not equal to	<>

Logical Operators AND and OR

OPERATION	OPERATOR
For the condition to be true:	
Both sub-conditions must be true	AND
At least one subcondition must be true	OR

FIGURE S-17
Relational and Logical Operators

The result in an IF function can be a number, a character string, or even another formula. The logical operators AND and OR (see Figure S-17) permit us to combine relational expressions in an IF function.

Suppose that Monroe wanted to include some data entry validation procedures in his spreadsheet template. He could ensure that realistic values are entered for the forecast variables by displaying a warning message in C40 in Figure S-10 if any of the values is above 25 percent. The following formula would perform the check on the data entered for the forecast variables.

```
@IF(C36>.25#OR#C37>.25#OR#C38>.25,"ABOVE 25% LIMIT","")
```

In the case of Figure S-10, where all forecast variables are less than 25 percent, no message ("" represents a null entry) is displayed because the condition is false. If any of the three forecast variables exceeds 25 percent, as in the case in Figure S-18, the message "ABOVE 25% LIMIT" is displayed in C40.

Adding and Deleting Rows and Columns. You can insert or delete entire rows and columns. For example, Monroe Green deleted rows in a duplicate copy of the income statement of Figure S-10 to produce the basis for compiling the spreadsheet of Figure S-16. If Monroe so desired, he could insert another "Year After Next" column in Figure S-10 such that what is now in columns B, C, and D would be moved over one column to columns C, D, and E. The "Year After Next" data would be in column B. The spreadsheet software automatically adjusts the relative cell addresses in the original spreadsheet data.

Viewing Data in a Spreadsheet. What if the spreadsheet template of Figure S-10 reflected data for the past five years? Since the screen on the monitor can display only a certain amount of information, Monroe would need to *scroll* horizontally through the spreadsheet to the first three years. To view spreadsheet areas that extend past the bottom of the screen, he

```
C40: @IF(C36>0.25#OR#C37>0.25#OR#C38>0.25, "ABOVE 25% LIMIT","")

                          A                    B              C            D
   33 =================================================================================
   34 FORECAST VARIABLES FOR NEXT YEAR'S PRO RATA INCOME STATEMENT
   35 ---------------------------------------------------------------------------------
   36 Projected change in sales                                50.00%
   37 Projected change in cost of goods sold                    1.00%
   38 Projected change in administrative expenses               0.00%
   39 =================================================================================
   40                                                 ABOVE 25% LIMIT
```

FIGURE S-18
Electronic Spreadsheet: Logical Operations
An IF function in C40 (see discussion in text) serves as a data entry validation
procedure. If any of the three forecast variables exceeds 25 percent, as is the case
in this figure, the message, "ABOVE 25% LIMIT," is displayed in C40.

would need to scroll vertically (e.g., the two parts of Figure S-10). Scrolling
through a spreadsheet is much like looking through a magnifying glass
as you move it around a page of a newspaper. You scroll left-right and/
or up-down to view various portions of a large spreadsheet (see Figure
S-19).

If Monroe were to scroll horizontally to view data from past years,
row headings (e.g., Net sales, TOTAL INCOME, etc.) disappear from the

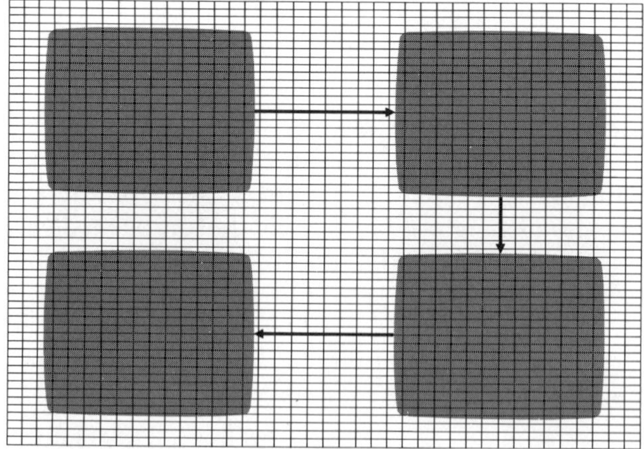

FIGURE S-19
Electronic Spreadsheet: Scrolling
Scroll vertically and horizontally to view those portions
of a spreadsheet that do not fit on a single screen.

screen to make room for other years of data. As you can imagine, data without labels can be very confusing. However, spreadsheet software has a solution to this dilemma: You can *freeze* selected columns or rows. In the example of Figure S-20, Monroe has frozen the leftmost column (A), the row headings, at the left side of the screen so that they are always visible when scrolling horizontally through the income statements. When you freeze a portion of the screen, you are creating a new border with labels, and everything moves on the screen but the labels. Notice in Figure S-20 that the the "Next Year" and "This Year" columns are off the screen, but the row labels remain. These columns are returned to the screen when Monroe scrolls in the other direction. The pointer cannot be positioned in a frozen area.

You can also freeze the rows at the top of the screen, the ones that usually label a column. The freeze feature is particularly helpful when the spreadsheet contains many rows or columns of data and you want to work with only a few columns at a time.

Use

Spreadsheet Templates.   The electronic spreadsheet of Figure S-10 is a *template*, or a model, of past years' income statements and a pro rata income statement. It can be used over and over for different purposes by different financial analysts. A template is analogous to a production program and a data base. It can be used again and again by different people with different sets of data. Next year the data now in the "This Year" column will be moved to the "Last Year" column and a new set of data will be entered for "This Year."

```
D10:   +D4-D6-D7-D8
                               A                      D
 1  =================================================
 2  ZIMCO INCOME STATEMENT ($1000)         Last Year
 3  -------------------------------------------------
 4  Net sales                               $144,780
 5  Cost of sales & op. expenses
 6     Cost of goods sold                    117,345
 7     Depreciation                            1,500
 8     Selling and admin. expenses           15,000
 9                                          ----------
10      Operating profit                    $10,935
```

FIGURE S-20
Electronic Spreadsheet: Freeze Column
When column A is frozen at the left of the screen, it is always visible when scrolling horizontally. In the figure, column D is now adjacent to column A.

With electronic spreadsheets, a template is easily modified to fit a variety of situations. Another analyst may wish to modify the template slightly to handle quarterly income statements (only the column headings would be changed).

"What If" Analysis.   The real beauty of an electronic spreadsheet is that if you change the value of a cell in a spreadsheet, all other affected cells are revised accordingly. This capability makes spreadsheet software the perfect tool for "what if" analysis. For example, by using the spreadsheet template of Figure S-10, Monroe Green, Zimco's VP of Finance and Accounting, was able to answer the question: "What if sales increased by 20 percent, the cost of goods sold increased by 1 percent, and everything else remained the same for the coming year?" To produce the pro rata income statement (the "Next Year" column of Figure S-10), he entered appropriate values for the three forecast variables in C36, C37, and C38 (i.e., 0.2, 0.01, and 0 in Figure S-10).

Besides the pro rata income statement for "Next Year," Monroe wanted to monitor the *price-earnings ratio*, or the relationship that exists between the *earnings per share* and the *market price* of Zimco's stock. Data and the calculations for the price-earnings ratios are in the range B25 . . D29 in Figure S-10. The formulas and entries in the range B25 . . D29 are shown in Figure S-15. The earnings per share is calculated by dividing the net profit by the number of shares outstanding [e.g., for "This Year," $6,645,000/6,000,000 = $1.11, which is calculated by the formula in C27: (C20*1000)/C25]. The price-earnings ratio is calculated by dividing the current market price of Zimco stock by the earnings per share [e.g., for "This Year," $14.00/$1.11 = 12.64, which is calculated by the formula in C29: +C26/C27].

In the "Next Year" column of the price-earnings (P-E) ratio section of the spreadsheet, Monroe asked: "What if Zimco issued 300,000 new shares of stock and the market price of Zimco stock reached $21.25, what would the P-E ratio be?"

Over the years Zimco's president, Preston Smith, has learned to temper the optimistic estimates of his VPs with a touch of reality, so he used the spreadsheet template of Figure S-10 to create his own pessimistic pro rata income statement. This income statement reflects what he called the "worst-case scenario." Preston Smith needed only to change the three forecast variables (C36 . . C38) to get the results of Figure S-21. The results confirmed Preston's belief that the estimated P-E ratio is very sensitive to the estimates for sales and expenses. Compare the price-earnings ratio of the optimistic pro rata income statement in Figure S-10 (5.87) with the pessimistic pro rata income statement in Figure S-21 (17.94).

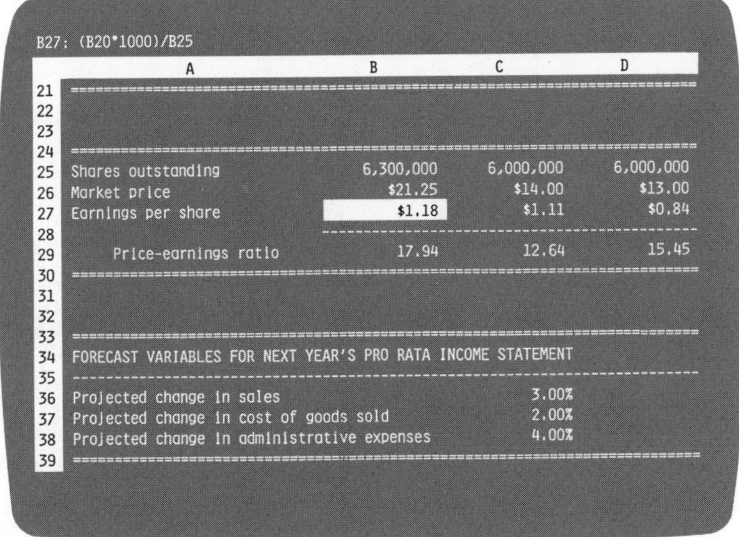

FIGURE S-21
Electronic Spreadsheet: An Income Statement Template
This electronic spreadsheet display is the same as the one in Figure S-10 except that the forecast variables in C36..C38 have been changed from 20%, 1%, and 0% to 3%, 2%, and 4%, respectively.

```
C53:   @SUM (C47..C51)

              A                          B            C            D
41  ===============================================================
42  ZIMCO BALANCE SHEET ($1000)                    This Year    Last Year
43  ---------------------------------------------------------------
44  ASSETS
45  ---------------------------------------------------------------
46  Current assets
47    Cash                                          $6,750       $4,500
48    Marketable securities @ cost                  $12,750      $6,900
49    Accounts receivable
50      Less: bad debt allowance                    $30,000      $28,500
51    Inventories                                   $40,500      $45,000
52                                          ----------------
53       Total current assets                       $90,000      $84,900
54
55  Fixed assets
56    Land                                          6,750        $6,750
57    Building                                      $55,500      $52,500
58    Machinery                                     $14,250      $12,750
59    Office equipment                              $1,500       $1,425
60                                                  --------------------
```

```
C71:   +C53+C64+C67+C69

              A                          B            C            D
61                                                   $78,000      $73,425
62         Less: accum. depreciation                 $27,000      $22,500
63                                                   --------------------
64         Net fixed assets                          $51,000      $50,925
65
66
67  Prepayments & deferred charges                   $1,500       $1,350
68
69  Intangibles (goodwill, patents)                  $1,500       $1,500
70                                                   --------------------
71  TOTAL ASSETS                                     $144,000     $138,675
72                                                   ====================
73
74  ---------------------------------------------------------------
75  LIABILITIES
76  ---------------------------------------------------------------
77  Current liabilities
78    Accounts payable                               $15,000      $14,100
79    Notes payable                                  $12,750      $15,000
80    Accrued expenses payable                       $4,950       $4,500
```

C100: +C89+C98

	A	B	C	D
81	Federal income taxes payable		$4,800	$4,350
82			----------------	----------------
83	Total current liabilities		$37,500	$37,950
84				
85	Long-term liabilities			
86	First mortgage bonds;			
87	9% interest, due 2000		$40,500	$40,500
88			----------------	----------------
89	Total liabilities		$78,000	$78,450
90	--	----------------	----------------	----------------
91	STOCKHOLDERS' EQUITY			
92	--	----------------	----------------	----------------
93	Common stock, $5 par;			
94	6,000,000 shares outstanding		$30,000	$30,000
95	Capital surplus		$10,500	$10,500
96	Retained earnings		$25,500	$19,725
97			----------------	----------------
98	Total stockholders' equity		$66,000	$60,225
99	--	----------------	----------------	----------------
100	TOTAL LIABILITIES & STOCKHOLDERS' EQUITY		$144,000	$138,675

FIGURE S-22
Electronic Spreadsheet: A Balance Sheet Template
The electronic spreadsheet representation of the Zimco balance sheets for the last two years is included in rows 41 through 100 of a spreadsheet template. The income statement template of Figures S-10 and S-21 is on rows 1 through 40 of the same spreadsheet.

Spreadsheet Summary

The possibilities of what Monroe Green, Preston Smith, you, and others can do with electronic spreadsheet software and micros are endless. For example, Monroe can add the Zimco balance sheets for the last two years (see Figure S-22) to the spreadsheet of Figure S-10 to create even more "what if" scenarios. With the income statement and the balance sheet in the same spreadsheet, he can change values in Zimco's financial statements to see how various financial indices, such as the net working capital (current assets minus current liabilities), the current ratio (current assets divided by current liabilities), and the inventory turnover (net sales divided by inventories), are affected. The formulas for the "This Year" balance sheet in Figure S-22 are listed in Figure S-23 to give you one more example of how formulas are used in an electronic spreadsheet template.

Cell	Formula
C53	@ SUM (C47 . . C51)
C61	@ SUM (C56 . . C59)
C64	+C61−C62
C71	+C53+C64+C67+C69
C83	@ SUM (C78 . . C81)
C89	+C83+C87
C98	@ SUM (C94 . . C96)
C100	+C89+C98

FIGURE S-23
Electronic Spreadsheet: Formulas in Balance Sheet Template of Figure S-22
These are the formulas for the "This Year" column of the balance sheet spreadsheet in Figure S-22.

REVIEW EXERCISES (S-4)

1. Describe the layout of an electronic spreadsheet.

2. Give an example cell address. Which portion of the address depicts the row and which portion depicts the column?

3. On what is a relative cell address based?

4. Give an example of each of the four types of ranges.

5. Give examples of the three types of entries that can be made in an electronic spreadsheet.

6. What types of operators are used to compare numeric and string values?

7. Write the equivalent formula for @AVG(A1 . . D1) without the use of functions.

8. If the formula B2*$B$1 is copied from C1 to E3, what is the formula in E3? If the formula in E3 is copied to D45, what is the formula in D45?

9. What is the difference between the pointer and the cursor?

10. List three alternatives descriptors for the range A4 . . P12.

11. When do you "anchor the pointer"?

12. What would you use in a formula to override the priority rules for arithmetic operators?

13. What formula would be entered in A5 to sum all numbers in the range A1 . . A4?

14. When would you need to scroll horizontally? Vertically?

15. What is a spreadsheet template?

HANDS-ON EXERCISES

1. The following data represent the unit sales data for the past year for Diolab, Inc., a manufacturer of a diagnostic laboratory instrument that is sold primarily to hospitals and clinics.

| | DIOLAB INC. SALES (UNITS) | | | |
REGION	QTR1	QTR2	QTR3	QTR4
NE REGION	214	300	320	170
SE REGION	120	150	165	201
SW REGION	64	80	60	52
NW REGION	116	141	147	180

Enter the title, headings, and data in an electronic spreadsheet. Place the title in the range B1, the column headings in the range A2 . . E2, the row headings in the range A3 . . A6, and the sales data in the range B3 . . E6.

If the following assignments are to be handed in, print out the initial spreadsheets, then print them out again for each revision.

2. Add another column heading called SALES/YR in F2 of the Diolab spreadsheet. Enter a formula in F3 that sums the sales for each quarter for the northeast region. Copy the formula to the range F4 . . F6. SALES/YR should be 1004 for the NE Region and 636 for the SE Region.

3. Add average sales per quarter, AVG/QTR, in column G. AVG/QTR should be 251 for the NE Region and 159 for the SE Region.

4. Add two more columns that reflect sales per salesperson. In column H, add number of salespersons per region, PERSONS: 5, 3, 2, and 4, respectively. In column I, add formulas that compute sales per person, SALES/PER (from the data in SALES/YR and PERSONS columns). SALES/PER should be 200.8 for the NE Region and 212 for the SE Region.

5. In the range B8 . . F8, use functions to total sales for each quarter and for the year. The total sales for all regions should be 2480.

6. Copy the range A2 . . A6 to A12 . . A16 and B2 . . E2 to B12 . . E12. Diolab, Inc., sales are estimated to be 120 percent of last year's sales. Complete the newly created spreadsheet by multiplying last year's quarterly sales data by 1.2 and placing the result in the spreadsheet. Title this set of data ESTIMATED DIOLAB INC. SALES - NEXT YEAR. The NE Region first-quarter sales should be 257 (rounded) and the SE Region second-quarter sales should be 180.

7. Each of the lab analysis units sells for $2000. Add formulas in column F to compute estimated GROSS sales ($2000 times the total of the estimated quarterly sales) for each region. Also format the GROSS sales values as currency with no decimal places such that the NE Region amount appears as $2,409,600 (SE Region is $1,526,400). You may need to expand the width of column F to 11 positions.

S-5   DATA MANAGEMENT

Function

With data management software, you can create and maintain a data base and extract information from the data base. To use data management or "database" software, you first identify the format of the data, then design a display format that will permit interactive entry and revision of the data base. Once the data base is created, its *records* (related data about a particular event or thing) can be deleted or revised and other records can added to the data base. "Data base," as one word, is an alternative terminology for data management software. "Data base," as two words, refers to the highest level of the hierarchy of data organization.

All database software packages have the following fundamental capabilities:

1. Create and maintain (e.g., add, delete, and revise records) a data base.
2. Extract and list all records or only those records that meet certain conditions.
3. Make an inquiry (e.g., the average value of a particular field in a series of records).
4. Sort records in ascending or descending sequence by primary, secondary, and tertiary fields.
5. Generate formatted reports with subtotals and totals.

The more sophisticated packages include a variety of other features, such as spreadsheet-type computations, graphics, and programming.

Concepts

Many similarities exist between commercially available word processing packages and between commercially available electronic spreadsheet packages. With word processing, the user sees and manipulates lines of text. With electronic spreadsheets, the user sees and manipulates data in numbered rows and lettered columns. This is not the case with data management packages. All commercial software packages permit the creation and manipulation of data bases, but what the user sees on the screen may be vastly different for the various packages. However, the concepts embodied in these database packages are very similar. The conceptual coverage that follows is generic and can be applied to all database packages; however, the examples are oriented to dBASEII and dBASEIII products of Ashton-Tate. The organization of the data in a microcomputer data base is similar to the traditional hierarchy of data organization. Related **fields,** such as course identification number, course title, and course type are grouped to form **records** (e.g., the course record in the COURSE data base in Figure S-24). A collection of related records make up a data **file** or a **data base.** In data management software terminology, "file" and "data base" are often used interchangeably.

The best way to illustrate and demonstrate the concepts of data management software is by example. Ed Cool, Zimco's education coordinator, uses a micro-based data management software package to help him with his record-keeping tasks. To do this, Ed created two data bases. The COURSE data base (see Figure S-24) contains a record for each course

```
Record#  ID     TITLE                 TYPE      SOURCE      DURATION
      1  100    MIS Orientation       in-house  Staff             24
      2  201    Micro Overview        in-house  Staff              8
      3  2535   Intro to Info. Proc.  media     Takdel Inc        40
      4  310    Programming Stds.     in-house  Staff              6
      5  3223   BASIC Programming     media     Takdel Inc        40
      6  7771   Data Base Systems     media     Takdel Inc        30
      7  CIS11  Business COBOL        college   St. Univ.         45
      8  EX15   Local Area Networks   vendor    HAL Inc           30
      9  MGT10  Mgt. Info. Systems    college   St. Univ.         45
     10  VC10   Elec. Spreadsheet     media     VidCourse         20
     11  VC44   4th Generation Lang.  media     VidCourse         30
     12  VC88   Word Processing       media     VidCourse         18
```

```
Record#  ID     EMPLOYEE           DEPARTMENT START     STATUS
      1  VC10   Bell, Jim          Marketing  01/12/87  I
      2  VC10   Austin, Jill       Finance    01/12/87  I
      3  VC10   Targa, Phil        Finance    01/12/87  C
      4  VC88   Day, Elizabeth     Accounting 03/18/87  C
      5  VC88   Fitz, Paula        Finance    04/04/87  I
      6  MGT10  Mendez, Carlos     Accounting 01/15/87  I
      7  EX15   Adler, Phyllis     Marketing  02/10/87  W
      8  100    Targa, Phil        Finance    01/04/87  C
      9  100    Johnson, Charles   Marketing  01/10/87  C
     10  100    Klein, Ellen       Accounting 01/10/87  C
```

FIGURE S-24
Data Management: COURSE Data Base and TRAINING Data Base
The COURSE data base contains a record for each course that Zimco offers to its employees. The TRAINING data base contains a record for each Zimco employee who is enrolled in or has taken a course.

that Zimco offers to their employees and for several courses at State University, for which Zimco provides tuition reimbursement. Each record in the COURSE data base contains the following fields:

- Identification number (supplied by Zimco for in-house courses, by vendors, and by State University)
- Title of course
- Type of course (in-house seminar, multimedia, college or vendor seminar)
- Source of course (Zimco staff or supplier of course)
- Duration (number of hours required to complete course)

The TRAINING data base (see Figure S-24) contains a record for each Zimco employee who is enrolled in or has taken a course. Each record contains the following fields:

- Identification number (cross-reference to COURSE data base)
- Employee (name of Zimco employee)
- Department (department affiliation of employee)
- Start (datc course was begun)
- Status (employee's status code: I = incomplete, W = withdrawn from course, C = completed course)

Creating a Data Base.   To create a data base, the first thing you do is to set up a *screen format* that will enable you to enter the data for a record. The data entry screen format is analogous to a hard-copy form that contains labels and blank lines (e.g., medical questionnaire, employment application). Data are entered and edited (deleted or revised) with data management software one record at a time, like they are on hard-copy forms.

The Structure of the Data Base.   To set up a data entry screen format you must first specify the *structure* of the data base by identifying the characteristics of each field in the data base. This is done interactively, with the system prompting you to enter the field name, field type, and so on (see Figure S-25). For example, the ID field in Figure S-25 is a five-character field. The *field name* is ID; the *field length* is five characters; and the *field type* is character. A character field type can be a single word or any alphanumeric (i.e., numbers, letters, and special characters) phrase up to several hundred characters in length. For numeric field types, you must specify the maximum number of digits (field length) and the number of decimal positions that you wish to have displayed. Since the course durations are all defined in whole hours, the number of decimal positions for the DURATION field is set at zero (see Figure S-25).

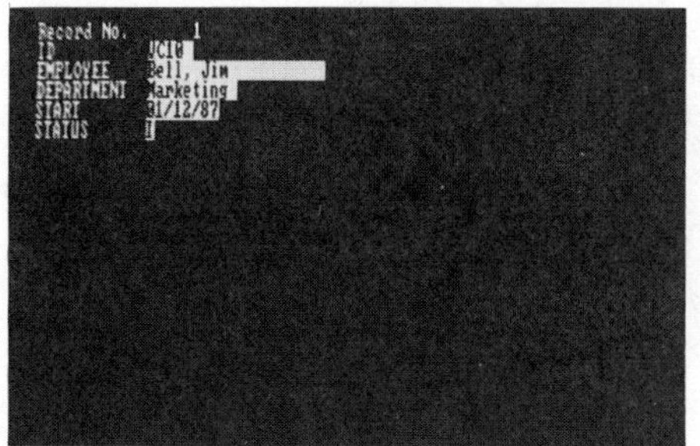

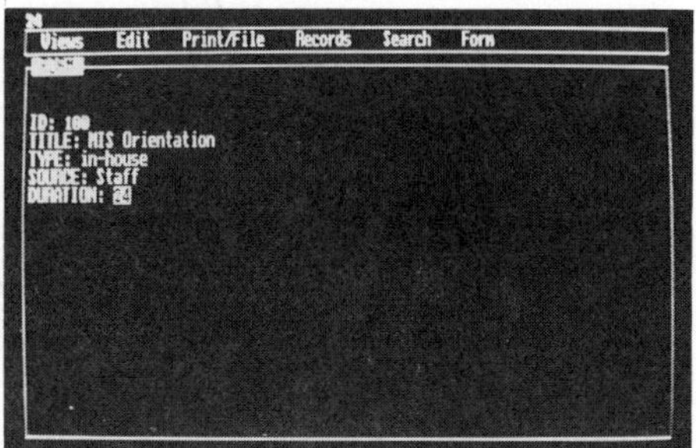

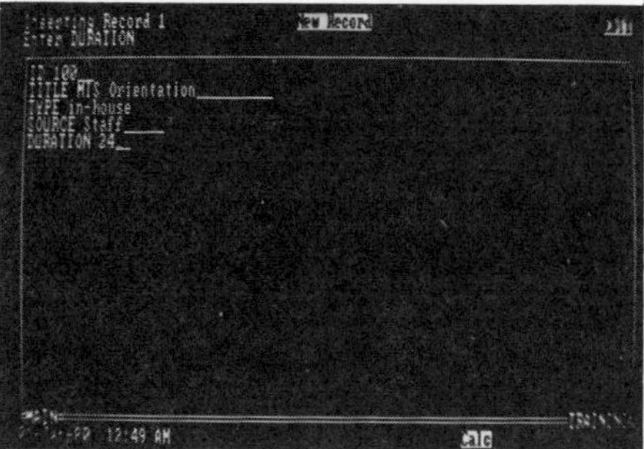

The data entry screen for the training data base of Figure S-24 is shown as it would appear for three popular data management packages. The first photo illustrates how the data entry screen would be displayed using dBASE III (dBASE III is a trademark of Ashton-Tate). The second photo illustrates how the data entry screen would be displayed using Reflex, an integrated package (Reflex-The Analyst is a trademark of BORELAND Analytica, Inc.). The third photo illustrates how the data entry screen would be displayed using Symphony, also an integrated package (Symphony is a trademark of the Lotus Development Corporation).
(Long and Associates)

Entering and Editing a Data Base.   The screen format for entering, editing, and adding records to the COURSE data base is shown in Figure S-26. This screen is generated automatically from the specifications outlined in structure of the COURSE data base (see Figure S-25). To create the

Field no.	Field name	Field type	Field length	Decimal positions
1	ID	Character	5	
2	TITLE	Character	20	
3	TYPE	Character	8	
4	SOURCE	Character	10	
5	DURATION	Numeric	4	0

FIGURE S-25
Data Management: Structure of the COURSE
Data Base

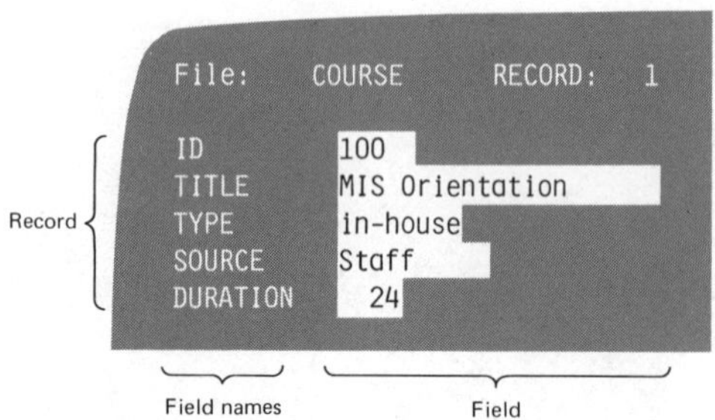

FIGURE S-26
Data Management: Data Entry Screen Format
Illustrated is the screen format for entering, editing, and adding records to the COURSE data base. This screen is automatically generated from the specifications outlined in structure of the COURSE data base (see Figure S-25).

COURSE data base, Ed Cool issued a command that called up the data entry screen of Figure S-26, then he entered the data for first record, then the second record, and so on. On most data management systems, the records are automatically assigned a number as they are entered. The reverse video portion of the screen in Figure S-26 comprises the data for the five fields in record "1."

To add a record to an existing COURSE data base, Ed would issue a command such as *append* or *add*. This command displays the format screen of Figure S-26 (without data) so that he can enter the data for the new record(s). Each additional record is assigned the record number that is one greater than the current total. To edit a record, Ed would issue a command such as *edit* in conjunction with the desired record number (e.g., record 1) or a qualifier (e.g., ID='100'). The desired record would then appear superimposed over the format screen, as in Figure S-26. Changes are made to fields in the format screen in much the same way that you would change text in a word processing document.

Setting Conditions for Record Selection.   Data management software also permits you to retrieve, view, and print records based on preset conditions. You set conditions for the selection of records by composing a *relational expression* that reflects the desired conditions. The relational expression normally compares one or more field names to numbers or character strings using the *relational operators* discussed in the skills section on electronic spreadsheet software (see Figure S-17). Several expressions can be combined in a single condition with *logical operators* (see Figure S-17).

Ed Cool wanted a listing of all in-house seminars, so he issued commands to *locate* (*search* for) then *list* the records of all courses that are of TYPE "in-house" in the COURSE data base (see Figure S-24). To retrieve these records, he set the condition to

TYPE='in-house'

Depending on the data management package, the *search* string is enclosed in single or double quotes (e.g., "in-house"). We'll use single quotes. To produce the output of Figure S-27, Ed keyed in the command

```
. LIST FOR TYPE='in-house'

Record#  ID     TITLE                TYPE      SOURCE      DURATION
      1  100    MIS Orientation      in-house  Staff             24
      2  201    Micro Overview       in-house  Staff              8
      4  310    Programming Stds.    in-house  Staff              6
```

FIGURE S-27
Data Management: Conditional Search and List

For the command, LIST FOR TYPE='in-house,' only the records from the COURSE data base (Figure S-24) for which TYPE='in-house' are displayed.

> LIST FOR TYPE='in-house'

Of course, one of the options is to route the output to a display screen or to a printer. If Ed wanted only the ID and TITLE for those records that meet the condition TYPE='in-house', he would enter a command like this:

> LIST ID, TITLE FOR TYPE='in-house'

Figure S-28 shows the output.

Data Base Inquiries. You can "page" through the data base by moving from record to record. You can view a particular record by entering the record number that is supplied by the software or by entering certain selection condition(s) (e.g., ID='EX15'). Database software also permits inquiries that involve parts or all of one or more records. To extract, then list (display, print, or edit) selected records from a data base, you must first establish the condition or conditions. The following relational expressions establish conditions that will select or extract records (noted to the right of the expression) from the COURSE data base of Figure S-24.

TYPE='in-house' .AND. DURATION<=10	records 2, 4 (see Fig. S–29)
SOURCE='VidCourse' .OR. SOURCE='Takdel Inc'	records 3, 5, 6, 10, 11, 12
DURATION>15 .AND. DURATION<25	records 1, 10, 12
ID='CIS11'	record 7

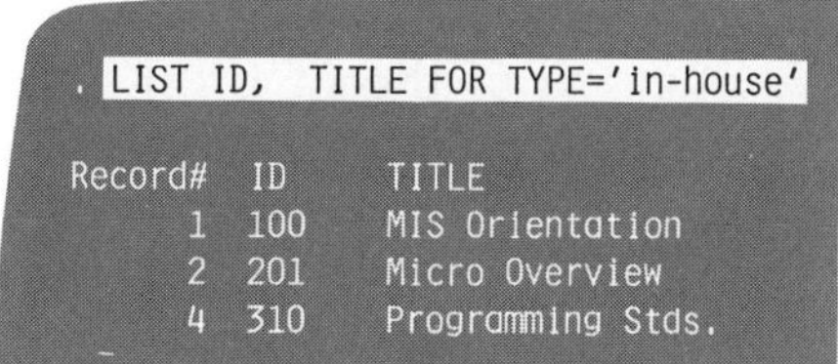

FIGURE S-28
Data Management: Conditional Search and List, Specified

Fields Only For the command, LIST ID, TITLE FOR TYPE='in-house,' only the ID and TITLE fields for the records from the COURSE data base (Figure S-24) for which TYPE='in-house' are displayed.

```
. LIST FOR TYPE='in-house' .AND. DURATION<=10
Record# ID       TITLE                    TYPE       SOURCE      DURATION
     2 201    Micro Overview          in-house Staff              8
     4 310    Programming Stds.       in-house Staff              6
```

FIGURE S-29
Data Management: Conditional Expression with AND
Operator
For the command, TYPE='in-house' .AND.
DURATION<=10, only the records from the COURSE data
base (Figure S-24) for which TYPE='in-house' *and*
DURATION < = (less than or equal to) 10 are displayed.

The process of selecting records by setting conditions is sometimes called
filtering; that is, those records or fields that you don't want are "filtered
out" of the display.

Besides filtering, you can also make inquiries to the data base that
result in a display of calculated information. For example, Ed Cool wanted
to know the total number of in-house seminar hours that are made available
to Zimco employees. To do this, he issued the following command for
the COURSE data base:

SUM DURATION FOR SOURCE='Staff'

The result, 38 (24+8+6), is displayed on the screen. To obtain the average
duration of all courses, Ed issued this command:

AVERAGE DURATION

This command causes the average of all course durations (28) to be displayed on the screen. Similarly, Ed issued this command to COUNT
the number of 'VidCourse' courses in the COURSE data base:

COUNT FOR SOURCE='VidCourse'

The result of 3 is displayed on the monitor.

Sorting Records.   Data can also be sorted for display in a variety of formats.
For example, the COURSE data base in Figure S-24 has been sorted and
is displayed in ascending order by course identification number (ID).
To obtain this sequencing of the data base records, Ed Cool selected ID
as the *key field* and requested an ascending sort of the COURSE data
base. Numbers are considered "less than" alphabetic characters; therefore,
the numeric IDs are listed before those that begin with a letter.

Ed also wanted a presentation of the COURSE data base that was
sorted by ID within SOURCE. This involves the selection of a *primary*
and a *secondary key field*. Ed selected SOURCE as the primary key field,
but he wanted the courses offered by each source to be listed in ascending

```
     Record#  ID    TITLE                  TYPE       SOURCE      DURATION
           1  EX15  Local Area Networks    vendor     HAL Inc          30
           2  CIS11 Business COBOL         college    St. Univ.        45
           3  MGT11 Mgt. Info. Systems     college    St. Univ.        45
           4  100   MIS Orientation        in-house   Staff            24
           5  201   Micro Overview         in-house   Staff             8
           6  310   Programming Stds.      in-house   Staff             6
           7  2535  Intro to Info. Proc.   media      Takdel Inc       40
           8  3223  BASIC Programming      media      Takdel Inc       40
           9  7771  Data Base Systems      media      Takdel Inc       30
          10  VC10  Elec. Spreadsheet      media      VidCourse        20
          11  VC44  4th Generation Lang.   media      VidCourse        30
          12  VC88  Word Processing        media      VidCourse        18
```

FIGURE S-30
Data Management: COURSE Data Base Sorted by ID within SOURCE
This display is the result of a sort operation on the COURSE data base with the
SOURCE field as the primary key field and the ID field as the secondary key field.

order by ID. To achieve this record sequence, he selected ID as the secondary key field. In most database packages, the issuing of a sort command
results in the compilation of a temporary data base. After the sort operation,
the temporary data base contains the records in the order described in
the sort command (see Figure S-30). Notice in Figure S-30 that the SOURCE
field entries are in alphabetical order and the three "Staff" records (i.e.,
records 4, 5, and 6) are in sequence by ID (e.g., 100, 201, 310).

Ed used the temporary data base of Figure S-30 to produce the listing
of Figure S-31. To do this he issued the following command:

LIST SOURCE, ID FOR TYPE='vendor' .OR. TYPE='media'

Because the entries in the SOURCE field are alphabetized in Figure
S-30, the selected SOURCE entries in Figure S-31 are also alphabetized.

Report Generation

"Quick and Dirty" Reports.   A data base is a source of information and
data management software provides the facility to get at this information.
A *report* is the presentation of information that is derived from one or
more data bases. The simple listings of selected records and fields in
Figures S-27 through S-30 are "quick and dirty" reports. Such reports
are the bread and butter of data base capabilities. These listings may
not be fancy, but in most instances the user is more interested in the
information than the format in which it is displayed. The generation of
formatted reports is discussed in a later section.

Combining Two Data Bases.   Ed Cool wanted to produce a "quick and
dirty" status report that contained an alphabetical listing of those employ-

```
. LIST SOURCE, ID FOR TYPE='vendor' .OR. TYPE='media'
Record#   SOURCE       ID
      1   HAL Inc      EX15
      7   Takdel Inc   2535
      8   Takdel Inc   3223
      9   Takdel Inc   7771
     10   VidCourse    VC10
     11   VidCourse    VC44
     12   VidCourse    VC88
```

FIGURE S-31
Data Management: Conditional Expression with OR Operator
For the command, LIST SOURCE, ID FOR TYPE='vendor' .OR. TYPE='media,' only the records from the COURSE data base (as sorted in Figure S-30) for which TYPE='vendor' *or* TYPE='media' are displayed.

ees who had completed courses (i.e., STATUS='C' on TRAINING data base of Figure S-24) along with the IDs and TITLEs of the courses they had taken. He also wanted a similar status report for those employees whose STATUS was incomplete (i.e., STATUS='I'). Producing these reports is a little more challenging because the data required are on two different data bases. The EMPLOYEE name and STATUS fields are on the TRAINING data base and the course ID and TITLE fields are on the COURSE data base. Since the two data bases have a common field (ID), Ed can *join* the two data bases to get the reports he wants.

The following command "joins" the TRAINING data base with the COURSE data base and generates the temporary data base (TEMP1) of Figure S-32.

```
JOIN [TRAINING] WITH COURSE TO TEMP1 FOR COURSE->ID=ID
FIELDS EMPLOYEE, ID, TITLE, STATUS
```

Since Ed wants the employee names to be listed alphabetically, he had to sort the resultant data base (TEMP1) on the EMPLOYEE field and create another temporary data base called TEMP2. He then issued the following commands to get the reports he wanted (Figure S-33):

```
LIST FOR STATUS='C'
LIST FOR STATUS='I'
```

The resultant reports are shown in Figure S-33.

Customized Reports.   Data management software provides the capability to create customized or formatted reports. This capability allows you to design the *layout* of the report. This means that you have some flexibility

TRAINING data base

```
Record#   ID     EMPLOYEE          DEPARTMENT  START      STATUS
      1   VC10   Bell, Jim         Marketing   01/12/87   I
      2   VC10   Austin, Jill      Finance     01/12/87   I
      3   VC10   Targa, Phil       Finance     01/12/87   C
      4   VC88   Day, Elizabeth    Accounting  03/18/87   C
      5   VC88   Fitz, Paula       Finance     04/04/87   I
      6   MGT10  Mendez, Carlos    Accounting  01/15/87   I
      7   EX15   Adler, Phyllis    Marketing   02/10/87   W
      8   100    Targa, Phil       Finance     01/04/87   C
      9   100    Johnson, Charles  Marketing   01/10/87   C
     10   100    Klein, Ellen      Accounting  01/10/87   C
```

+

COURSE data base

```
Record#   ID     TITLE               TYPE       SOURCE       DURATION
      1   100    MIS Orientation     in-house   Staff              24
      2   201    Micro Overview      in-house   Staff               8
      3   2535   Intro to Info. Proc. media     Takdel Inc         40
      4   310    Programming Stds.   in-house   Staff               6
      5   3223   BASIC Programming   media      Takdel Inc         40
      6   7771   Data Base Systems   media      Takdel Inc         30
      7   CIS11  Business COBOL      college    St. Univ.          45
      8   EX15   Local Area Networks vendor     HAL Inc            30
      9   MGT10  Mgt. Info. Systems  college    St. Univ.          45
     10   VC10   Elec. Spreadsheet   media      VidCourse          20
     11   VC44   4th Generation Lang. media     VidCourse          30
     12   VC88   Word Processing     media      VidCourse          18
```

TEMP1 data base

```
Record#   EMPLOYEE          ID     TITLE                STATUS
      1   Bell, Jim         VC10   Elec. Spreadsheet    I
      2   Austin, Jill      VC10   Elec. Spreadsheet    I
      3   Targa, Phil       VC10   Elec. Spreadsheet    C
      4   Day, Elizabeth    VC88   Word Processing      C
      5   Fitz, Paula       VC88   Word Processing      I
      6   Mendez, Carlos    MGT10  Mgt. Info. Systems   I
      7   Adler, Phyllis    EX15   Local Area Networks  W
      8   Targa, Phil       100    MIS Orientation      C
      9   Johnson, Charles  100    MIS Orientation      C
     10   Klein, Ellen      100    MIS Orientation      C
```

FIGURE S-32
Data Management: Combining Two Data Bases
A common ID field enables the "joining" of the TRAINING
data base with the COURSE data base to produce the
TEMP1 data base.

in spacing and can include titles, subtitles, column headings, separation
lines, and other elements that make a report more readable. The user
describes the layout of the *customized* report interactively, then stores
it for later recall. The result of the description, called a *report form*, is
recalled from disk storage and merged with a data base to create the
customized report. Managers often use this capability to generate periodic
reports (e.g., weekly training status report).

Once a month Ed Cool generates four reports that summarize the
courses being offered for each type of course; that is, one report summarizes
Zimco's course offerings for TYPE='in-house', another for TYPE='media'
(multimedia), and so on. One of these formatted reports is shown in

```
. LIST FOR STATUS='C'
  Record#   EMPLOYEE              ID       TITLE               STATUS
        4   Day, Elizabeth        VC88     Word Processing     C
        6   Johnson, Charles      100      MIS Orientation     C
        7   Klein, Ellen          100      MIS Orientation     C
        9   Targa, Phil           VC10     Elec. Spreadsheet   C
       10   Targa, Phil           100      MIS Orientation     C

. LIST FOR STATUS='I'
  Record#   EMPLOYEE              ID       TITLE               STATUS
        2   Austin, Jill          VC10     Elec. Spreadsheet   I
        3   Bell, Jim             VC10     Elec. Spreadsheet   I
        5   Fitz, Paula           VC88     Word Processing     I
        8   Mendez, Carlos        MGT10    Mgt. Info. Systems  I
```

FIGURE S-33
Data Management: Reports Made Possible by Combining Two Data Bases
For the command, LIST FOR STATUS='C,' only the records from the TEMP1 data
base (Figure S-30) for which STATUS='C' (completed course) are displayed in the
first list. For the command, LIST FOR STATUS='I,' only those records for which
STATUS='I' (incomplete) are displayed in the second list.

Figure S-34. This summary report of "MULTIMEDIA COURSES" was
compiled by merging a predefined report format with the COURSE data
base (as sorted in Figure S-30). The layout of the report form called
for a title, column headings, subheadings (for each SOURCE of
TYPE='media'), plus subtotals and a total for DURATION. The formatted

```
              MULTIMEDIA COURSES

  Title of Course          ID     Duration


  ** Source: Takdel Inc
   Intro to Info. Proc.    2535        40
   BASIC Programming       3223        40
   Data Base Systems       7771        30
  ** Subtotal **

                                     110


  ** Source: VidCourse
   Elec. Spreadsheet       VC10        20
   4th Generation Lang.    VC44        30
   Word Processing         VC88        18
  ** Subtotal **

                                      68

  *** Total ***

                                     178
```

FIGURE S-34
**Data Management: Formatted
Reports**
This formatted report was compiled by
merging a predefined report format
with the COURSE data base (as sorted
in Figure S-30).

report of Figure S-34 is one of dozens that Ed Cool generates on a weekly and monthly basis by using data management software.

Use

Data management software earns the "productivity tool" label by providing users with the capability to organize data into an electronic data base that can be easily maintained and queried (permit user inquiries). The examples illustrated and discussed in the "concepts" section merely scratch the surface of the potential of database software. With relative ease, you can generate some rather sophisticated reports that involve subtotals, calculations, and even programming. You can change the structure of a data base. For example, if Ed Cool wanted to add and END field (data course was completed) to structure of the TRAINING data base in Figure S-24, he could do so without having to recreate the data base.

Many of the capabilities of electronic spreadsheet software are embodied in data management software. For example, you can also make "what if" inquiries with database software. For example, Ed Cool might ask: "What if we discontinued the VidCourse contract, how many courses would we have left to offer." You might observe that this and some other queries illustrated in this section might best be answered by simply examining a hardcopy of the 10- and 12-record data bases. But what if Ed Cool had 120 different courses in his COURSE data base and 1500 employees in his TRAINING data base? These numbers are much more realistic for a company the size of Zimco, but procedures for making the inquiries to a data base with 1500 records are no more difficult than making inquiries to a data base with 10 records.

REVIEW EXERCISES (S-5)

1. Describe the capabilities of data management software.
2. What characteristics describe a field in a data base record?
3. What is the purpose of setting conditions for a data base?
4. In data base terminology, what is meant by the term "filtering"?
5. Describe two types of inquiries to a data base that involve calculations.
6. What is the relationship between a field, a record, and the structure of a data base?
7. Give examples and descriptions of at least three other fields that might be added to the record for the COURSE data base.
8. Give examples and descriptions of at least three other fields that might be added to the record for the TRAINING data base.

9. What would be the employee name for the third record if the TRAIN-
ING data base were sorted such that the primary and secondary key
fields were DEPARTMENT and EMPLOYEE, respectively?

HANDS-ON EXERCISES

1. **(a)** Design a data entry screen to accept the following sales data for
Diolab, Inc., a manufacturer of a diagnostic laboratory instrument
that is sold primarily to hospitals and clinics.

	DIOLAB INC. SALES (UNITS)			
REGION	QTR1	QTR2	QTR3	QTR4
NE REGION	241	300	320	170
SE REGION	120	150	165	201
SW REGION	64	80	60	52

   (b) What is the data base record?

   (c) What are the field names, types, and lengths?

2. **(a)** Enter the Diolab data above into a data base.

   (b) Revise the NE Region first-quarter sales to be 214.

   (c) Add the following NW Region record to the data base.

REGION	QTR1	QTR2	QTR3	QTR4
NW REGION	116	141	147	180

   (d) Obtain a printout of the data base and store the data on a disk
file named DIOLAB.

3. **(a)** What conditions would be needed to select all Diolab regions
(records) that sold more than 150 units in the fourth quarter (all
but SW Region)?

   (b) What conditions would be needed to select all Diolab regions
(records) that sold more than 150 units in the fourth quarter *and*
for which fourth-quarter sales are greater than third-quarter sales
(SE and NW Regions)?

   (c) What command and conditions would be needed to select and display only the REGION and QTR4 fields of those Diolab regions for which the average sales for the first three quarters is less than the sales for the fourth quarter (SE and NW Regions)?

4. **(a)** Make an inquiry to the Diolab data base that results in a display of the average unit sales for each quarter (QTR1=128).

   (b) Make an inquiry to the Diolab data base that results in a display of the total unit sales for each quarter (QTR1=514).

5. **(a)** Sort the Diolab data base in ascending order by QTR1 sales. What regions are first and last?

   (b) Sort the Diolab data base in descending order by QTR4 sales. What regions are first and last?

6. Generate a formatted report from the sorted data base of Exercise 5(a) that is entitled "DIOLAB INC. SALES (UNITS) and has the following column headings: Sales Region, 1st Qtr, 2nd Qtr, 3rd Qtr, and 4th Qtr. The report should include the total sales for each quarter.

S-6 GRAPHICS

Function

With the graphics software, you can create a variety of presentation graphics from data in an electronic spreadsheet of a data base. Among the most popular presentation graphics are **bar charts, pie charts,** and **line charts** (as seen in Figures S-36, S-39, and S-40, respectively). Other types of charts are possible. Each of these charts can be annotated with chart *titles, labels* for axes, and *legends.*

Some graphics software lets you create and store original drawings. To do this, however, your personal computer must be equipped with a mouse, joystick, digitizing board, or some type of device that permits the input of curved and angular lines. To make drawing easier to do, such software even offers a data base filled with a variety of frequently used symbols, such as rectangles, circles, cats (yes, even cats), and so on. Some companies draw and store the image of their company logo so it can be inserted on memos, reports, and charts.

Graphic representations of data have proven to be a very effective means of communication. It is easier to recognize problem areas and trends in a chart than it is in a tabular summary of the same data. For many years, the presentation of tabular data was the preferred approach to communicating tabular information. This was because it was simply too expensive and time consuming to produce presentation graphics manually. Today, you can use graphics software to produce perfectly proportioned, accurate, and visually appealing charts in a matter of seconds.

Prior to the introduction of graphics software, the turnaround time was at least a day, and often a week.

Concepts

The data needed to produce a chart already exist in a spreadsheet or data base. The graphics software leads you through a series of prompts, the first of which asks you what type of graph is to be produced: bar chart, pie chart, line chart, and so on. You then select the spreadsheet ranges (or data base fields) that are to be plotted. You can also select spreadsheet ranges or data base field names for the labels. Once you have identified the source of the data and labels, and perhaps added a title, you can display, print, or plot the graph. Any changes made to data in a spreadsheet or data base are reflected in the charts as well.

Use

Sally Marcio, the VP of Sales and Marketing at Zimco, is an avid user of spreadsheet and graphics software. The spreadsheet of Figure S-35 is an annual summary of the sales for each of Zimco's four products by sales region. This spreadsheet is used in the following sections to demonstrate the compilation of bar, pie, and line charts.

Bar Charts. To prepare the bar chart of Figure S-36, Sally first had to specify appropriate ranges; that is, the values in the "Total" column (range F5 . . F8 of Figure S-35) are to be plotted and the values in the

```
F10: @SUM(F5..F8)
```

	A	B	C	D	E	F
1		ANNUAL SALES FOR ZIMCO ENTERPRISES BY REGION ($1000)				
2						
3	Sales Region	Stibs	Farkles	Teglers	Qwerts	Total
4	-----------	-----	-------	-------	------	-----
5	Southern	$7,140	$5,460	$3,150	$5,250	$21,000
6	Western	$14,790	$11,310	$6,525	$11,875	$44,500
7	Northern	$13,260	$10,140	$5,850	$10,750	$40,000
8	Eastern	$15,810	$12,090	$6,975	$12,625	$47,500
9	-----------	-----	-------	-------	------	-----
10	Totals	$51,000	$39,000	$22,500	$40,500	$153,000

FIGURE S-35
Graphics: Sales Data
These data are used to produce the bar, pie, and line charts of Figures S-36 through S-40.

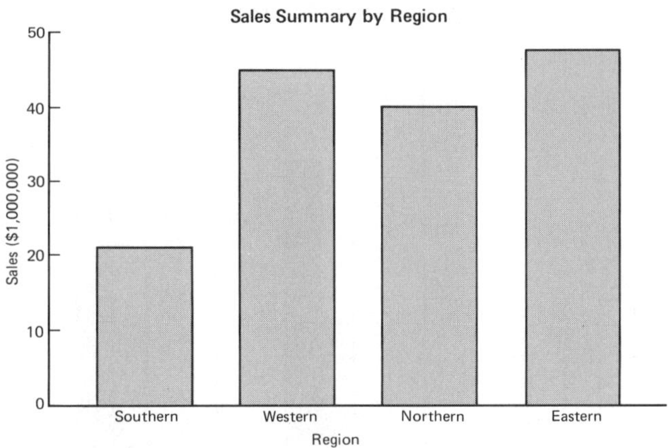

FIGURE S-36
Graphics: Bar Chart
The "Total" sales for each region in Figure S-35 are
graphically represented in this bar chart.

"Sales Region" column (range A5 . . A8 of Figure S-35) are to be inserted
as labels along the horizontal or x axis. Sally also added a title for the
chart (Sales Summary by Region), titles for the x axis (Region) and the
vertical or y axis [(Sales ($1000)].

The sales figures for each region in Figure S-35 (range B5 . . E8)
can be plotted in a *clustered-bar chart*. The resultant chart, shown in

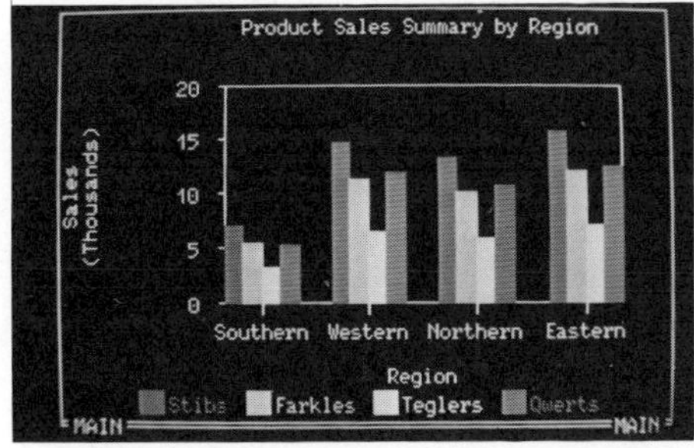

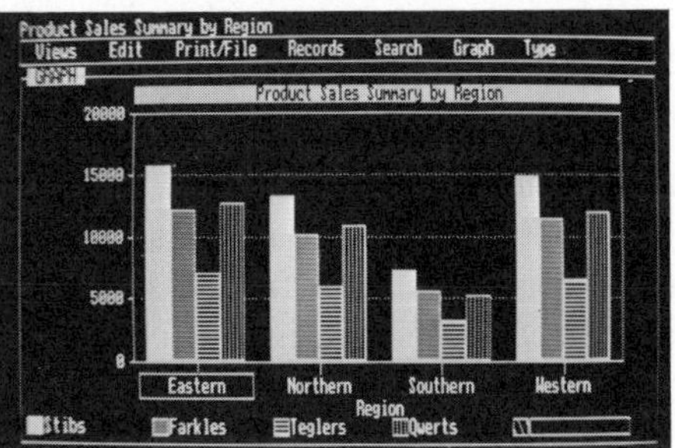

The bar chart of Figure S-37 was prepared using two popular graphics packages.
The first photo illustrates how the chart would be displayed using Symphony, an
integrated package (Symphony is a trademark of the Lotus Development Corporation).
The second plot illustrates how the chart would be displayed using Reflex, also an
integrated package (Reflex-The Analyst is a trademark of BORELAND Analytica,
Inc.).

(Long and Associates)

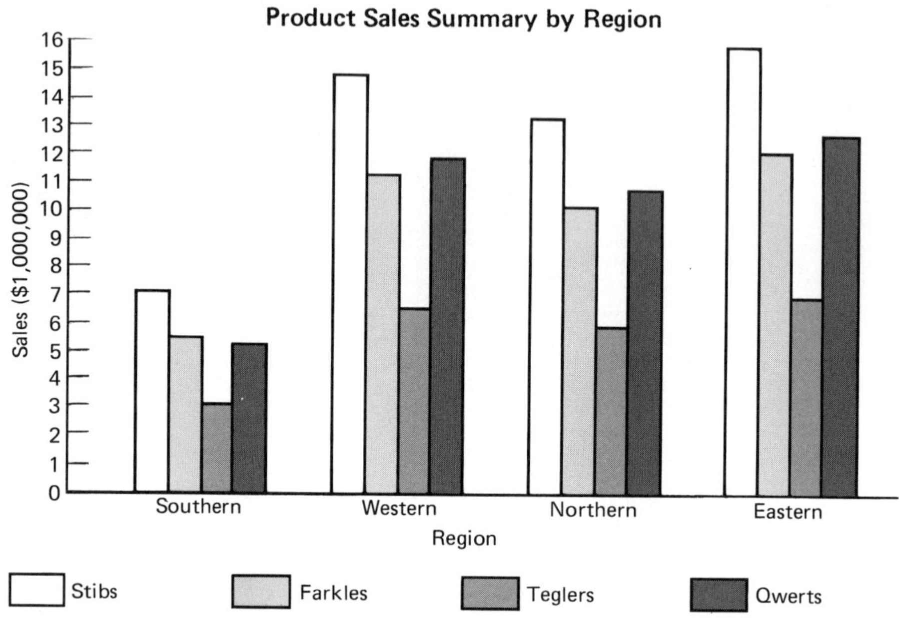

FIGURE S-37
Graphics: Clustered-Bar Chart
Regional sales for each of the four products in Figure S-35 are graphically
represented in this clustered-bar chart.

Figure S-37, permits Sally to better understand the regional distribution
of sales. The *stacked-bar chart* in Figure S-38 is an alternative presentation
to the clustered-bar chart in Figure S-37. The clustered-bar chart visually
highlights the relative contribution that each product made to the total
sales for each region.

Pie Charts.   Pie charts are the most basic of presentation graphics. A
pie chart graphically illustrates each "piece" of data in its proper relationship to the whole "pie." To illustrate how a pie chart is constructed
and used, refer again to the "Annual Sales" spreadsheet in Figure S-35.

Sally Marcio produced the sales-by-product pie chart in Figure S-39
by specifying that the values in the "Totals" row (range B10 . . E10 of
Figure S-35) to be "pieces" of the pie. She specified further that selected
values in the column headings row (range B3 . . E3) be inserted as labels
and she added a title. The numbers in parentheses represent what percent
each piece (i.e., total sales for a particular product) is of the whole (i.e.,
total sales or the value of F10). To emphasize the product with the greatest
contribution to total sales, Sally decided to *explode* (or separate) the
Stibs piece of the pie.

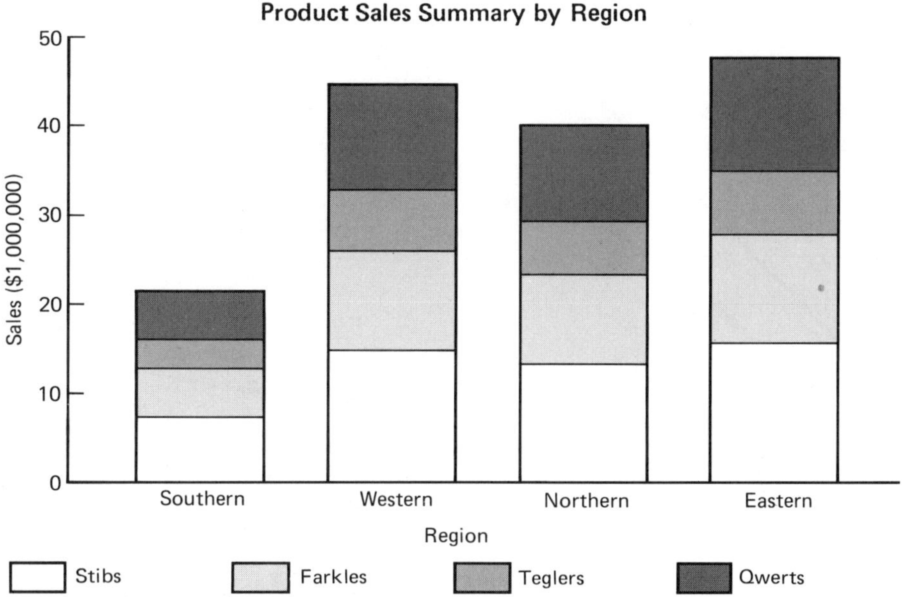

FIGURE S-38
Graphics: Stacked-Bar Chart
Regional sales for each of the four products in Figure S-35 are graphically represented in this stacked-bar chart.

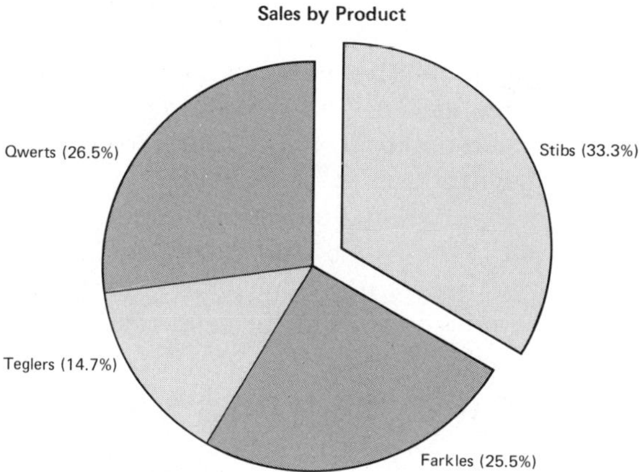

FIGURE S-39
Graphics: Pie Chart
Total sales by product (i.e., the "Totals" row, B10..E10) in Figure S-35 are graphically represented in this pie chart. The "Stibs" piece of the pie is exploded for emphasis.

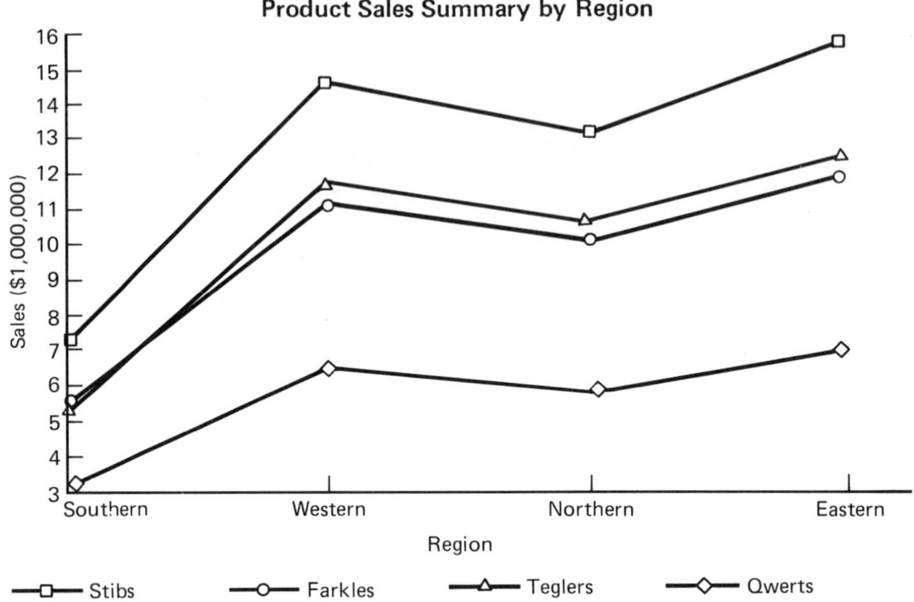

FIGURE S-40
Graphics: Line Chart
This line chart shows a plot of the data of Figure S-37. A line connects the sales
for each product by region.

Line Charts.   A line chart connects similar points on a graph with one
or several lines. Sally Marcio used the clustered-bar chart of Figure
S-37 to visually highlight relative product sales by region. She used the
same data in the spreadsheet of Figure S-35 to generate the line chart of
Figure S-40. The line chart makes it easy for Sally to compare sales between
regions for a particular product.

In the line chart of Figure S-40, four ranges of data from the spreadsheet
of Figure S-35 (B5 . . E5, B6 . . E6, and so on) are plotted and connected
with a line, one for each product. The chart clearly indicates that the
proportion of product sales is similar for each region.

REVIEW EXERCISES (S-6)

1. Name three types of charts commonly used for presentation graphics.
2. What is the source of the data needed to produce the charts?
3. Name and graphically illustrate (by hand) two variations on the bar
   chart.
4. What types of input devices enable you to produce original line drawings?

5. Under what circumstances is a graphic representation of data more effective than a tabular presentation of the same data?

6. What is meant when a portion of a pie chart is exploded?

7. Is it possible to present the same information in a stacked bar and a line chart? How about stacked bar and pie charts?

HANDS-ON EXERCISES

1. The following Diolab, Inc., sales data are reproduced from the Hands-on Exercises in Sections S-5 and S-6. Produce the accompanying bar chart showing the total unit sales by region for Diolab, Inc. Label the y and x axes as shown.

DIOLAB INC. SALES (UNITS)

REGION	QTR1	QTR2	QTR3	QTR4
NE REGION	214	300	320	170
SE REGION	120	150	165	201
SW REGION	64	80	60	52
NW REGION	116	141	147	180

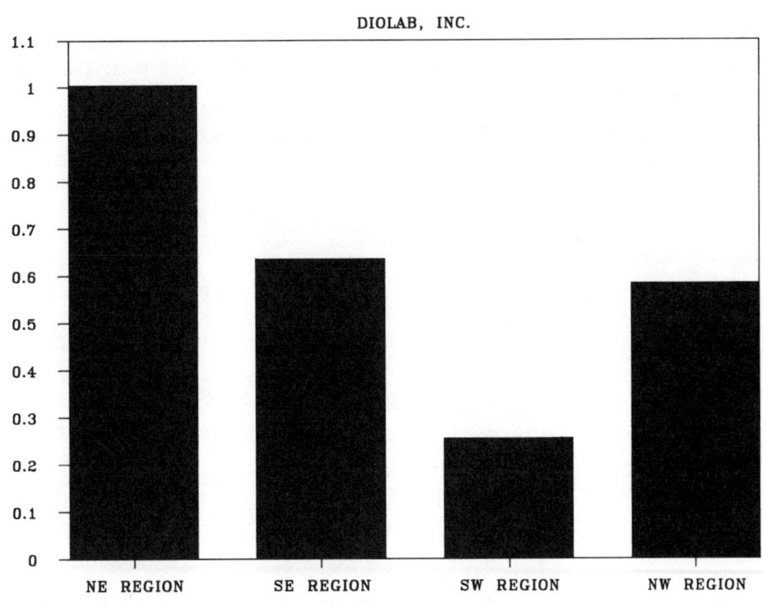

2. Produce the accompanying pie chart showing the total unit sales by region for Diolab, Inc. Title the chart and label each piece as shown.

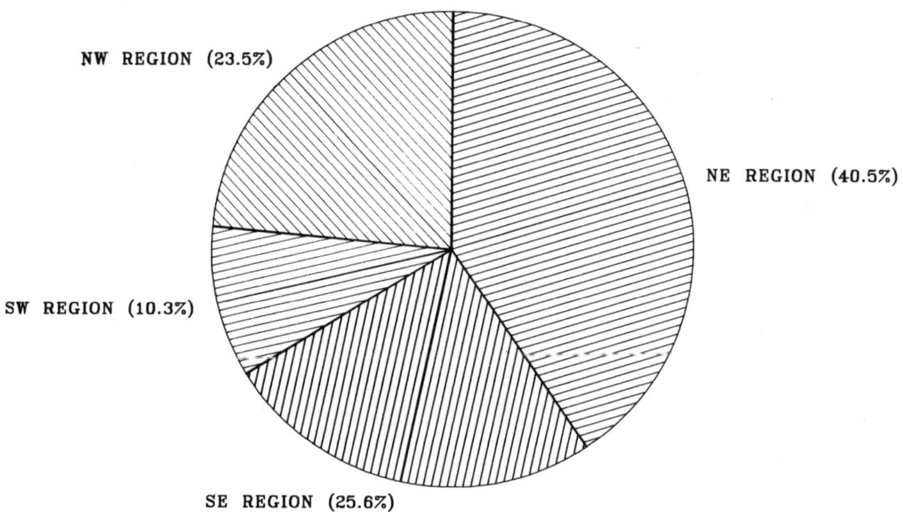

3. Compare the information portrayed in the bar and pie charts above.

4. Produce the accompanying clustered-bar chart showing quarterly unit sales by region for Diolab, Inc. Title the chart, label the axes, and include a legend as shown.

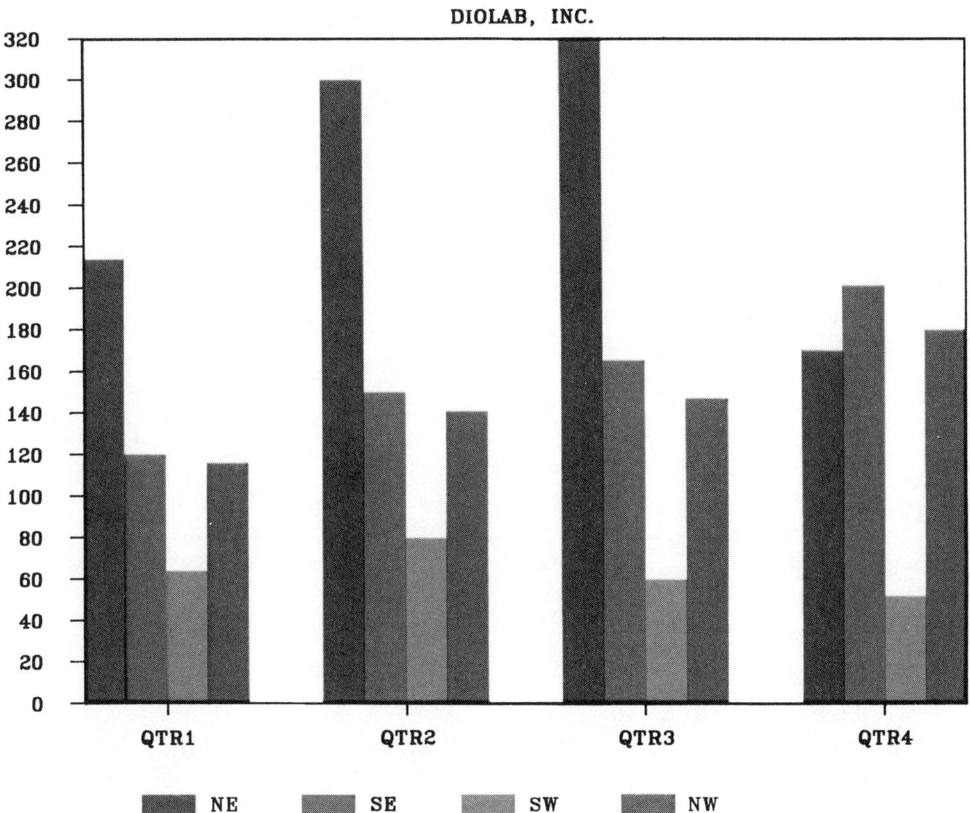

5. Produce the accompanying line chart showing quarterly unit sales by region for Diolab, Inc. Title the chart, label the axes, and include a legend as shown.

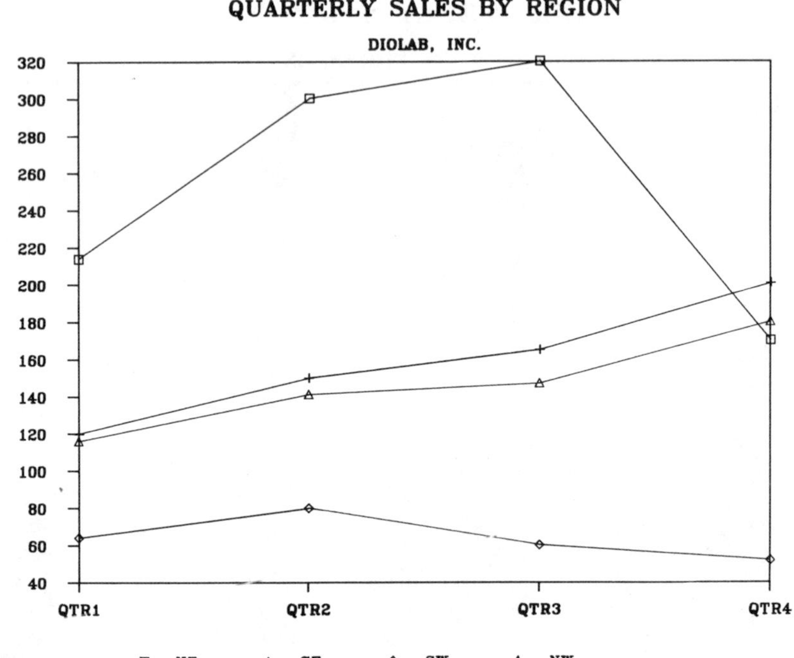

6. Compare the information portrayed in the clustered-bar and line charts above.

S-7   IDEA PROCESSORS

Function

An idea processor is a productivity tool that allows you to organize and document your thoughts and ideas. Such software can be used for brainstorming, outlining project activities, developing speeches and presentations, compiling notes for meetings and seminars, and a myriad of other uses. Idea processors let you work with one idea at a time within a hierarchy of other ideas such that you can easily organize and reorganize your ideas.

Some people have referred to idea processor software as an electronic version of the yellow note pad. When you use an idea processor, you can focus your attention on the thought process by letting the computer help with the task of documenting your ideas.

Concepts

Like word processing software, idea processor packages permit the manipulation of text, but with a different twist. They deal with one-line explanations of *items*: "ideas," points, notes, things, and so on. Idea processors, which are also called *outliners*, can be used to organize these single-line items into an outline format. You create an outline by entering items, then using the capabilities of the software to arrange them into a well organized outline.

Preston Smith, Zimco's president, dictates his letters, memos, and reports from outlines that he prepares using idea processor software. He also prepares notes for his meetings with an idea processor. For example, he prepared the agenda outlined in Figure S-41 for an "executive planning session." This example is the basis for demonstrating outliner concepts.

```
1  2  3  4 - Level

Issues to be resolved
    Planning horizon
        5 years
        10 years
    Expansion of product line
    Decentralization of information services functions
        Hardware
            Personal Computers
            Minis
            Mainframes
        Personnel
Approach to long-range planning at Zimco
    Mission statement
    Objectives
        Qualitative results
        Quantitative results
    Goals
    Strategies
    Task identification and scheduling
    Preparation of plan
```

FIGURE S-41
Idea Processor: Display of an Outline
The outline shown is an example of an agenda for an "executive planning session." The levels of the items can be equated to the level indicators in the top left corner of the display.

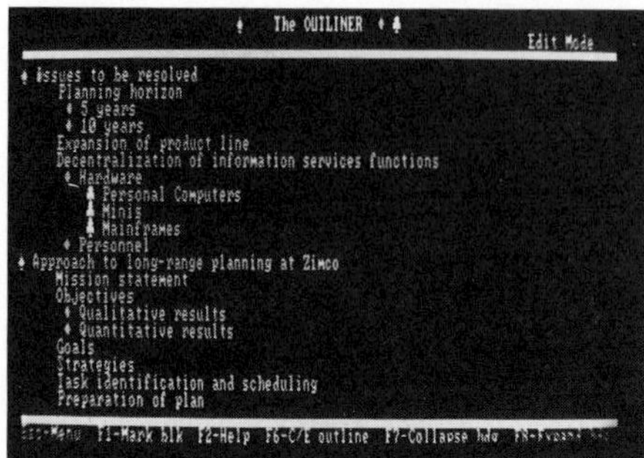

The outline of Figure S-41 was prepared using two popular idea processor packages.
The first photo illustrates how the outline would be displayed using The OUTLINER
(Long and Associates). The second photo illustrates how the outline would be
displayed using ThinkTank. (ThinkTank is a trademark of Living Videotext, Inc.)
(Long and Associates)

The Item Orientation of Outliners.   Just as a block of text in a word processing document can be moved, copied, and deleted, one or more items in
an outline can be moved, copied, or deleted. First-level items are flush
with the left margin. Second-level items are indented to show subordina-
tion to a first-level item. Third-level items are indented under second-
level items, and so on (see Figure S-41 and the level indicators at the
top left corner of the display). One of the handy features of an outliner
is that you can easily change the level of an item by shifting it to the
left or to the right. For example, the "5 year" and "10 year" items in
Figure S-41 were originally fourth-level items under a third-level heading
called "Alternatives," but Preston decided to delete the "Alternatives"
heading and shift the "Planning horizon" options to the third level.

The first draft of Preston's agenda outline did not include any third-
level headings under "Approach to long-range planning at Zimco." However, Preston wanted to emphasize two types of "Objectives," so he inserted the two third-level headings, "Qualitative results" and "Quantita-
tive results" (see Figure S-41).

Until moments before the planning session, Preston had the "Approach to long-range planning at Zimco" as the first item on the session's
agenda. Once he decided to make "Issues to be resolved" the first item,
he made the revision to the outline by *marking* the lines to be moved,
then issuing a block move command. The resultant outline is shown in
Figure S-41.

Collapsing/Expanding an Outline.   In outliner terminology, the relationship between an item and its subordinate items is that of a *parent* and
children. An item, no matter what level, is a parent if it has subordinate
items, or children. For example, in Figure S-41, the second-level heading

"Planning horizon" is the parent to its children "5 years" and "10 years." Notice that the "Planning horizon" item is also a child to "Issues to be resolved." Thus it is both a child and a parent.

The user can selectively *collapse* an outline to "hide" the children of a particular parent. That is, the children are deleted from the visual display of the outline, but they remain in main memory as part of the complete outline. This feature enables a user to "hide" children from the view of the user for those circumstances where all that is needed is a display of the parent item. For example, Preston Smith collapsed his entire outline (see Figure S-41) to the second-level (see Figure S-42). In most outliner packages, the parents with hidden children are marked with a "+" (see Figure S-42). His plans were to print out the more detailed outline of Figure S-41 for himself and the overview outline of Figure S-42 for the VPs attending the planning session.

An entire outline can be collapsed to a given level or the children of a single item can be hidden. To redisplay the hidden children, you issue an *expand* command. Again, the expand can be applied to any item marked with a plus or it can be applied collectively to an entire outline.

Printing an Outline.   While organizing your thoughts, a meeting, the day's activities, and so on, by using an idea processor, the relationship between the ideas is purely positional (sequence and level of heading). However, on output (to a printer or a text file), the hierarchical display of items on the monitor is transformed into a traditional outline format. The hardcopy output of the Figure S-41 is shown in Figure S-43. The outline in Figure S-43 is presented in the traditional outline format. Some outliner

FIGURE S-42
Idea Processor: Display of an Outline with Hidden Children
The outline of Figure S-41 is displayed after being collapsed to the second level.

```
          EXECUTIVE PLANNING SESSION

 I.       Issues to be resolved
          A.  Planning horizon
              1.  5 years
              2.  10 years
          B.  Expansion of product line
          C.  Decentralization of information services functions
              1.  Hardware
                  a.  Personal Computers
                  b.  Minis
                  c.  Mainframes
              2.  Personnel
 II.      Approach to long-range planning at Zimco
          A.  Mission statement
          B.  Objectives
              1.  Qualitative results
              2.  Quantitative results
          C.  Goals
          D.  Strategies
          E.  Task identification and scheduling
          F.  Preparation of plan
```

FIGURE S-43
Idea Processor: Printout of an Outline
On output, the hierarchy of items displayed in Figure
S-41 is transformed to a traditional outline format.

packages use the alternative format (i.e., 1, 1.1, 1.1.1, 1.1.2, 1.2, 1.3, and
so on, versus I, A, 1, 2, B, C, and so on).

Use

People use idea processors or outliners to organize their thinking, their
meetings, their presentations, their dictation, and anything else that can
be documented in the hierarchical style of an outline. The number and
variety of applications for an idea processor are limitless. Sybil Allen,
Zimco's manager of the Systems Analysis Department, has created an
outline template for her weekly team meeting. The outline contains a
generic list of topics (items) that are common to all meetings, such as
progress reports, problem areas, work schedules for coming week. Prior
to the meeting, she fills in the details (e.g., itemizing problems). Like
Preston Smith, Sybil works from the detailed outline and hands out an
overview outline to members of the team.

REVIEW EXERCISES (S-7)

1. Describe what advantages an idea processor has over a yellow note
   pad during brainstorming sessions.
2. Relate the parent/children concept to collapsing and expanding an
   outline.
3. Describe a business, a domestic, and a student application for idea
   processors.

H A N D S - O N   E X E R C I S E S

1. Using idea processor software, create an outline that you might use to deliver a 10-minute verbal presentation on word processing, electronic spreadsheet, and data management software. Make these three productivity tools the first-level headings and give each of them the following children: function, concepts, and use. Fill in third- and fourth-level headings to complete the outline. Print the outline.

2. Use block moves to rearrange the outline that you prepared in Exercise 1 such that data management is first, followed by electronic spreadsheet and word processing. Edit the outline if necessary. Print the outline.

3. Collapse the outline that you prepared in Exercise 2 to the second level, then expand the "function" items. Print the outline.

S-8   COMMUNICATIONS

Function

Communications software makes the microcomputer more than a small stand-alone computer. With communications software, a micro can transmit and receive data to/from a remote computer. Communications software automatically "dials up" a remote computer (another micro or a mainframe), then "logs-on" (establishes a link with a remote computer). Once on-line, you can communicate and share data with a remote computer.

After logging on, communications software allows you to **download** files; that is, you can request and receive data or program files that are transmitted from a remote computer. Once the files have been downloaded to your micro, you can select any of the microcomputer productivity tools to work with the files. Once processing is complete, you can use the communications software to **upload** the file to a remote computer. Uploading is the opposite of downloading.

Concepts

You use the communications software to link your microcomputer via telephone lines to another computer system anywhere in the world. However, to do this, your micro must be equipped with a *modem*. The modem links your micro with the telephone line that connects the two computers. On most microcomputers the modem is an optional plug-in circuit board. You can purchase it with your micro or you can add it later as the need arises. A modem can also be purchased as a separate unit and connected to the micro with an electrical cable.

The communications software can be set up to dial and log-on automatically to frequently accessed computer systems. It will even redial if a busy signal is detected.

A micro with a modem and communications software can be on the receiving end as well. That is, it can automatically answer "calls" from other computers.

Use

Many *information services*, such as flight and hotel information, stock quotes, and even restaurant menus, are available to microcomputer owners with communications capabilities. A few information services are gratis, but most require a fee. The fee normally consists of a set monthly charge plus an amount based on usage.

Just about every city with a population of 25,000 or more has at least one *computer bulletin board*, often sponsored by a local computer club. Members "post" messages, announcements, for-sale notices, and so on, to the computer bulletin board by transmitting them to a central computer, usually another micro. To scan the bulletin board, members again use communications software to link up to the central computer. This software component also opens the door to sending and receiving *electronic mail*.

In the coming years, we'll probably see a shift to smaller briefcases. Why? With communications software and an ever-growing number of home computers, people won't need to lug their paperwork between home and office every day. For a great many white-collar workers, at all levels, much of their work is on computers. Continuing their work at home is simply a matter of establishing a link between their home and office computers.

The combination of microcomputers and communications software has fueled the growth of *cottage industries*. The world has been made a little more compact with the computer revolution. Stock brokers, financial planners, writers, programmers, and people from a wide variety of professions may not need to "go to the office." They can live wherever they choose. Micros make it possible for these people to access needed information, communicate with their clients, and even deliver products of their work (e.g., programs, stories, or recommendations).

REVIEW EXERCISES (S-8)

1. What is the function of communications software?
2. Why would you download data? Upload data?
3. Why is a modem needed to upload data via telephone lines?

4. Some communications software has automatic dial and redial capabilities. Describe these capabilities.

5. One popular information service is home banking. Describe an interactive session with at least one transaction to both a checking and savings account. Begin from the time you turn on your microcomputer.

HANDS-ON EXERCISES

1. Upload the text file of the memo you created in the Hands-on Exercises in Section S-3 to another computer. Download the same file to your microcomputer.

2. Send a message via electronic mail to a friend.

3. Tap into and scan a local computer bulletin board. Respond to one of the messages.

S-9 INTEGRATED MICRO SOFTWARE: A "WINDOW" TO INFORMATION

Function

Seldom do we produce a chart (graphics) without adding some explanatory text (word processing). Producing a hard copy of a memo (word processing) may be unnecessary if we can send it via electronic mail (communications). If you think about it, all of the micro productivity tools can be integrated to increase the capabilities of the individual software packages.

In contrast to software that is designed for a *specific* application, **integrated microcomputer software** is *general-purpose* software and provides the framework for a great number of business and "personal" applications. Integrated micro software, or simple **integrated software,** is the integration of two or more of the six major productivity tools (i.e., word processing, electronic spreadsheet, data management, graphics, idea processors, and communications software). These integrated packages permit us to work as we always have—on several projects at a time—but with the assistance of a computer.

Concepts

Integrated software lets you work the way you think, and think the way you work. Several projects are at the tips of your fingers, and you can switch easily between them with relative ease. When you do this, you are switching from one *window* (e.g., spreadsheet) to another window (e.g., word processing). You can even "look through" several windows on a single display screen; however, you can only manipulate text or data in one window at a time. This is called the "current" window. Windows can overlap one another on the display screen.

You can perform work in one of several windows on a display screen or you can **zoom** in on a particular window. That is, the window you select is expanded to fill the entire screen. Press a key and you can return to a multiwindow display. A multiwindow display permits you to view how a change in one window affects another window. For example, as you change the data in a spreadsheet, you can view how an accompanying pie chart is revised to reflect the new data.

You can even create **window panes!** As you might expect, a window is divided into panes so that you can view several parts of the same window subarea at a time. For example, suppose that you were writing a long report in a word processing window; then you might wish to write the conclusions to the report in one window pane while viewing portions of the report in another window pane.

A handy feature available with most micro software packages is the **macro.** A macro is a sequence of frequently used operations or keystrokes that can be recalled as you need them. You create a macro by entering the sequence of operations or keystrokes, then storing them on disk for later recall. To *invoke* or execute the macro, you either refer to it by name (perhaps in the text of a word processing file) or enter the series of keystrokes that identify the desired macro (e.g., ALT-8, CTRL-F4). Three common user-supplied macros in word processing could be the commands necessary to format the first-, second- and third-level headings in a report. For example, the first-level heading is centered, boldface, and followed by two spaces; the second level is flush left, boldface, and followed by an indented paragraph; and the third level is flush left, underlined, and followed on the same line by the beginning of the first paragraph. In electronic spreadsheets, macros are commonly used to produce charts "automatically" from spreadsheet data.

Use

A manager might use all micro productivity tools to handle a variety of administrative duties. In one window, a manager might use electronic spreadsheet software to track product sales by region. At the end of each week the manager might summarize and plot sales data in a bar chart in another window. In still another window the manager might write a memo recommending the top field sales representatives for special recognition. Another window might contain personal "things-to-do" notes in an outline format. The manager can distribute the memo via electronic mail by uploading it to the company's mainframe (via communications software). This example illustrates how the capabilities of the individual software packages complement the capabilities of the others.

S-10 SUMMARY

Several hundred micro "productivity" software packages are available commercially. Over 30 integrated micro software packages are available. Commercially available software packages vary greatly in capabilities and price. Before buying, have an idea of how you plan to use the software, then check it out thoroughly to make sure it has the features you want. Ask the salesperson to demonstrate the package.

Software with essentially the same capabilities may be priced as much as several hundred dollars apart. Some graphics software creates displays of charts in seconds, while others take minutes. Some software packages are easy to learn and are accompanied by good documentation; others are not. Considering the amount of time that you might spend using micro software, any extra time you spend in evaluating the software will be time well spent.

Not all micro software packages are as "user friendly" as vendors would have us believe. Vendors are sometimes overzealous in their use of the phrase "easy to learn." However, hundreds of thousands of computer novices and experts have mastered the use of these valuable productivity tools, and with a little study and practice, you will too.

During the learning stages, keep a list of error messages handy; you will probably need them. A word of warning: Manuals and disk tutorials tell you everything you *can* do but say very little about what you *cannot* do. That may take a bit of "trial and error" to learn.

Perhaps the best way to learn micro software is to use it. Anticipate some frustrations, but before you know it, you too will be a software wizard. What you do with the software, though, is 10 percent skills and 90 percent imagination.

REVIEW EXERCISES (S-9 and S-10)

1. Briefly describe the concept of integrated microcomputer software.
2. Why would a user of an integrated software package use the zoom feature?
3. What is a macro and how can the use of macros save time?
4. What do you look for when buying a microcomputer software package?
5. If you are in the market for micro software, test out at least two packages at a computer store and write up a brief comparison, noting the strengths and weaknesses of each.

Index